Mastering Java EE Development with WildFly

Create Enterprise-grade Java applications with WildFly

Luca Stancapiano

BIRMINGHAM - MUMBAI

Mastering Java EE Development with WildFly

First published: June 2017

Production reference: 1160617

Published by Packt Publishing Ltd.
Livery Place
35 Livery Street
Birmingham
B3 2PB, UK.

ISBN 978-1-78728-717-4

www.packtpub.com

Credits

Author
Luca Stancapiano

Reviewers
Alexandre Arcanjo de Queiroz
Deepak Vohra

Commissioning Editor
Amarabha Banerjee

Acquisition Editor
Shweta Pant

Content Development Editor
Mohammed Yusuf Imaratwale

Technical Editor
Murtaza Tinwala

Copy Editors
Shaila Kusanale
Vikrant Phadkay

Project Coordinator
Ritika Manoj

Proofreader
Safis Editing

Indexer
Tejal Daruwale Soni

Graphics
Jason Monteiro

Production Coordinator
Shantanu Zagade

About the Author

Luca Stancapiano has been working in the IT industry since 2000. He specializes in Java EE and JBoss, and has collaborated with Apache, Alfresco, Atliassian, EXo, and JBoss communities on several open source products for many years. He lives in Italy and collaborates with leading consulting companies for design and implementation of applications for both government and private companies dealing with information, finance, and transport. Abroad, he is known for his interventions at the Daily Telegraph in portals. He brings projects such as Wildfly, Alfresco ECM, Activiti, JGroups, Arquillian, Exo Portal, Solr, Infinispan, JBoss Portal ,Gatein, Jira, and Confluence, and manages Vige, an open source community specializing in open government and smart cities. He is one of the authors of the Gatein Cookbook, showing Gatein's portal and how to develop portlets with it, published in 2012 by Packt.

I want to thank the people who have been close to me and supported me, especially my wife Gladys and my parents.

About the Reviewers

Alexandre Arcanjo de Queiroz is a Brazilian software developer who graduated from the Faculty of Technology of São Paulo, a renowned institution in his country. He has experience in developing applications using Java EE and Spring Framework.

He currently works as senior software engineer for Geofusion. Geofusion is the leader in geomarketing in Brazil, and offers an online platform called OnMaps, which is indispensable for companies seeking expansion and assistance in more accurate decision making.

He worked as a technical reviewer for the books *Spring Cookbook*, *Advanced Java EE Development with WildFly*, and *Enterprise Application Development with ExtJS*, and in the *Building Applications with ExtJS* video course.

> *I would like to thank my family who supported me in every moment of my life and my friends who believed in my potential.*

Deepak Vohra is a consultant and principal member of the NuBean.com software company. Deepak is a Sun Certified Java programmer and Web component developer, and has worked in the fields of XML, Java programming, and Java EE for 10 years. Deepak is the co-author of the Apress book *Pro XML Development with Java Technology* and was the technical reviewer for the O'Reilly book *WebLogic: The Definitive Guide*. He was also the technical reviewer for the course technology PTR book *Ruby Programming for the Absolute Beginner*. Also, he is the author of Packt's books *JDBC 4.0* and *Oracle JDeveloper for J2EE Development*, *Processing XML Documents with Oracle JDeveloper 11g*, *EJB 3.0 Database Persistence with Oracle Fusion Middleware 11g*, *Java EE Development in Eclipse IDE*, *Advanced Java EE Development with WildFly*.

www.PacktPub.com

For support files and downloads related to your book, please visit `www.PacktPub.com`.

Did you know that Packt offers eBook versions of every book published, with PDF and ePub files available? You can upgrade to the eBook version at `www.PacktPub.com` and as a print book customer, you are entitled to a discount on the eBook copy. Get in touch with us at `service@packtpub.com` for more details.

At `www.PacktPub.com`, you can also read a collection of free technical articles, sign up for a range of free newsletters and receive exclusive discounts and offers on Packt books and eBooks.

`https://www.packtpub.com/mapt`

Get the most in-demand software skills with Mapt. Mapt gives you full access to all Packt books and video courses, as well as industry-leading tools to help you plan your personal development and advance your career.

Why subscribe?

- Fully searchable across every book published by Packt
- Copy and paste, print, and bookmark content
- On demand and accessible via a web browser

Customer Feedback

Thanks for purchasing this Packt book. At Packt, quality is at the heart of our editorial process. To help us improve, please leave us an honest review on this book's Amazon page at `https://www.amazon.com/dp/1787287173`.

If you'd like to join our team of regular reviewers, you can e-mail us at `customerreviews@packtpub.com`. We award our regular reviewers with free eBooks and videos in exchange for their valuable feedback. Help us be relentless in improving our products!

Table of Contents

Preface

Java EE is the main tool used over the last few decades to develop **Information Technology** (**IT**) applications. Java EE has evolved during these years according to the needs of large customers. Large companies such as Oracle, Redhat, and IBM have invested in Java EE by improving it over time, providing feedback and workflows for the JCP specifications, making it more suitable for ever stringent requests from around the world. The **Java Community Process** (**JCP**) has favored Java EE, thanks to the contribution of not only these companies but of anyone who is interested in the now-consonant open source philosophy. Many people and companies contribute to open source by providing their expertise and contributing to the design and development of well-known products in information technology. The development of important open source products has also helped improve Java EE. Implementations of Java EE specifics come mainly from the Apache and JBoss communities. JBoss initially emerged as a product implementing Java EE and later became a true open source community; it was the first community to invest in Java EE. WildFly is the evolution of JBoss, an application server that implements Java EE 7 specifications. In this book, we will show all the opportunities that this product can provide customers by focusing on Java EE implementations and some extensions that make WildFly a great alternative to proprietary application servers.

What this book covers

Chapter 1, *Introducing Java EE and Configuring the Development Environment*, gives an introduction to Java EE, focusing on the novelties introduced in version 7. The book provides several examples, and this chapter will explain how to install and use them when reading the various chapters.

Chapter 2, *Working with Dependency Injection*, states that dependency injection has brought innovation to the way of programming. The instantiation of automatically rendered objects at the configuration level has made it simpler and more performative in the development of applications, avoiding the problems of lack of memory and memory leaks. Thanks to annotations almost completely replacing XML configurations, development has become even simpler and more portable. In this chapter, we'll see how to use the CDI inside WildFly 10.

Chapter 3, *Persistence,* explores the significant novelties annotations have brought to the development of entities. It has now become very easy to create objects and make them persistent in a relational database. The JPA deals with this. We will look at the JPA 2.1 features on WildFly 10 in detail, with related examples.

Chapter 4, *Implementing Business Logic,* says that EJBs are the historical components provided by Java EE to implement the business logic. This chapter will show the novelties and all types of EJBs so that the reader can choose the most suitable component for their needs.

Chapter 5, *Working with Distributed Transactions,* teaches that distributed transactions are the key element of Java EE. **Java Transaction Architecture (JTA)** does not need much work to handle transactional operations; it is very easy to handle transactions not only between different applications, but also between different databases and application servers. In this chapter, we will show Narajana, the open source product that implements JTA within WildFly 10 and the possible transaction scenarios.

Chapter 6, *Creating REST Services,* explains that the latest specifications have conveyed the use of REST as the key to building services. REST is very easy to use, fast, and fits very well with the latest requirements of HTML 5. In this chapter, we will focus on the use of JAX-RS 2.0 implemented by RESTEasy and featured on WildFly since its inception.

Chapter 7, *Implementing Web Sockets,* states that the main innovation introduced by Java EE 7 is the web sockets that revolutionized the web world as it did in its AJAX times. With web sockets, we finally have a direct channel between the browser and web applications, so asynchronous mechanisms, such as notifications and messaging, make it simpler, safer, and faster.

Chapter 8, *Working with Messaging,* says that JMS is a historical framework for Java EE. JMS provides good support for writing clients who receive messages from queues or topics. Version 7 introduces improvements in development by leveraging annotations to write a lot less code. In this chapter, we will analyze the development and configuration of the messaging server implemented by ActiveMQ Artemis.

Chapter 9, *Implementing a Mail Client,* teaches you to send emails with JavaMail. WildFly provides a dedicated session for mails to be included in enterprise applications. We will see several examples and how to test them with the open source SubEtha Mail product.

Chapter 10, *Asynchronous REST,* finishes the work on REST by dwelling on the asynchronous mechanisms introduced in the last two Java EE specifications, such as timeouts and callbacks. We will write examples of clients using REST asynchronous.

Chapter 11, *Asynchronous EJB*, continues the discussion of EJBs by focusing on new asynchronous mechanisms, such as timers, schedulers, and timeouts, described in Java EE 6 and 7. We will also provide examples of listener and message-driven beans and explain how to support transactions.

Chapter 12, *Batches and Workflows*, discusses the scheduler's speech by analyzing new batch specifications introduced in Java EE 7. With WildFly 10, you can write rather complex batches and workflows by competing with highly consolidated BPM specifications.

Chapter 13, *Working with Servlets and JSP*, is entirely dedicated to the web and its Java components. We'll see how undertow, the new engine that implements web connectors, implements servlets 3.1 and JSP 2.3 through several examples of web pages.

Chapter 14, *Writing a JSF Application*, outlines how to develop Java Server Faces 2.2 applications with the help of the Mojarra engine present in WildFly 10. We will show examples of configurations, navigation, and major JSF components.

Chapter 15, *Sharing the Web Sessions*, covers how to set up a cluster with WildFly using standalone and domain mode. This chapter will also teach us how the data is propagated with the help of Infinispan, the product that implements the second-level cache, and which allows us to replicate the data in the WildFly cluster.

Chapter 16, *WildFly in Cloud*, showcases how to install and use WildFly in a cloud machine provided by OpenShift; the chapter will provide details on this product used to manage cloud machines in an open context.

Chapter 17, *Share your Data*, analyzes Infinispan components and displays network configurations in order to have special configurations depending on the network used.

Chapter 18, *Deployment*, looks at deployment as a key part of the application server. We will see examples of deploying different applications and custom configurations in this chapter.

Chapter 19, *Working with OSGI,* takes you through the modular structure of WildFly provided by JBoss modules, a framework that allows a strong personalization of the components that make up WildFly. In addition, we will see an extension of JBoss modules, JBoss OSGI, which allows us to deploy applications through OSGI.

What you need for this book

To try the examples, it is important to have an internet connection and a PC or notebook with at least 8 GB of RAM and free space of about 3 GB on the hard drive. The preferred operating system is Linux, but other operating systems that are based on Linux core or have at least one bash shell is also good.

Who this book is for

Given the wide array of examples, those who read the book should know the Java language. The knowledge of Java EE is not indispensable as the book proposes to make it known to both bases and details.

Conventions

In this book, you will find a number of text styles that distinguish between different kinds of information. Here are some examples of these styles and an explanation of their meaning.

Specific commands or tools from the interface will be identified as follows:

Select the **Save** button.

Code words in text, database table names, folder names, filenames, file extensions, pathnames, dummy URLs, user input, and Twitter handles are shown as follows: "We can include other contexts through the use of the `include` directive."

A block of code is set as follows:

```
INFO   [org.jboss.as] (Controller Boot Thread) WFLYSRV0025: WildFly Full
10.1.0.Final (WildFly Core 2.2.0.Final) started in 20718ms - Started 580 of
816 services (405 services are lazy, passive or on-demand)
```

When we wish to draw your attention to a particular part of a code block, the relevant lines or items are set in bold:

```
asyncInvoker.get(new InvocationCallback<Response>() {
   @Override
   public void completed(Response response) {
    ...
```

Any command-line input or output is written as follows:

```
vi $USER_HOME/.bash_profile
```

New terms and important words are shown in bold. Words that you see on the screen, for example, in menus or dialog boxes, appear in the text like this: "Clicking the **Next** button moves you to the next screen."

Warnings or important notes appear in a box like this.

Tips and tricks appear like this.

Reader feedback

Feedback from our readers is always welcome. Let us know what you think about this book—what you liked or disliked. Reader feedback is important for us as it helps us develop titles that you will really get the most out of.

To send us general feedback, simply e-mail feedback@packtpub.com, and mention the book's title in the subject of your message.

If there is a topic that you have expertise in and you are interested in either writing or contributing to a book, see our author guide at .www.packtpub.com/authors

Customer support

Now that you are the proud owner of a Packt book, we have a number of things to help you to get the most from your purchase.

Downloading the example code

You can download the example code files for this book from your account at http://www.packtpub.com. If you purchased this book elsewhere, you can visit http://www.packtpub.com/support and register to have the files e-mailed directly to you.

You can download the code files by following these steps:

1. Log in or register to our website using your e-mail address and password.
2. Hover the mouse pointer on the **SUPPORT** tab at the top.
3. Click on **Code Downloads & Errata**.
4. Enter the name of the book in the **Search** box.
5. Select the book for which you're looking to download the code files.
6. Choose from the drop-down menu where you purchased this book from.
7. Click on **Code Download**.

You can also download the code files by clicking on the **Code Files** button on the book's webpage at the Packt Publishing website. This page can be accessed by entering the book's name in the **Search** box. Please note that you need to be logged in to your Packt account.

Once the file is downloaded, please make sure that you unzip or extract the folder using the latest version of:

- WinRAR / 7-Zip for Windows
- Zipeg / iZip / UnRarX for Mac
- 7-Zip / PeaZip for Linux

The code bundle for the book is also hosted on GitHub at `https://github.com/PacktPublishing/Mastering-Java-EE-Development-with-WildFly`. We also have other code bundles from our rich catalog of books and videos available at `https://github.com/PacktPublishing/`. Check them out!

Errata

Although we have taken every care to ensure the accuracy of our content, mistakes do happen. If you find a mistake in one of our books—maybe a mistake in the text or the code—we would be grateful if you could report this to us. By doing so, you can save other readers from frustration and help us improve subsequent versions of this book. If you find any Errata, please report them by visiting `http://www.packtpub.com/submit-Errata`, selecting your book, clicking on the Errata submission form link, and entering the details of your Errata. Once your Errata are verified, your submission will be accepted and the Errata will be uploaded to our website or added to any list of existing Errata under the Errata section of that title.

To view the previously submitted Errata, go to `https://www.packtpub.com/books/content/support`and enter the name of the book in the search field. The required information will appear under the Errata section.

Piracy

Piracy of copyrighted material on the internet is an ongoing problem across all media. At Packt, we take the protection of our copyright and licenses very seriously. If you come across any illegal copies of our works in any form on the internet, please provide us with the location address or website name immediately so that we can pursue a remedy.

Please contact us at `copyright@packtpub.com` with a link to the suspected pirated material.

We appreciate your help in protecting our authors and our ability to bring you valuable content.

Questions

If you have a problem with any aspect of this book, you can contact us at `questions@packtpub.com`, and we will do our best to address the problem.

1
Introducing Java EE and Configuring the Development Environment

WildFly 10 is an open source application server compliant with Java EE 7. Once called EJB-OSS and then JBoss, it was always one of the most used in the world. Redhat acquired JBoss and all of the community committed to it in 2005, with effect from version 5. Thanks to an internal Redhat policy, JBoss become WildFly in 2012; since version 8, WildFly is the first implementation of EE 7 by Redhat.

This application server is built with different architectures. Luckily WildFly maintains the same core architecture of the previous JBoss 7, adding some innovation from EE 7, a new set of competitive open source products and a very modular core, which simplify sharing libraries through applications.

So WildFly can be thought of as a set of sub-products all tied together by the same system.

Each of these products has its configuration in an XML file only, so we avoid redundant configurations. There is a web page for each module of these products. Moreover we can use all independent instruments provided if we want a detailed configuration.

The application server is made to maintain applications. A Java application server must be able to manage all classes from the applications; for example, it must deal with duplication classes, managing a more sophisticated class loading system. It must able to cache more frequently used objects to guarantee the fast loading of classes. Since the last enterprise specification, an application server simplifies the developing of real time services providing a wide set of instruments so the developer does not have to write voluminous code to manage asynchronous messages, concurrency, or multi-thread requests.

WildFly remains the best solution as a repository of web applications. These applications become more advanced year after year thanks to a continuous upgrade of the Java enterprise specifications.

This chapter will cover the following points:

- Introduction to the new stuff of Java EE included in WildFly 10, showing the major details in the next chapters.
- The Java EE specification certified by WildFly 10 is Java EE 7. We will cover the main features of EE 7 and the starting points for the next chapters.
- A step by step guide to install the examples.

In WildFly, across configurations, it is very important to be able to develop applications. Many books explain the patterns and strategies of programming, and the user must be able to choose the right developing strategy according the need of the client. Each chapter will get its downloadable examples of web apps and enterprise components, and step by step we will strive to use them.

JSON and HTML5

Good news from EE 7! JSON is included in the specification. HTTP always becomes more default, not only for writing web applications but also for services! REST through JSON confirms the HTML 5 approach and becomes the guideline for not only the frontend but also the service tier.

Undertow is the new substitute for Tomcat, becoming not only a servlet container but the infrastructure that manages all Java EE 7 web technologies as JSON, REST, and WebSockets.

WebSockets

Finally the asynchronous messaging system available through a browser becomes the standard. It's the WebSocket. Each site has its own chat available. For example, banking applications have online support through chat, with an operator ready to help. All this can be used without boring authentications and waits. We will dedicate `Chapter 7`, *Implementing WebSockets* to it.

Simplified JMS 2.0 API

JMS APIs provide an interface to send, receive, and authenticate asynchronous messages through Java. They let you develop a client connecting to a message engine. The message engine used in WildFly is **Active MQ Artemis**, a substitute for the deprecated **JBoss Messaging**. The difference between this specification and the older one is simplicity of use and development thanks to the new annotations. These annotations will be covered in detail in Chapter 8, *Working with Messaging*.

Groundwork for Cloud environments

Every new feature and update is done here to get free access to the Cloud. By guaranteeing much simplicity to an interface, the interface becomes a candidate to be used in a Cloud system.

Standard paths or the simplest JNDI names too help to implement this. **Infinispan** is a distributed cache product and contributes to configuring a cluster better in a Cloud system. Clustering will be analyzed in Chapter 15, *Sharing the Web Sessions* and Chapter 16, *Wildly in Cloud*.

Batch applications

A very important contribution in these years is from workflows. With a workflow, you can develop complex systems in very little time.

An air reservation application is a workflow, for example. There are steps such as the choice of a flight, booking, and confirming the flight that can be configured and then executed without developing much code. Java EE 7 gets a new role for the Java enterprise, giving the opportunity to work with XML files to configure steps to add in web applications.

Schedulers too are part of it and they are finally standard. Frontend technologies now include flows with a strategy very similar to the workflows. Schedulers and flows will be discussed in Chapter 12, *Batches and Workflows*.

Updated web profiles

JBoss 5 introduced the web profile. A web profile is a configuration including only the technology base representing the Web. Java EE 7 included WebSockets and JSON together with old technologies as servlets, JSF, and CDI. Web profiles are a good mode to simply configure an application server in a Cloud machine.

Concurrency utilities

Java EE always gives an alternative to the developer instead of working with threads. Threads are always denied in Java EE because they are dangerous. They risk compromising the correct execution of a Java enterprise component, especially concurrent components. With these utilities, we can use threads with more simplicity, minus the dangers concerning stability of our applications.

Context dependency injection

Many new features are provided by interfaces and annotations in our context dependency injection container. New scopes and new **Service Provider Interface** (**SPI**) were added to guarantee much stability to our injected objects. Chapter 2, *Working with Dependency Injection* will analyze the new features provided by Weld.

Java API for RESTful web services (JAX-RS) 2.0

As for JMS, REST APIs are very flexible and simple to use. Get and post calls become more simple using the annotations. REST is now asynchronous too! RESTEasy is the product candidate to implement these APIs. REST will be seen in detail in Chapter 6, *Creating REST Services* as synchronous services and in Chapter 10, *Asynchronous REST* as asynchronous ones.

Servlet 3.1

Java servlet technologies were made for the web developers as an extension to the functionalities of the web server functionality using Java and as access to business systems. There are new good features that we will show, for example the non-blocking I/O, an HTTP protocol upgrade mechanism, and new updates to security. Servlets and how WildFly implements them will explored seen in `Chapter 13`, *Working with Servlets and JSP*.

JNDI

JNDI is the protocol for resolving names in WildFly. This is a standard specification ready since the birth of Java. All enterprise components can be called through JNDI. Here is the syntax to call an EJB:

```
java:global[/<app-name>]/<module-name>/<bean-name>[!<fully-qualified-
interface-name>]
```

The `java:global` JNDI reference is used for the shared name. A name inside this path is accessible by all components inside the same application server.

Other paths include `java: app` to specify the path for a web or backend application and `java: module` to specify the path for a module. A module is a simple JAR file that has no lifecycle of its own, so it needs to be used by a third component.

Asynchronous invocation

The increase in asynchronous features is very high in Java EE 7. Each component can now be invoked in an asynchronous manner. With it, EJB and servlets add some major power, which will be seen in Part 3 - Asynchronous and real time of this book.

Timers

Now we can use our annotations to schedule events and processes. In any part of our component, we can create a timer and configure its time execution, configure the date and time to start it, and implement a set of operations. We will cover these in detail in `Chapter 11`, *Asynchronous EJB*.

EJB Lite

EJB's are very complex architectures, including different EE technologies such as transactions, persistence, remote interfaces, security, and CORBA. Never in a web application do we need all of the stack that an EJB takes with itself.

To make the business logic less bulky, EJB Lite is introduced and can be used in lighter applications. It excludes the following technologies:

- Message-driven beans
- 2.x remote home components
- 2.x local home components
- 3.x remote home components
- Timers
- RMI-IIOP

We will explore globally these components in detail in Chapter 4, *Implementing Business Logic*.

Development in WildFly

In this section, we will look at the mandatory inventory used to start development with WildFly 10.

Operating system

WildFly is open source. Open source is a vast world of applications and ideas. So an open source operating globally system will get a regard point by us. In this book, we will work with Linux, a very important open source operating system. So we will guide you through bash console samples. Bash is the most used command line tool for managing an operative system, mainly Linux. Of course, any OS can work.

Java

Usually Java EE and Java Standard globally follow the same path. For example Java EE 7 specifications recommend Java standard 7 as the JDK but none denies to use a major version of Java. A JDK version greater than 7 respect the EE never gave problems, even WildFly recommends using the last version of Java 8 and WildFly 10 denies to use Java 7. So we assume in our exercises that Java standard 8 is installed in your machine.

Application server

Of course, we will use the latest version of WildFly to work with enterprise components and web applications. WildFly, as an application server, provides a deploy system that you can install inside your application and use. It can be done through a filesystem, adding a package in the deploy directory, or through the console. The deployment system will be seen in detail in `Chapter 18`, *Deployment*.

The new version is 10.1.0. It can be downloaded from `http://download.jboss.org/wildfly/10.1.0.Final/wildfly-10.1.0.Final.zip`. The installation is very simple. Just extract the downloaded ZIP and put it in your preferred folder.

Before we start the application server, we need to create a default admin user so that we can use the management web console. Through the command line, go to the WildFly root folder under the `bin` directory and execute this command:

`./add-user.sh`

After you will get the following output:

```
What type of user do you wish to add?
a) Management User (mgmt-users.properties)
b) Application User (application-users.properties)
(a): a
Enter the details of the new user to add.
Using realm 'ManagementRealm' as discovered from the existing property
files.
Username : admin
The username 'admin' is easy to guess
Are you sure you want to add user 'admin' yes/no? yes
Password recommendations are listed below. To modify these restrictions
edit the add-user.properties configuration file.
- The password should be different from the username
- The password should not be one of the following restricted values {root,
admin, administrator}
- The password should contain at least 8 characters, 1 alphabetic
```

```
character(s), 1 digit(s), 1 non-alphanumeric symbol(s)
Password : admin
WFLYDM0098: The password should be different from the username
Are you sure you want to use the password entered yes/no? yes
Re-enter Password : admin
What groups do you want this user to belong to? (Please enter a comma
separated list, or leave blank for none)[  ]:
About to add user 'admin' for realm 'ManagementRealm'
Is this correct yes/no? yes
Added user 'admin' to file
'/Users/lucastancapiano/wildfly-10.1.0.Final/standalone/configuration/mgmt-
users.properties'
Added user 'admin' to file
'/Users/lucastancapiano/wildfly-10.1.0.Final/domain/configuration/mgmt-
users.properties'
Added user 'admin' with groups  to file
'/Users/lucastancapiano/wildfly-10.1.0.Final/standalone/configuration/mgmt-
groups.properties'
Added user 'admin' with groups  to file
'/Users/lucastancapiano/wildfly-10.1.0.Final/domain/configuration/mgmt-
groups.properties'
Is this new user going to be used for one AS process to connect to another
AS process?
e.g. for a slave host controller connecting to the master or for a Remoting
connection for server to server EJB calls.
yes/no? yes
To represent the user add the following to the server-identities definition
<secret value="YWRtaW4=" />
```

Now you have an admin user with credentials--,user: admin and password: admin

Once you have created the user you can start WildFly with the following command inside the bin directory of the root of WildFly:

`./standalone.sh`

When you log in, the console will show the row:

```
INFO  [org.jboss.as] (Controller Boot Thread) WFLYSRV0025: WildFly Full
10.1.0.Final (WildFly Core 2.2.0.Final) started in 20718ms - Started 580 of
816 services (405 services are lazy, passive or on-demand)
```

This means that the WildFly application server has started.

The web management console can be used by connecting from http://localhost:9990/console.

In the next chapter, we will see how to work with it.

Build system

Many tools can be used in Java to build applications. Open source products are Ant, Ivy, Maven, and the more recent Gradle. For convenience, as Maven the most popular in this book we will use it to build our examples.

Apache Maven is a software project management and comprehension tool. Based on the concept of **project object model** (**POM**), Maven can manage a project's build, reporting, and documentation from a central piece of information.

We will use Maven to manage our projects. With Maven we will get a simple starting point to build, execute, and test our projects. Maven 3.3.9 is downloadable from https://maven.apache.org/download.cgi.

Since we have installed JDK 8 in our machine, we can extract the downloaded Maven ZIP and put it in any folder that we prefer. After that, we will need a system variable, MAVEN_HOME, for our system. In Linux, you can set MAVEN_HOME by editing the .bash_profile file in your home directory:

```
vi $USER_HOME/.bash_profile
export MAVEN_HOME=/$your_home_path/apache-maven-3.3.9
export path:$MAVEN_HOME/bin
```

The second row lets you use Maven in any folder path. So, for example, in /etc, you can run the Maven command mvn. A Maven guide is not given in this book, but for those who don't know Maven, we will use only three commands:

- mvn clean: Used to clean the project
- mvn install: Used to build, install, and test the project and create the packages to deploy in WildFly
- mvn test: Used only to execute test cases

All the commands can be used together. For example:

The mvn clean install command will execute both the commands, first cleaning the project and then installing it. If you avoid tests it's enough add the property:

```
mvn clean install -DskipTests
```

Maven can be used only in the folder for Maven projects. A Maven project is recognized by a file contained in the root of the folder, pom.xml. It is the key descriptor of the Maven projects. For example in this POM file you put the dependency libraries of the projects. When you install a project, it automatically downloads the mandatory dependencies if they are not present and it compiles with them.

Structure of the exercises

This book provides different examples structured by projects divided by part and chapter. Each chapter excluding the introduction has its own project Maven sample. The exercises can be downloaded from the link provided in the Preface of this book.

Once you have downloaded the project, you will notice a tree similar to this:

```
Wildfly-book
    Business-components
        Injection
            pom.xml
Persistence
            pom.xml
...
        pom.xml
    Class-loading
        ...
        pom.xml
    ...
    pom.xml
```

If you are interested only in testing the examples inside the Chapter 3, *Persistence*, you need only to go in the persistence folder and start the Maven commands seen before.

Tests

All our examples are testable inside WildFly containers. A good test framework to execute the tests inside components is Arquillian. Arquillian is the official test framework of WildFly. With Arquillian, by starting simple JUnit integration tests by command line or an IDE, we can see the execution inside a container. So in a hide mode, Arquillian starts the WildFly containers, deploys the components, and in the end executes the tests inside the containers. It's a very important product for the integration tests.

Arquillian is configured through Maven in the `pom.xml` files. Now, we see the details of the `wildfly-book root pom.xml` and see the dependencies introduced before in the build system paragraph:

```
<dependency>
    <groupId>junit</groupId>
    <artifactId>junit</artifactId>
    <scope>test</scope>
</dependency>
<dependency>
    <groupId>org.jboss.arquillian.junit</groupId>
    <artifactId>arquillian-junit-container</artifactId>
    <scope>test</scope>
</dependency>
<dependency>
    <groupId>org.wildfly.arquillian</groupId>
    <artifactId>wildfly-arquillian-container-managed</artifactId>
</dependency>
```

There are three important dependencies to work with Arquillian and integration tests:

- JUnit is one of the most important frameworks used to write repeatable tests. It is the first Java framework that introduces test-driven development. It uses assertion concepts and Java annotations as configuration. Here's a basic test case:

```
public class MyTestCase {
    @Test
    public void shouldSumMyNumbers() {
        Assert.assertEquals(10, Numbers.sum(8,2));
    }
}
```

This class can be executed directly through Maven or the IDE using its instruments:

- The Arquillian JUnit container provides the components to hook to JUnit. It provides the `Arquillian` class configuration. Simply add this configuration to your JUnit test case and it will work inside a container:

```
@RunWith(Arquillian.class)
public class MyTestCase {
    ....
}
```

- The Arquillian WildFly container manager tells Arquillian what container to start when the unit test is launched. Through system or Maven properties, it automatically starts a WildFly instance if the deployment is configured. Here a sample deploy configuration in our test:

```
@Deployment
public static WebArchive createWebDeployment() {
        final WebArchive war = ShrinkWrap.create(WebArchive.class,
"resource-injection-test.war");
        war.addAsWebInfResource(MyTestCase.class.getPackage(), "web.xml",
"web.xml");
        return war;
}
```

Through the @Deployment annotation, we ask Arquillian to create an empty enterprise package to deploy. Once the JUnit test is launched, Arquillian automatically deploys the enterprise package and puts it inside the test class so that it can be executed inside the WildFly container exposed in the type of package, in this case, a WAR (web archive).

 Although the idea of a framework test working inside a container can be applied to any application server, Arquillian limits its scope to inside WildFly. So it never works in an application server different from JBoss or WildFly.

IDE

Three IDEs are recommended.

Netbeans IDE

You can quickly and easily develop desktop, mobile, and web applications with Java, JavaScript, HTML5, PHP, C/C++, and very importantly Java EE 7 support.

NetBeans IDE is free, open source, and has a worldwide community of users and developers.

IntelliJ IDEA

Each aspect of IntelliJ IDEA is exclusively organized to enhance the productivity of the developer. It provides a complete support for Java EE 7.
Moreover, the analysis and the design of the code make development a comfortable experience and very productive.

Eclipse IDE

Eclipse is a *moduleable* open source IDE written in Java to work in Java and other languages thanks to a good plugin management. It was started by IBM and later donated to the community. It manages all the Java EE components with good graphics tools. In this book, we will use Eclipse, the Neon.2a Release (4.6.2) version. It can be downloaded from `https ://www.eclipse.org/downloads/`.

Importing exercises

Now, see how to import the exercises inside Eclipse. Eclipse works with a workspace and working sets. The workspace is a physical directory where we put our projects.

Working sets are logical folders used inside Eclipse as collectors of projects usually organized by argument.

For example, a set of projects that describe a forum can all be put together in a working set and we can call it `forum`. Another set of projects can be used for an air reservation application, so we can put them in another working set called `air-reservation`.

The exercises projects, as we mentioned before, are written as a modular tree structure with parents and children. The parent folders are used as collectors of chapters, so they are not important in our system environment. We now create two Eclipse working sets, one for the children (book) and one for the parents (book-parent).

So, when we start Eclipse for the first time, we should set the workspace by choosing the directory we want to use:

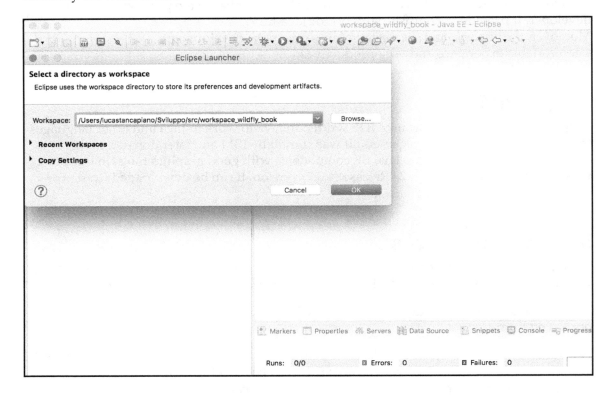

Okay, the workspace is ready. Now configure the view with the working sets. Click on the little down arrow near the **Project Explorer** title and choose **Working Sets**:

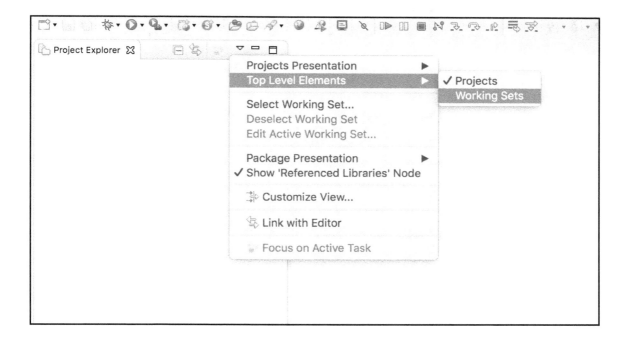

A new window will be opened. In this window, choose the following dialog so we can start to create the working sets:

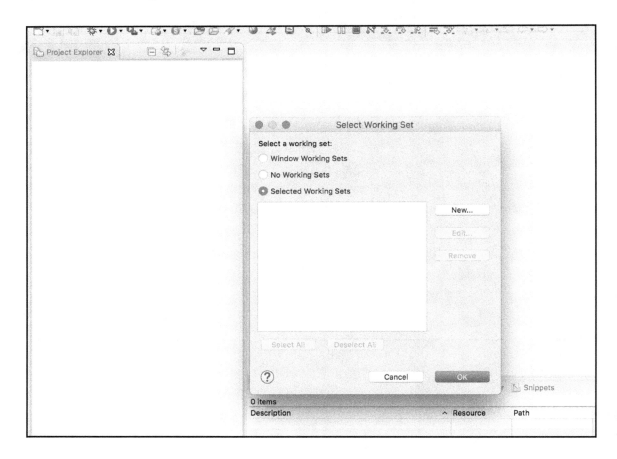

After that click on the **New...** button and choose the working set type:

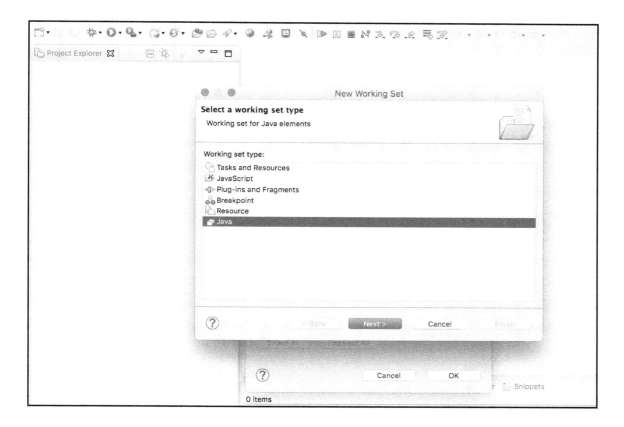

Java is the better type for us. After you have done this, click on the **Next >** button and create the new book working set:

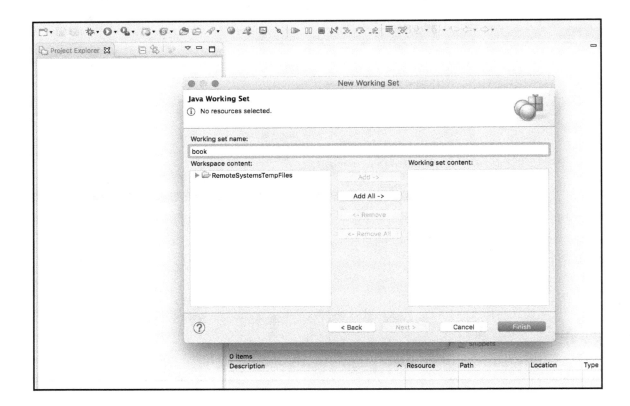

Repeat the same operations for the second working set: `book-parent`:

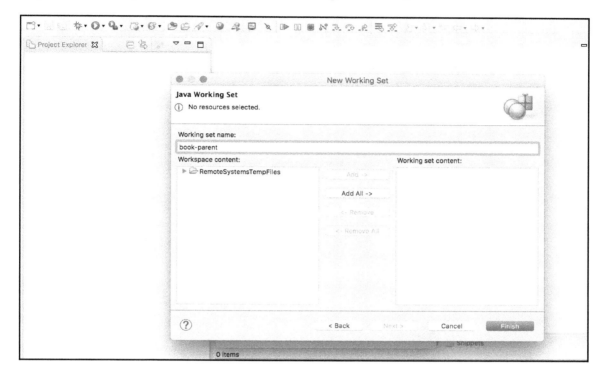

Now select all the created working sets and click on **OK** to end the configuration of the working sets:

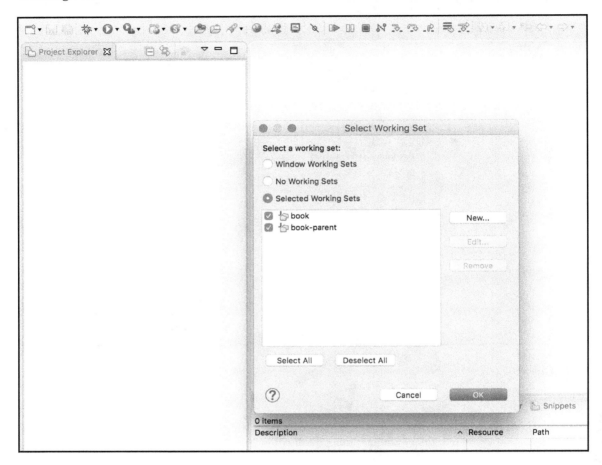

Now we have to import the exercises. Click on **File** | **Import**:

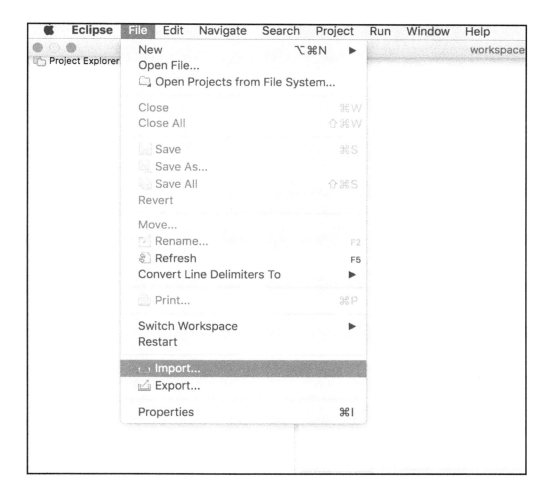

We are importing a Maven project so select **Maven** | **Existing Maven Projects**:

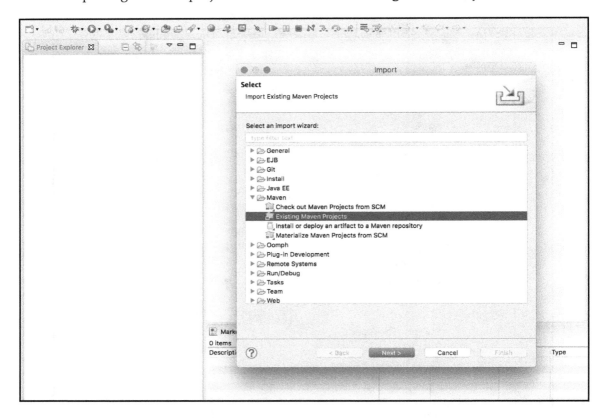

Click on Next; you should select the root directory for the exercises that you have downloaded. Once you have selected it, you will see a list of all sub- projects. By default the first working set you have created is selected, so choose child projects to add to it and click on **Next >**:

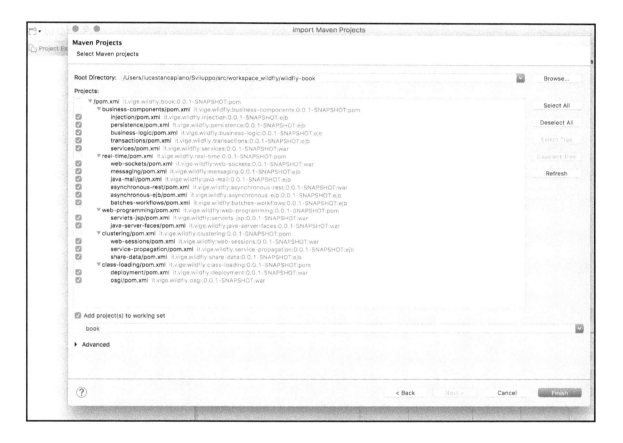

The same operation must be done with the parent projects. So now select the **book-parent** working set and click on **Next >**:

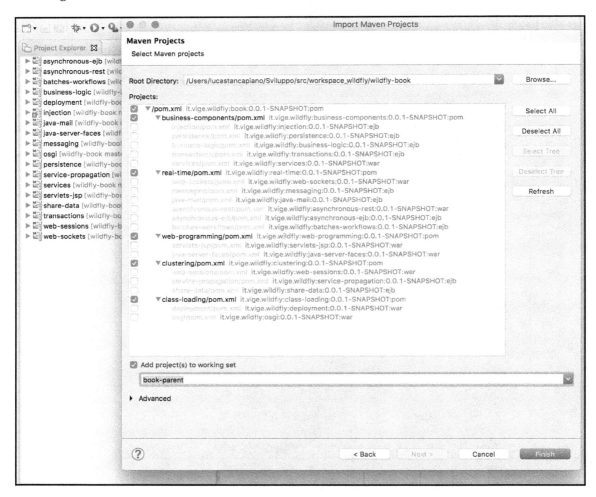

Once done, go to the **Select Working Set** screen again and click on **OK** to refresh:

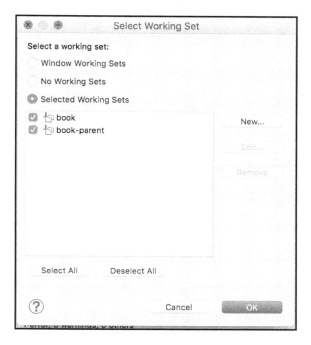

Now we will see a list of working sets:

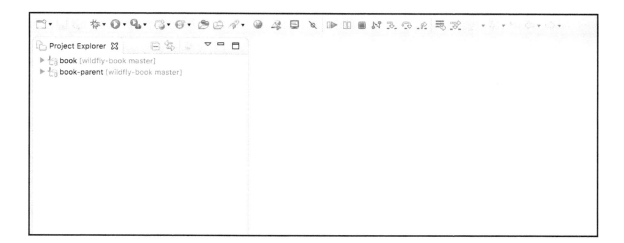

If we open the working set we can see all ordered parent and child projects:

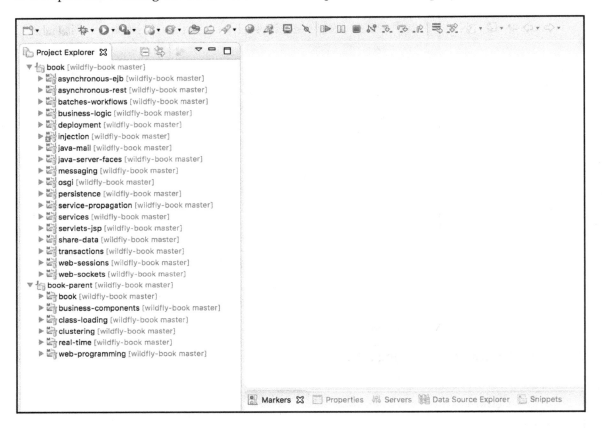

Debug exercises

With this environment, we can debug our components too. It would be very useful to see how our components work inside the WildFly container. To start the debug process, simply enter the sub-project you want to test and enter, for example, the following command:

```
mvn test -Djboss.options="-Xdebug -
Xrunjdwp:transport=dt_socket,address=8001,server=y,suspend=y"
```

`Jboss.options` is a property used by the Arquillian container managed subproject to add external properties to the start of WildFly startup process. So you can pass Java properties to set the debug environment.

In our case, we force WildFly to use the following parameters:

- `debug`: This activates debug mode. If set to `false`, the next parameters will not be considered.

- `runjdwp`: transport JDWP is the common communication protocol used to start the debug. The transport can be of type `DT_SOCKET` used in Linux or `DT_SHMEM` used in Windows.

Other parameters to add in the transport are:

- **Address**: The client/server connection URL. It can be valorized as `8001`. Adding only the port we presume the transport running on localhost, the same machine we will start the debug. When WildFly starts, after setting these properties, a JDWP server automatically starts on the specified port:

- **Server**: It must be set to `y` or else no server can be started:

- **Suspend**: If set to `y`, WildFly will wait for one connection by a JDWP client; otherwise it will be waiting. If set to `n`, WildFly will start anyway, leaving the connections free to start at another time.

Here is the complete command you need to start the debug:

```
-Xdebug -Xrunjdwp:transport=dt_socket,address=8001,server=y,suspend=n
```

Once the test starts, thanks to the suspend property. WildFly will be suspended till we start the JPDA client. This client is ready to work in Eclipse. Here's how to configure and start it.

Click on the row near the **debug figure** and select **Debug Configurations...**:

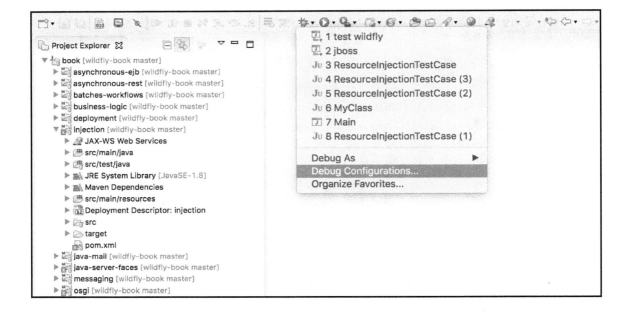

On, the item **remote Java debugger** right-click and select **New**:

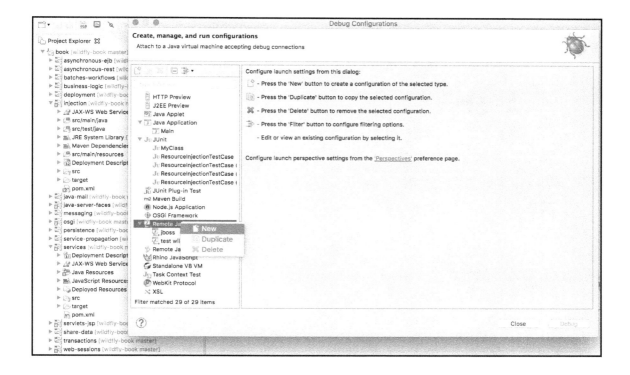

You will see a new window. Fill in the fields like this:

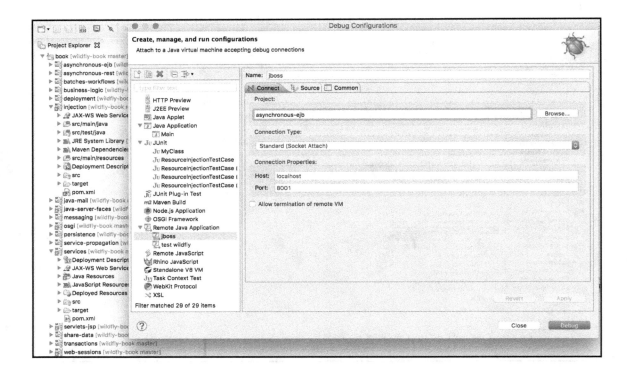

The field port must be the same as the one used in `jboss.options` so that the client can connect to the JPDA server that was started in the test. The Project field can be one of the subprojects inside our exercises.

Now close the window. We need to put in a breakpoint, so we show the debugger at work. Simply, take a code class of the project you would like to test and click twice on a row, for example:

Again launch **Debug Configurations** and start the debugger:

Your breakpoint is now active!

Now we have all of the environment ready to work. In the next chapter, we will see tests and how to start them depending on the argument.

In other samples, you will find that Arquillian uses an annotation called `@RunAsClient` that lets you start test cases outside the container as remote clients. In that case, you cannot use `jboss.options` to start the debug because it starts the debug only inside the container.

To debug remote clients annotated with the `@RunAsClient` annotation, use this script:

```
mvn test -Dmaven.surefire.debug
```

And configure your JPDA client with the default port, `5005`.

Summary

We have finished the configuration of our examples. We now know all the focal points of WildFly that we will explore in subsequent chapters. We are ready to start the examples while working through this book. In the next chapter we will start the first focal point in WildFly 10: injection. Read it well and practice!

2
Working with Dependency Injection

Dependency injection is a very important design principle for working simply and at the same time with major security. It lets us write a very simple code to test. Java uses this principle since Java EE 5 through the CDI specifications.

The first Java frameworks to host this technology were the following:

- **Seam**: Firstly, it was a set of utilities to work better with web applications. Next, it was discontinued and integrated in the Java EE 5 specifications; now it represents the main standard that a developer must use.
- **Spring**: This was the first Java dependency injection framework born exclusively for complex Java applications. Now it is an evolved set of plugins where you can build anything through dependency injection. It remains an alternative to Java EE.

Contexts and Dependency Injection (**CDI**) is a set of annotations and services that make it easy for developers, when used together, to work with enterprise technologies in services, web applications and enterprise beans. CDI works fine with stateful objects too and also has many larger uses. It gives developers much flexibility to integrate various types of components in a loosely coupled but type safe way.

Weld 2.3 is the injection engine used by WildFly 10.1. We can consider it as the evolution of JBoss Seam because the idea was initiated by the same authors. All Java EE 7 interfaces and annotations we have seen are fully supported by Weld. It is integrated with other applications servers too, such as JBoss **Enterprise Application Platform** (**EAP**), GlassFish, Oracle WebLogic Server, and WebSphere Application Server.

Weld can be started standalone too, thanks to an external module called **Weld SE**. Of course, you can use it only as a pure injection engine. All the integration with enterprise components doesn't work outside the containers.

Weld has no interfaces and annotations of its own because the CDI specifications 1.2 provide a rather complete set of tools. So, you will never see in your application custom classes with a package name containing the weld name. However, it's the real meat of Weld, a very transparent engine fully compliant with Java EE.

The CDI specifications involved in Java EE 7 will be described in the next paragraphs. Here you can see what we will show:

- All the annotations available in CDI and how to use them
- All the bean types available in CDI
- How to use CDI in standalone and inside the enterprise components
- Available scopes and when use them
- Java patterns used in CDI as interceptors and Decorators
- Introduction to Weld and monitoring of the beans through Weld

Dependency injection 1.0 for Java

This specification is provided by the javax.inject API. This is a set of packages specifying a means of getting objects in such a way as to achieve major reusability, testability, and maintainability compared to traditional approaches such as constructors, factories, and service locators. This process, known as dependency injection, is beneficial to most non-trivial applications.

With CDI, you don't instantiate the classes. CDI takes care of it. An internal management of the instances lets the developer create better features for the application. Instances are a point of work where we resolve performance problems. All this becomes simpler using a CDI engine.

Take, for example, a book service:

```
class BookService {
    final List<Book> books;
   BookService () {
     books = new ArrayList(...);
    }
  }
```

Using the `new` construct, we are adding health to our application. A good developer knows the correct time to instantiate own objects. By using this annotation, he/she doesn't need to worry about it:

```
class BookService {
    @Inject
    final List<Book> books;
  }
```

Weld will work to instantiate the list of books and cache the result according to its scope.

Qualifiers

A qualifier identifies an injection. Through qualifiers, we establish a custom achievement for the injected object. In this case, `@Random` is a qualifier:

```
@Random
@Inject
private Instance<Integer> randomInt;
```

A qualifier type is annotated through the `@Qualifier` annotation. Qualifiers can be used at class level, field or method. Here is a sample of a qualifier declared in a method:

```
@Produces
@Random
private int next() {
    ...
}
```

Here's the declaration of the qualifier:

```
@Target( { TYPE, METHOD, PARAMETER, FIELD })
@Retention(RUNTIME)
@Documented
@Qualifier
public @interface Random {
}
```

If a bean does not explicitly declare a qualifier other than @Named, the bean will take the qualifier @Default as default.

EL name resolution

EL is a specification used often, but not only in web applications. It defines expressions to call injected beans and operate with them. Through EL, you can find and execute instances by different parts of your business components or web pages.

It will be seen in detail in Chapter 14, *Writing a JSF Application*.

The @Named annotation can name a bean under an EL expression so that the bean can be called through this name:

```
@Named("my_named_test")
public class NamedBean { ... }
```

Here's how to call the named bean:

```
@Inject
@Named("my_named_test")
private NamedBean nb;
```

If the @Named annotation does not specify the value member, the EL name of the class will be taken as default. So, it will be injected:

```
@Inject
@Named("namedBean")
private NamedBean nb;
```

Note that, in this case, the `@Named` annotation is not important because if we have only `NamedBean`, the CDI engine succeeds in finding it anyway. Therefore, we could simply inject the bean:

```
@Inject
private NamedBean nb;
```

Resources

A resource does not have its own life cycle and that can only be called up. A resource can be, for example, an image, a CSS file, or a Word document. In CDI, we can also inject a resource through the `@Resource` annotation. It is very similar to the `@Inject` annotation, the difference being that we can specify a URL to call it.

Here are the main configurable parameters used to call the resource:

- **Lookup**: The identifier URL to call the resource. Usually this is done by a **Java Naming and Directory Interface (JNDI)** name.
- **Authentication type**: The authentication type where we internally authenticate to take the resource. It can be done through application or container.
- **Shareable**: Indicates whether this resource can be private or public. If true, the resource can be shared in all components of the application.

Here's a resource annotation that takes a DataSource:

```
@Resource(lookup = "java:comp/ds1", authenticationType = APPLICATION,
shareable=false)
private DataSource myData1;
```

DataSources will seen in detail in `Chapter 3`, *Persistence*.

Context and dependency injection 1.1 for Java

This includes advanced SPI interfaces and annotations for CDI development.

Injection and contexts

When we inject a bean, we participate in a context. The context is declared in the CDI specifications as an environment based on the scope. The scope represents how the instances are registered and the type of visibility. If a bean is part of a context representing a session, it will work only in the session. If the same bean is called outside of its context, that bean excluding memory errors could become a part of another context. All instances inside a context are called contextual instances. A bean and a resource are contextual instances.

Managed beans

All **Plain Old Java Object** (**POJO**) in CDI are managed beans by default. A managed bean is an injectable object with a particular scope called dependent. A dependent object, usually marked with the @Dependent annotation, is always instantiated to each injection. The annotation provided by CDI is @ManagedBean. By default, Weld doesn't need to annotate the bean with it because the engine automatically scans the POJO and marks it as annotated. This provision can be deleted through custom configuration. We will see it when we see the standard descriptor file.

Producer methods and fields

A producer method or field is a method or field of a bean class annotated as @Produces. It generates beans after the deployment time of the application hosting the CDI engine.

Here's a sample producer method:

```
@Published
@Produces
public List<Book> getPublishedBooks() {
    Book[] books = new Book[] { new Book("Mastering Java EE Development
with WildFly 10", "Luca Stancapiano", PUBLISHED),
    new Book("Gatein Cookbook", "Luca Stancapiano", PUBLISHED) };
    return asList(books);
}
```

We have a @Published qualifier used to identify the list of books and the @Produces annotation. Thanks to this last annotation, we can inject a list of books from a bean and it will be automatically populated with the books:

```
@Inject
@Published
private List<Book> publishedBooks;
```

Bean types

Generics are introduced in Java EE 5 and they are propagated in different Java technologies. CDI supports generics too but it needs a particular declaration to restrict a type for a bean.

The annotation is `@Typed`. Here we will see its use. It's important to declare `@Typed` when you would inject a typed bean. For example:

```
public class TransientOrderManager implements Comment<String>, Serializable
{...}
```

Suppose we try to inject it into another bean as follows:

```
@Inject
private Comment<String> orderManager;
```

It will not be recognized and an exception will be thrown. To resolve the problem, you need to put the annotation:

```
@Typed
public class TransientOrderManager implements Comment<String>, Serializable
{...}
```

The BeanManager object

The `BeanManager` is the interface to the CDI engine. It can be injected in any bean as follows:

```
@Inject
BeanManager beanManager
```

Through it, you can programmatically operate the managed beans. For example, you can do an injection or a disposal of the bean, or you can annotate it at runtime and declare it. Here is a sample of manual injection:

```
Set<Bean<?>> beans = beanManager.getBeans(CommonBean.class);
assertEquals("One injected common bean", 1, beans.size());
@SuppressWarnings("unchecked")
Bean<CommonBean> bean = (Bean<CommonBean>) beanManager.resolve(beans);
CommonBean cb = beanManager.getContext(bean.getScope()).get(bean,
beanManager.createCreationalContext(bean));
final String greeting = cb.sayHello(user);
```

It can be invoked manually through Java Naming and Directory Interface (JNDI) too:

```
BeanManager bm = null;
  try {
     InitialContext context = new InitialContext();
     bm = (BeanManager) context.lookup("java:comp/BeanManager");
  } catch (Exception e) {
     e.printStackTrace();
  }
```

Or through the `@Resource` annotation:

```
@Resource(lookup = "java:comp/BeanManager")
private BeanManager beanManager;
```

Java EE 7 introduces two new service provider interfaces for the CDI engine with the same features of the BeanManager, but they can be used statically without being injected.

CDI

This is an abstract class that uses Java Service Loader to retrieve a concrete `CDI` class from the implementation:

```
CDI<Object> cdi = CDI.current();
```

CDI gives faster access to the BeanManager with the `CDI.getBeanManager()` method, but more interestingly, a simple way to request a contextual instance is provided without using the impactful code through the BeanManager.

Because CDI extends `Instance<Object>`, the contextual instance resolution is naturally provided through a programmatic lookup.

To make it simple, the access to CDI in our non CDI code, the specifications provide an alternative to the injection. Here you can see the injection of a bean:

```
@Inject @Any Instance<Object> cdi;
```

The same thing can be done through the `CDI` class as:

```
CDI<Object> cdi = CDI.current();
  MyService service = cdi.select(MyService.class).get();
```

Unmanaged

The CDI specification adds a new feature to use CDI into a code that works outside the CDI container.

Though this feature does not use those CDI can still use the callback (@PostConstruct and @PreDestroy) and injection with @Inject record within its class. Keep in mind that these annotations are not part of the CDI specifications but of @Inject.

For example, this class included in a non-CDI archive will work anyway:

```java
public class Car {
    @Inject
    SomeClass someInstance;
    @PostConstruct
    public void init()   {
        . . .
    }
    @Predestroy
    public void cleanUp() {
        . . .
    }
}
```

Here's how we can obtain an instance of an object through Unmanaged:

```java
Unmanaged<Car> unmanaged = new Unmanaged(Car.class);
UnmanagedInstance<Car> unmanagedCar = unmanaged.newInstance();
Car car = unmanagedCar.produce().inject().postConstruct().get();
```

Enabled and disabled beans

In WildFly, injection is enabled by the XML descriptor. For example if you are in a web application, you deploy web.xml, and in EJB, ejb-jar.xml. Considering that these descriptors are now optional, the same thing is not true for the CDI. If you don't deploy an almost empty XML descriptor, CDI doesn't work because the CDI engine is not started. For a simple CDI injection you must also deploy the standard beans descriptor, the beans.xml. Here is an empty sample of beans.xml that lets the CDI engine to start:

```xml
<beans xmlns="http://xmlns.jcp.org/xml/ns/javaee"
xmlns:xsi="http://www.w3.org/2001/XMLSchema-instance"
xsi:schemaLocation="http://xmlns.jcp.org/xml/ns/javaee
http://xmlns.jcp.org/xml/ns/javaee/beans_1_1.xsd" bean-discovery-
mode="all">
</beans>
```

The **bean-discovery-mode** tag lets us identify implicit and explicit archives. An implicit archive defining as *annotation* tells that only the annotated classes will manage beans. When we said earlier that all POJO is a managed bean, that is because the all value is used. The all value identifies an explicit archive, so the not annotated classes will also be managed beans. The none value will not accept the annotated beans but only beans declared in the XML descriptor.

A bean is said to be enabled if:

- It is deployed in a bean archive
- It is not a producer method or field of a disabled bean
- It is not specialized for any other enabled bean, and either
- It is not an alternative, or it is a selected alternative of at least one bean archive

Let's now see an alternative bean.

Here's a simple bean interface:

```
public interface Coder {
    String codeString(String s, int tval);
    Bean<Coder> getBean();
}
```

And here is its implementation:

```
public class CoderImpl implements Coder {
    @Override
    public String codeString(String s, int tval) {
        return "hi";
    }
    @Override
    public Bean<Coder> getBean() {
        return null;
    }
}
```

We can inject the `Coder` in any bean through the following code:

```
@Inject
private Coder coder;
```

Executing the `codeString` method:

```
coder.codeString("Hello", 3);
```

We get `hi`.

Presuming we don't want this implementation, we can write an alternative implementation:

```
@Alternative
public class CoderBrutalImpl implements Coder {
    @Override
    public String codeString(String s, int tval) {
        return "hiiiiiiii";
    }
    @Override
    public Bean<Coder> getBean() {
        return null;
    }
}
```

We want to ensure that when the codeString method is executed, this new implementation is executed. To do this, we need to add the script in beans.xml:

```
<alternatives>
        <class>
  it.vige.businesscomponents.injection.alternative.CoderBrutalImpl
        </class>
</alternatives>
```

Now we will view as a result the value hiiiiiiii.

To an alternative bean (and only to it), the @Specializes annotation can be added.

@Specializes indicates that a bean directly specializes another bean. This may be applied to a bean class or producer method. If a bean directly specializes a second bean, it inherits:

- All qualifiers of the second bean
- The name, if any, of the second bean

To use it, we need to modify CoderBrutalImpl:

```
@Specializes
@Alternative
public class CoderBrutalImpl extends CoderImpl
```

And add some annotation to the CoderImpl class. For example:

```
@Named
public class CoderImpl implements Coder...
```

The specialized class using the @Specializes annotation needs to extend another class so it can inherit its properties.

Now execute this code:

```
@Inject
private BeanManager beanManager;
...
Bean<?> bean =
beanManager.getBeans(CoderBrutalImpl.class).iterator().next();
bean.getQualifiers();
```

We will see that this class has imported the qualifier @Named. In the next section, we will see this annotation in detail.

Another good annotation is @Stereotype.

The @Stereotype establishes a role for the annotated beans. It can contain other annotations to define a set of achievements.

Here is a @Stereotype annotation sample:

```
@Stereotype
@Alternative
@Audit
@Logging
@Retention(RUNTIME)
@Target(TYPE)
public @interface ServiceStereotype {
}
```

In an alternative use, bean is very useful to switch according to the used annotation instead of the class as seen before. We can have two different beans annotated with two different stereotypes and switch, thanks to the beans.xml that annotated beans use:

```
<alternatives>
    <stereotype>
it.vige.businesscomponents.injection.alternative.stereotype.ServiceStereoty
pe
    </stereotype>
</alternatives>
```

CDI 1.1 introduces a new annotation to disable beans so that they cannot be injectable. It is @Vetoed. This annotation was done for the first time in the Seam project called @Veto. Now it is introduced in Java EE 7.

@Vetoed can hide a class by the injection, a method with a simple annotation, or even a whole package. See now how to hide a package.

Create two simple beans in the package it.vige.businesscomponents.injection.inject.veto:

```
public class MockBean {
}
public class TestBean {
}
```

Now, in the same package, add the package-info.java package descriptor:

```
@Vetoed
package it.vige.businesscomponents.injection.inject.veto;
import javax.enterprise.inject.Vetoed;
```

Now try a manual injection through the beanManager:

```
beanManager.getBeans(MockBean.class).iterator().next();
beanManager.getBeans(TestBean.class).iterator().next();
```

Both the invocations will fail, throwing a NoSuchElementException!

If you need the objects for injection, simply delete package-info.java from the package.

The injection target

Here is a sample to use manual injection through the inject.spi API:

```
BeanManager beanManager = current().getBeanManager();
```

CDI uses an AnnotatedType object to read annotations of a class:

```
AnnotatedType<String> type = beanManager.createAnnotatedType(String.class);
```

The extension uses an `InjectionTarget` to delegate instantiation, dependency injection, and lifecycle callbacks to the CDI container:

```
InjectionTarget<String> it = beanManager.createInjectionTarget(type);
```

Each instance needs its own CDI `CreationalContext`:

```
CreationalContext<String> ctx = beanManager.createCreationalContext(null);
```

Call the constructor:

```
String instance = it.produce(ctx);
```

Then call initializer methods and perform field injection:

```
it.inject(instance, ctx);
```

Here we call the the `@PostConstruct` method:

```
it.postConstruct(instance);
```

The instance is created; now we can destroy the framework component instance and clean up dependent objects.

Call the `@PreDestroy` method:

```
it.preDestroy(instance);
```

It is now safe to discard the instance:

```
it.dispose(instance);
```

Clean up dependent objects:

```
ctx.release();
```

Scopes

Scopes establish the lifecycle of a bean. A bean according to its scope can always exist in memory or be destroyed after the invocation.

A scope is an annotation that extends the `@Scope` or the `@NormalScope` annotations. The scope is defined in a bean by annotating the class, producer method or field with a scope type or a stereotype that defines a default scope. Here is an example:

```
@ConversationScoped
public class ConversationBean ...
```

A class, producer method or field of a bean can specify at most one scope annotation.

If the bean does not explicitly declare a stereotype with a default scope or another scope, the scope default becomes automatically @Dependent.

A normal scope is a scope annotated with @NormalScope. These are contextual scopes having a client proxy. A contextual scope implements a contextual interface, which provides operations to create and destroy contextual instances of a certain types (create() and destroy()). During create() and destroy(), the contextual interface uses the CreationalContext operations, push() and release(). Contextual instances with a particular scope of any contextual type are obtained via context interface operations (for example, get()). Samples of normal scopes are:

- @ApplicationScope
- @SessionScope
- @RequestScope
- @ConversationScope

A pseudo-scope is a scope annotated with @Scope. So, a dependent scope is a pseudo-scope. This is a non-contextual scope with no client proxy. Well, the "no client proxy" part should be highlighted, ... and it is! CDI managed beans can be successfully used in **JavaServer Faces** (**JSF**), but there is a problem with CDI managed beans annotated with @Singleton. They don't use proxy objects! Since there is a direct reference instead of a proxy we have some serialization issues. When singleton scoped beans are injected into client beans, the client beans will get a direct reference to the injected bean. So, if a client bean is serializable (for example, SessionScoped), it must ensure that the injected singleton bean serialization is accomplished correctly. Samples of pseudo-scopes are:

- @Dependent
- @Singleton

A singleton is taken by the common annotation specifications that we will see after javax.inject.Singleton. It is a simple singleton, not to be confused with the javax.ejb.Singleton, a more complex singleton working inside an EJB container. This annotation will be seen in Chapter 4, *Implementing Business logic*.

Session beans

The EJB specifications define the basic lifecycle and the rules of EJB session beans:

- A stateless session bean must be part of the `@Dependent` pseudo-scope
- A singleton must be part of either the `@ApplicationScoped` scope or the `@Dependent` pseudo-scope
- A stateful session bean can declare any scope

Session beans can be generic types. If the session bean class is a generic type, it is important it has scope `@Dependent`.

If a session bean is declared as stateful:

- If it has a `@Dependent` scope, the application can call the EJB `remove` method of an instance of the session bean
- Otherwise, the application cannot directly call the EJB `remove` method

The main feature of the session beans is passivation. With passivation, a bean is able to temporarily transfer the state of any idle instance to a secondary storage.

We are free to write session beans without EJB but they will use a mock passivation. Here is a session bean:

```
@SessionScoped
public class SessionBean extends CountBean implements Serializable
```

Service Provider Interfaces

Each scope type is associated with a context object. The context object is implemented by the CDI framework according the scope type. There usually exists a context object assigned for each scope type.

The CDI container collaborates with the context through the `javax.enterprise.context.cdi.Context` and `javax.enterprise.context.cdi.Contextual` interfaces to create and destroy the contextual instances.

CDI 1.1 adds a new context interface, the `AlterableContext`. It provides an operation for obtaining and destroying contextual instances passing a scope of any contextual type. An instance of context is defined as a **context object**.

`AlterableContext` was introduced in CDI 1.1 to allow bean instances to be destroyed by the application. Extensions should implement `AlterableContext` instead of context.

The context object can create or destroy contextual instances by calling operations extended with the class `javax.enterprise.context.Contextual`. Mostly, the context can destroy any created contextual instance passing the instance to the `Contextual.destroy(Object, CreationalContext)` method.

A custom context object can be registered in the container through the following method: `AfterBeanDiscovery.addContext(Context)`.

See now how Weld uses the context `spi`:

```
@Inject
private MethodScopedBean methodScopedBean;
```

All contexts in Weld are Alterable Contexts. Through this code, we get the context for a chosen bean choosing the scope:

```
AlterableContext dependentContext = (AlterableContext)
methodScopedBean.getBeanManager().getContext(Dependent.class);
```

In our code, we will create a custom contextual for the chosen bean. We can do it using an anonymous class:

```
Contextual<DependentBean> contextualDependentBean = new
Contextual<DependentBean>() {
    private DependentBean dependentBean;
    @Override
    public DependentBean create(CreationalContext<DependentBean>
creationalContext) {
        dependentBean = new DependentBean();
        creationalContext.push(dependentBean);
        return dependentBean;
    }
    @Override
    public void destroy(DependentBean instance,
CreationalContext<DependentBean> creationalContext) {
    creationalContext.release();
        dependentBean = null;
    }
};
```

A `CreationalContext` provides operations that are used by the contextual implementation during instance creation and destruction. Here's how to create a custom:

```
CreationalContext<T> creationalContext = new CreationalContext<T>() {
    private List<T> applicationBeans = new ArrayList<T>();
    private T currentInstance;
    @Override
    public void push(T incompleteInstance) {
        applicationBeans.add(incompleteInstance);
        currentInstance = incompleteInstance;
    }
    @Override
    public void release() {
        applicationBeans.remove(currentInstance);
    }
};
```

Now we have the contextual and the `CreationalContext`. With them we can operate with the context to do a manual injection:

```
DependentBean myCustomDependentBean =
dependentContext.get(contextualDependentBean, getCreationalContext());
```

These operations are done internally in any CDI compliant engine. Usually this API is not done for the developer but only for internal use because we have more intuitive instruments as the annotations. This sample teaches what a container does when an Inject annotation is used by the developer.

Events

CDI supports events. A bean can send an event representable by a simple POJO and another bean can receive it and execute the next operation tied to it. An event is a good manner to decoupling of the code because it works with transversal classes. The `Event` interface is used to inject the events with any bean we want.

Here's a simple event object:

```
public class Bill {
    ...
}
```

It can be injected in any bean:

```
@Inject
private Event<Bill> billEvent;
```

It can also be started:

```
Bill bill = new Bill();
bill.setId(0);
bill.setTitle("ticket for the concert of Franco Battiato");
billEvent.fire(bill);
```

Event qualifiers

Events work with qualifiers too. We could, for example, inject a different type of Bill, simply marking it with a qualifier.

Observer methods

Other than injecting the event, we can declare methods that observe the event; and when the event is started, they intercept the event and do operations.

Here is a sample of an observer:

```
public class AlwaysObserver {
    public void inProgress(@Observes Bill event) {
        . . .
    }
    . . .
}
```

When the fire method of the Bill Event is executed, the CDI engine automatically searches all methods with parameters marked as @Observes and with class Bill and executes them. In this sample, the observer method is executed in any case. See now the different cases of observer methods.

See this observer method:

```
public void inProgress(@Observes(notifyObserver = IF_EXISTS) Bill event) {
    . . .
}
```

The parameter value IF_EXISTS restricts the use of the observer method only if the observer class is created. To do this, you need the AlwaysObserver class injected in some context.

The during parameter works inside a transaction. It restricts the observer method depending on the transaction state. Here are the available transactional states:

- BEFORE_COMPLETION: The observer method is started shortly before the completion phase of the transaction
- AFTER_COMPLETION: The observer method is started shortly after the completion phase of the transaction
- AFTER_FAILURE: The observer method is started after the failure phase of the transaction, after the rollback
- AFTER_SUCCESS: When the transaction completes successfully, the observer method is started

To test execute annotated methods, simply start the event inside a transaction:

```
Try {
    userTransaction.begin();
    Bill bill = new Bill();
    billEvent.fire(bill);
    userTransaction.commit();
} catch (NotSupportedException | SystemException | SecurityException |
IllegalStateException | RollbackException
| HeuristicMixedException | HeuristicRollbackException e) {
    try {
        userTransaction.rollback();
    } catch (SystemException se) {}
}
```

If the commit succeeds, the following observer methods will be executed during the commit:

```
public void beforeCompletion(@Observes(during = BEFORE_COMPLETION) Bill
event) {...}
public void afterSuccess(@Observes(during = AFTER_SUCCESS) Bill event) {
...}
public void afterCompletion(@Observes(during = AFTER_COMPLETION) Bill
event) {...}
```

If the commit fails, the following observer methods will be executed during the rollback:

```
public void afterFailure(@Observes(during = AFTER_FAILURE) Bill event)
{...}
public void afterCompletion(@Observes(during = AFTER_COMPLETION) Bill
event) {...}
```

An important annotation introduced in the Java EE 7 is @Priority. If we have more interceptors or observer methods acting on the same resource or bean, we can annotate them forcing the priority, so we can decide who starts before whom. In our case, we can have two observer methods using the @Observes annotation annotated on the Bill event:

```
@Priority(PLATFORM_BEFORE + 1)
public class AlwaysObserver {
    public void inProgress(@Observes Bill event) {
        ...
    }
...}
@Priority(PLATFORM_BEFORE)
public class IfExistsObserver {
    public void inProgress(@Observes(notifyObserver = IF_EXISTS) Bill
event) {
        ...
    }
...}
```

If IfExistsObserver is injected, they will start both. The priority signifies that the inProgress method of IfExistsObserver will start earlier because the priority number is lower.

Container lifecycle events

An internal event management is inside the life cycle of the CDI container. For example, when the discovery system finds a bean, it sends a registration event. When the bean goes out of scope, an event is sent to destroy it. CDI lets us customize these processes thanks to the extensions.

The extensions are represented by classes extending the API Extension and declared as services in the folder META-INF/services of our application. An extension can override one of these events, BeforeBeanDiscovery, AfterBeanDiscovery, AfterDeploymentValidation, and BeforeShutdown.

Here's a sample of CDI extension:

```
import javax.enterprise.inject.spi.Extension;
class ObserverExtension implements Extension { ... }
```

Next, register our extension as a service provider through a file META-INF/services/javax.enterprise.inject.spi.Extension, which contains the name of our extension class:

```
it.vige.businesscomponents.injection.inject.spi.ObserverExtension
```

We have created an extension. Unlike the beans, the extensions start at deploy time but they can be injected in our beans anyway:

```
@Inject
private ObserverExtension observerExtension;
```

See now how to implement the beforeBeanDiscovery event:

```
import javax.enterprise.inject.spi.Extension;
class ObserverExtension implements Extension {
  void beforeBeanDiscovery(@Observes BeforeBeanDiscovery bbd) {
    ...
  }
  <T> void processAnnotatedType(@Observes ProcessAnnotatedType<T> pat) {
    logger.info
("scanning type: " + pat.getAnnotatedType().getJavaClass().getName());
  }
  void afterBeanDiscovery(@Observes AfterBeanDiscovery abd) {
    ...
  }
}
```

Thanks to the AfterBeanDiscovery object, we can register a bean at runtime. Here is a sample:

```
Void afterBeanDiscovery(@Observes AfterBeanDiscovery abd, BeanManager bm) {
```

This example reads annotations of the class:

```
AnnotatedType<SecurityManager> at =
bm.createAnnotatedType(SecurityManager.class);
```

This example creates an instance of the class and injects dependencies:

```
final InjectionTarget<SecurityManager> it = bm.createInjectionTarget(at);
abd.addBean(new Bean<SecurityManager>() {...}
```

In fact, the extension does more than just observe. An extension can modify the metamodel of the container too. Here's a very simple sample:

```
import javax.enterprise.inject.spi.Extension;
class ObserverExtension implements Extension {
<T> void processAnnotatedType(@Observes @WithAnnotations({Named.class})
ProcessAnnotatedType<T> pat) {
    /* tell the container to ignore the type if it is annotated
    @Ignore */
    if ( pat.getAnnotatedType().isAnnotationPresent(Named.class) )
    pat.veto();
  }
}
```

 The @WithAnnotations annotation causes the container to deliver the events only for the types that contain the annotation specified as a parameter.

The observer method may inject a BeanManager:

```
<T> void processAnnotatedType(@Observes ProcessAnnotatedType<T> pat,
BeanManager beanManager) { ... }
```

An extension observer method is not allowed to inject any other object.

Utilities

This contains shared, general-purpose helper classes and annotations. It contains two metadata classes, one to represent an annotaion, the AnnotationLiteral, and one to represent a type. An AnnotationLiteral represents an annotation as an abstract class and it is used mainly for manual injection through the BeanManager:

```
Set<Bean<?>> beans = beanManager.getBeans(ConfigurationBean.class, new
AnnotationLiteral<Default>() {});
```

Here's a representation of a named annotation as `AnnotationLiteral`:

```
public class NamedAnnotation extends AnnotationLiteral<Named> implements
Named {
     private final String value;
     public NamedAnnotation(final String value) {
         this.value = value;
     }
     public String value() {
         return value;
     }
}
```

The same goes for the `TypeLiteral`; you can represent a typed annotation as an abstract class. You can use it over than a manual injection, to create a list with declared types. Here is a sample:

```
TypeLiteral listBooleans = new TypeLiteral<List<Boolean>>() {};
List<Type> types = asList(Integer.class, String.class, listBooleans);
```

The util package provides an annotation too, Nonbinding. It can exclude a member of an annotation type (for example, an interceptor binding type or a qualifier type) when the container must compare two annotation instances. See these elements as an example. Here's an enum:

```
public enum ConfigurationKey {
DEFAULT_DIRECTORY, VERSION, BUILD_TIMESTAMP, PRODUCER
}
```

The following is a qualifier marked with the `@Nonbinding` annotation:

```
@Target({ FIELD, METHOD })
@Retention(RUNTIME)
@Qualifier
public @interface ConfigurationValue {
@Nonbinding
ConfigurationKey key();
}
```

We will inject a String qualified by the parametric annotation `@ConfigurationValue`:

```
@Inject
@ConfigurationValue(key = DEFAULT_DIRECTORY)
private String defaultDirectory;
```

At the same time, we have a produces method for the String qualified by
`@ConfigurationValue` but with a different key:

```
@Produces
@ConfigurationValue(key = PRODUCER)
public String produceConfigurationValue(InjectionPoint injectionPoint) {
        Annotated annotated = injectionPoint.getAnnotated();
        ConfigurationValue annotation =
annotated.getAnnotation(ConfigurationValue.class);
        if (annotation != null) {
            ConfigurationKey key = annotation.key();
            if (key != null) {
                switch (key) {
                    case DEFAULT_DIRECTORY:
                        return "/user/test";
                    case VERSION:
                        return "2.3.4";
                    case BUILD_TIMESTAMP:
                        return "10-10-2016:10:10:10";
                    default:
                        return null;
                }
            }
        }
    throw new IllegalStateException("No key for injection point: " +
injectionPoint);
}
```

The value of the injected `defaultDirectory` will be: `/user/test`. In this case if we delete
the `@Nonbinding` annotation in `ConfigurationValue`, `defaultDirectory` will never be
enhanced because the producer method will be active only for the `key = PRODUCER`. So,
thanks to `@Nonbinding`, the comparison of the `ConfigurationKey` enum is never done.

Decorators

A decorator is a class that intercepts a bean and overrides one or more its operations. It can
be used, for example, to add features without touching the original class, a more complex
log, an audit or by adding more information to the bean. A decorator is declared by the
`@Decorator` annotation.

Here is an example of a decorator. In the previous paragraphs, we have seen a simple bean
called **Coder** and its implementation `CoderImpl`.

Now, taking the Coder as a sample, create a decorator for the Coder:

```
@Decorator
public abstract class CoderDecorator implements Coder {
        @Inject
        @Delegate
        @Any
        private Coder coder;
        @Override
        public String codeString(String s, int tval) {
                int len = s.length();
                return "\"" + s + "\" becomes " + "\"" +
coder.codeString(s, tval) + "\", " + len + " characters in length";
        }
}
```

And try again to execute the `codeString` method. We will get as a result:

`Hello` becomes `hi`, 5 characters in length

Enabled decorators

To activate the decorators, the annotations are not enough. You need to update the `beans.xml` file adding the decorator classes list:

```
<Decorators>
 <class>

 it.vige.businesscomponents.injection.decorator.CoderDecor
 ator
 </class>
</Decorators>
```

And more...

CDI provides a very large set of annotations. See in this paragraph other important annotations.

Model

The @Model annotation is an exclusive qualifier for the **Model-View-Controller** (**MVC**) web applications. It's of use to mark the models with this annotation:

```
@Named
@RequestScoped
@Documented
@Stereotype
@Target(value={TYPE,METHOD,FIELD})
@Retention(value=RUNTIME)
public @interface Model
```

Here the properties inherited by the classes annotated with the @Model annotation are:

- Reachable through EL script (Named).
- Elaborated at runtime usually by a JSF engine (Retention).
- Active at request scope (Request scope).
- Stereotyped for internal use. A JSF could switch all models for a more stereotype, changing the configurations at runtime.

TransientReference

The following is a bean marked with the @TransientReference annotation:

```
@SessionScoped
@Typed(Comment.class)
public class TransientOrderManager implements Comment<String>, Serializable
{
        private Order order;
        public TransientOrderManager() {
        }
        @Inject
        public TransientOrderManager(@TransientReference Order order) {
                this.order = order;
        }
        @Inject
        public void initialize(@TransientReference Order order) {
                this.order = order;
        }
        @Override
        public Order getOrder() {
                return order;
        }
}
```

The order is a dependent object:

```
@Dependent
public class Order {...}
```

The comment is a simple interface:

```
public interface Comment<T> {
        Order getOrder();
}
```

Now inject the `orderManager`:

```
@Inject
private Comment<String> orderManager;
```

then call the order: `orderManager.getOrder()`

The order is marked as `@TransientReference` so, after it is created, it will be removed. A session scoped can inject a dependent bean only if there is this annotation. If we remove the annotation, we get an error because the order is not serializable.

Interceptors 1.2

This contains annotations and interfaces for defining interceptor methods and interceptor classes and for binding interceptor classes to target classes.

Interceptor classes

An interceptor class is a class that establishes a set of operations to carry out when a bean is invoked. It is marked with `@Interceptor`:

```
@Interceptor
public class AuditInterceptor {
...}
```

Or through the `beans.xml` file:

```
<beans xmlns="http://xmlns.jcp.org/xml/ns/javaee"
xmlns:xsi="http://www.w3.org/2001/XMLSchema-instance"
xsi:schemaLocation="http://xmlns.jcp.org/xml/ns/javaee
http://xmlns.jcp.org/xml/ns/javaee/beans_1_1.xsd" bean-discovery-
mode="none">
        <interceptors>
```

```
        <class>
  it.vige.businesscomponents.injection.Interceptor.AuditInterceptor
        </class>
      </interceptors>
</beans>
```

Look at the none in the bean-discovery-mode property. In WildFly, the file markup for the interceptors works only if set to none. It is done to encourage the use of annotations.

Associating an interceptor class with the target class

The `@AroundInvoke` annotation establishes the operations that an interceptor executes when the bean is intercepted. Here is a sample of an annotated operation for an interceptor:

```
@AroundInvoke
public Object aroundInvoke(InvocationContext ic) throws Exception {
    String methodName = ic.getMethod().getName();
    return ic.proceed();
}
```

To associate this interceptor to a bean, create a qualifier annotation:

```
@Retention(RUNTIME)
@Target({ METHOD, TYPE, CONSTRUCTOR })
@InterceptorBinding
public @interface Audit {
}
```

Add it on to the interceptor to identify the interceptor:

```
@Interceptor
@Audit
public class AuditInterceptor {
...}
```

And, at the end, add the qualifier in the method or field of the bean you want intercept:

```
@Audit
public List<Item> getList() {
    return items;
}
```

Now when the `getList()` method is invoked, automatically the method of the Interceptor marked as `@AroundInvoke` is invoked.

In the case of Timeout method interceptors, the interceptor applies to all Timeout methods of the target class:

```
@AroundTimeout
public Object aroundTimeout(InvocationContext ic) throws Exception {
    Object[] parameters = (Object[]) ic.getParameters();
    return ic.proceed();
}
```

To execute this method of the interceptor, we need a bean marked as EJB working with the time service. It will be seen in detail in `Chapter 4`, *Implementing Business logic*.

A new invocation method of the interceptor introduced in Java EE 7 is the invocation through constructor:

```
@AroundConstruct
public Object aroundConstruct(InvocationContext ic) throws Exception {
    Map<String, Object> data = ic.getContextData();
    data.forEach((k, v) -> logger.info("data key: " + k + " - value: " +
v));
    return ic.proceed();
}
```

To start it, simply add the qualifier annotation in a constructor of a bean:

```
public class ItemServiceBean ...{
   @Audit
   public ItemServiceBean() {
     items = new ArrayList<Item>();
   }
...
}
```

We can exclude the invocation of class-level interceptors through the `ExcludedInterceptors.class` annotation or through deployment descriptors different by `beans.xml`. An example of a descriptor is the `ejb-jar.xml` that lets us exclude default and class interceptors.

Here's a sample of exclusion of class interceptors through annotation:

```
@interceptors({ ExcludedInterceptor.class, IncludedInterceptor.class })
public class SimpleService {
    private Item item;
    @ExcludeClassInterceptors
```

```
    public Item getItem() {
        return item;
    }
    public void setItem(Item item) {
        this.item = item;
    }
}
```

The getItem method will never be intercepted by `ExcludedInterceptor` and `IncludedInterceptor`, while `setItem` will be intercepted by both.

Default interceptors

Default interceptors are configurable interceptors that apply to a chosen set of classes. To configure the default interceptors, you can use the deployment descriptor to define them and their relative execution order.

The `ExcludeDefaultInterceptors` annotation showed in the previous paragraph can be used to exclude the invocation of these interceptors for a chosen annotated class or method of a chosen class. In WildFly, they can be used only through the EJB context and the `ejb-jar.xml` descriptor that we will see in `Chapter 4` - *Implementing Business logic*, but the achievement of exclusion is the same as `@ExcludeClassInterceptors`.

Interceptors for lifecycle callbacks

An interceptor works inside the invocation context. In the invocation context are all the details of the invoked bean. The methods of the interceptor need to import it as a parameter. Here is a sample of a callback method that can be put in the invoked bean too. The `@PostConstruct` annotation declares that this method will start after the construction of the invoked bean. An interceptor will be invoked and it will execute the method:

```
@PostConstruct
    public void interceptPostConstruct(InvocationContext ctx) { ... }
```

We can add more callbacks too. Here is a sample of an event that starts after the construction and before the destruction of the bean:

```
@PostConstruct @PreDestroy
    public void interceptLifecycle(InvocationContext ctx) { ... }
```

Interceptor bindings

Interceptors can intercept any bean except other interceptors. To transform a bean in an interceptor, simply add the `@Interceptor` annotation to the bean:

```
@Interceptor
@Logging
@Priority(LIBRARY_BEFORE)
public class LoggingInterceptor {
    @Inject
    @Intercepted
    private Bean<?> bean;

    @AroundInvoke
    public Object aroundInvoke(InvocationContext ic) throws Exception {...}
```

An interceptor binding is a Java annotation annotated with the `@InterceptorBinding`. An interceptor binding of a bean can be declared as bean class level, or a method level of the bean class, through this annotation or with a stereotype that declares the interceptor binding. Here is a sample:

```
@Retention(RUNTIME)
@Target({ METHOD, TYPE, CONSTRUCTOR })
@InterceptorBinding
public @interface Logging {
}
```

In the following example, `LoggingInterceptor` will be applied at the class level and therefore applies to all business methods of the class:

```
@Logging
public class SimpleService {...}
```

Alternatively, we can use the interceptors annotation:

```
@interceptors({ ExcludedInterceptor.class, IncludedInterceptor.class })
public class SimpleService {...}
```

In this example, the `LoggingInterceptor` will be applied at the method level:

```
public class ItemServiceBean implements ItemService {
  @Logging
  @Override
  public void create(Item item) {
    items.add(item);
  }
...}
```

A new feature from CDI 1.2 in Java EE 7 is the `@Intercepted` annotation. With it, an interceptor can trace the injected bean, read its metadata, and manipulate the bean. Here's an example of the programmatic execution of an injected bean:

```
@Inject
BeanManager beanManager
...
beanManager.getContext(bean.getScope()).get(bean,
beanManager.createCreationalContext(bean));
```

In this case you need the `BeanManager`. It can be injected inside the interceptor. If a managed bean class is declared with the final construct, it cannot have any interceptor bindings. If it has a non-static, non-private, final method, it cannot have any class-level interceptor bindings, and no method-level interceptor bindings for its methods.

Common annotations for the Java platform 1.2

In common annotations, there are three feature sets.

Common annotation

Provided by the `javax.annotation` package, it is the basis of dependency injection. `ManagedBean` is the base used to make a POJO an injected object. By default, we don't need to use it because the CDI engine 1.2 automatically makes this annotation to the POJO. So, automatically each bean is injectable. The `@priority` annotation was added in this new specification. The `@Generated` annotation is very useful to mark autogenerated codes, so you can treat them in a different manner. Here is a sample of `PostConstruct`:

```
@PostConstruct
public void reset() {
      this.minimum = 0;
}
```

It will be executed after the creation of the managed bean that implements it.

@Resources lets us group a set of @Resource annotations and call them a second time through the @Resource annotation. Here's a sample of injection of a BeanManager:

```
@Resources({ @Resource(name = "beanManager", lookup =
"java:comp/BeanManager") })
public class CommonManagedBean {
    @Resource
    private BeanManager beanManager;
    ...
}
```

SQL utilities

Provided by the javax.annotation.sql package, these annotations can be injected directly in a DataSource in your bean. So now you are ready to make a database connection and all derived properties as connection pools, transactions, and security. Here is an example of injection of a DataSource:

```
@DataSourceDefinition(name = "java:comp/ds1", className =
"org.h2.jdbcx.JdbcDataSource", user = "sa", url =
"jdbc:h2:./target/test_wildfly")
private DataSource myData1;
```

If we have more DataSources, we can group them with a single annotation:

```
@DataSourceDefinitions({
@DataSourceDefinition(name = "java:comp/ds1", className =
"org.h2.jdbcx.JdbcDataSource", user = "sa", url =
"jdbc:h2:./target/test_wildfly"),
@DataSourceDefinition(name = "java:comp/ds2", className =
"org.h2.jdbcx.JdbcDataSource", user = "sa", url =
"jdbc:h2:./target/test_wildfly_2") })
public class DataBean {
...}
```

Inside, we can then inject them through the @Resource annotation:

```
public class DataBean {
        @Resource(lookup = "java:comp/ds1", authenticationType =
APPLICATION, shareable=false)
        private DataSource myData1;
        @Resource(lookup = "java:comp/ds2", authenticationType =
CONTAINER, shareable=true)
        private DataSource myData2;
...}
```

Web console for monitoring beans

WildFly 10 provides a tool to monitor CDI instances as interceptors, decorators, beans, and observer methods. This console is provided by Weld probe 2.3.5.

Weld probe provides the option for to any application to use an additional web console to monitor all CDI components of the web app.

Our example offers a complete web application where you can monitor all the components seen in this chapter.

Web applications will be seen in detail in `Chapter 14`, *Writing a JSF Application*. At the moment, just remember that in any web application, if you want to activate the weld console, add this script in your `web.xml` file:

```
<context-param>
 <param-name>org.jboss.weld.development</param-name>
 <param-value>true</param-value>
</context-param>
```

Always remember that you usually need a `beans.xml` to start the CDI container.

To use this console, execute these operations:

- Start your WildFly
- Go to the injection project directory
- Build it through the maven command--`mvn clean install -DskipTests`
- Copy the resulting injection.war in the WildFly deployment directory: `$JBOSS_HOME/standalone/deployments`
- Connect to `http://localhost:8080/injection/web-probe`

You are ready to play with the console. Enjoy!

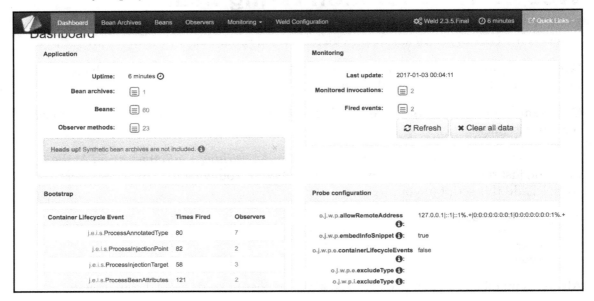

Summary

Now we know, in some depth, about the injections of the Java components and how to use them in WildFly. All Java enterprise components work with CDI to be injected or built. CDI Implementations are a good standalone framework, but they also provide a base to work with the other Java enterprise components. This chapter has introduced you to components that we will see in all of the following chapters. We are now ready for the next chapter, where we will see the Java persistence.

3
Persistence

Persistence is a key feature in the Java EE. Application servers compliant with the Java EE 7 specifications provide **Java Persistence API (JPA)** 2.1 implementations for it. JPA was born with Java EE 5 moving from the old Entity Beans 2.x with the goal to give standard specifications on how to persist objects inside relational databases.

There exists many JPA implementations such as EclipseLink, Oracle TopLink, OpenJPA, and Hibernate. WildFly since JBoss 4.x a is built under Hibernate.

Hibernate 5 is the community product that manages as default JPA provider the persistence in WildFly 10. Although WildFly is built with a modular architecture where you can choose the versions of the core products by configuration or automatic import of libraries, we will focus in this chapter on the default Hibernate version provided by WildFly 10.1.0. The default version is the 5.0.10. Here are the products involved in the persistence:

- **Hibernate core**: This annotation implements the JPA interface. It is one of the first persistence engines. This product is developed inside the JBoss community.

- **Hibernate Entity Manager**: The interface for using the JPA through Hibernate. You will only see the standard API, and only in a few cases will you need to use the Hibernate implementation directly.

- **Hibernate Search**: This lets you work with indexes. Indexes are an important feature of relational databases. Indexes are faster than queries. With this product, you obtain major performance boosts according to custom configurations of the indexes. It provides annotations to add to the data fields so that you can configure them to improve performance. It works together with Apache Lucene, the main Java index engine.

See now how JPA works in WildFly. In the next paragraphs we will focus on:

- Descriptions of all JPA annotations and how to use them
- Java connector architecture and DataSource
- Available query types and relationship types
- News in Java EE 7 about persistence
- How to add the indexes to the tables and Java beans

Common JPA annotations

In this chapter, we will create entities to represent a forum application. The main entities involved in a forum are the forum itself (which exposes the argument), the topic that exposes the questions of the argument, the posts (the responses), and the category of a forum.

So we can start with the upper level, the category:

```
@Entity
@Table(name = "JBP_FORUMS_CATEGORIES")
public class Category implements Serializable {
        @Id
        @Column(name = "JBP_ID")
        @GeneratedValue
        private Integer id;
}
```

The @Entity annotation specifies that the bean we have written is an entity. An entity is an object representing a table in a relational database. The @Table annotation maps the entity to the relational table of a database. If the @Table is not specified, the entity will be mapped with a relational table represented by the simple name of the class, in the case of the example it will be Category.

In this sample we have specified the primary key of the table thanks to the `@Id` annotation that declares a field as primary key. The `@Column` annotation maps the Java field to the field name of the relational table. The `@GeneratedValue` specifies that the key is automatically generated. This annotation follows the configurations of the database. So you can choose how to generate the key according to a strategy for example as SEQUENCE, IDENTITY, or TABLE. The default AUTO simply follows the configuration of the mapped table. You can also specify a custom generator that you can annotate as @TableGenerator or @SequenceGenerator. Here's a sample:

```
@TableGenerator(
        name="empGen",
        table="ID_GEN",
        pkColumnName="GEN_KEY",
        valueColumnName="GEN_VALUE",
        pkColumnValue="EMP_ID",
        allocationSize=1)
@Id
@GeneratedValue(strategy=TABLE, generator="empGen")
private Integer id;
```

The `@Column` annotation can be used for all fields of the table too. Here is a sample of the title field of the category:

```
@Column(name = "JBP_TITLE")
private String title;
```

The category has a one-to-many relationship with the Forum entity. Here is the forum:

```
@Entity
@Table(name = "JBP_FORUMS_FORUMS")
public class Forum implements Serializable {
        private Category category;
...}
```

See now the `Embeddable` objects. Create a message object:

```
@Embeddable
public class Message implements Serializable, Cloneable {
        @Column(name = "JBP_SUBJECT")
        private String subject = "";
        @Column(name = "JBP_TEXT")
        private String text = "";
        ...
    }
```

And a post entity:

```
@Entity
@Table(name = "JBP_FORUMS_POSTS")
public class Post implements Serializable {
        @Embedded
        private Message message;
}
```

`@Embeddable` is an alternative to the entity. An annotated class with `@Embeddable` doesn't represent a table on a database. It can be defined as a part of a table depending on who imports it. In this case, the post entity encapsulates the message, so in the end the fields of the post table will be JBP_SUBJECT and JBP_TEXT because they are imported by the Embeddable message.

All entities are inheritable. Consider the following sample:

```
@Entity
public class Pet {
...}
```

And an entity that extends pet:

```
@Entity
public class Dog extends Pet {
...}
```

As a result in the database, we will get one table called PET, and all data inserted through the Dog and Pet entity will end up in the PET table. By default, the entities use a inheritance strategy called `SINGLE_TABLE`. We can change this strategy through the `@Inheritance` annotation. There are two other inheritance strategies as well:

- **TABLE PER CLASS:** It works like SINGLE_TABLE except that the annotated class will create a new table. A sample:

  ```
  @Entity
  @Inheritance(strategy = TABLE_PER_CLASS)
  public class Vehicle {...}
  @Entity
  public class Car extends Vehicle {...}
  ```

- **JOINED**: The extended class will be represented as a `JOIN` table while the extending class will provide a foreign key versus the `JOIN` table. Here is a sample of an inheritable class:

```
@Entity
@Table(name = "JBP_FORUMS_WATCH")
@Inheritance(strategy = JOINED)
public class Watch implements Serializable {
    @Id
    @Column(name = "JBP_ID")
    @GeneratedValue
    private Integer id;
    @Column(name = "JBP_MODE")
    private int mode;
}
```

A class extending Watch can be:

```
@Entity
@Table(name = "JBP_FORUMS_TOPICSWATCH")
public class TopicWatch extends Watch implements Serializable {..}
```

During the creation of the database, the Entity Manager engine will create two tables:

- `JBP_FORUMS_WATCH`: With ID and mode columns
- `JBP_FORUMS_TOPICSWATCH`: With a `fk_TopicsWatch_Watch` foreign key versus the `JBP_FORUMS_WATCH` table

Named queries

See now how to interrogate our entities. JPA supports different types of query. Here are some:

- **Native**: These work directly in SQL. All caching is managed by the database.
- **Simple**: According to the JPA specification, it lets you use **Java Persistence Query Language (JPQL)**, a language that is more object-oriented with respect to SQL. These queries as for the native queries are created at the moment of the query. All caching is managed by the database.

Here is a simple query sample:

```
TypedQuery<Forum> query = entityManager
    .createQuery("select f from Forum f left outer join fetch f.topics
where f.id = :forumId", Forum.class);
query.setParameter("forumId", 1);
List<Forum> forumList = query.getResultList();
```

Named: These are queries created at deploy time at the start of the session factory. They are invoked by name. They are managed in a system caching of the entities very useful for clustering too. The caching system is managed by Infinispan 8.2, a good distributed caching software; Infinispan automatically avoid redundant queries. When you execute a named query, all of the environment is already in session, so it is faster.

Named queries represent a better mode to increase performance in an Entity Manager. See how to use them in the following code block.

Each entity by routine should have its named query declared in its class. Here is a sample for the forum entity:

```
@NamedQueries({
    @NamedQuery(name = "findForumByIdFetchTopics", query = "select f from
Forum f left outer "
    + "join fetch f.topics where f.id = :forumId"),
    @NamedQuery(name = "findPostsFromCategorydesc", query = "select p from
Forum as f join f.topics as "
    + "t join t.posts as p where f.category.id = :categoryId order by
p.createDate desc") })
@Entity
...
public class Forum implements Serializable {...}
```

As you can see, the named queries are declared at the beginning of the class and they are marked with a name. See now how to execute a named query:

```
@PersistenceContext
private EntityManager entityManager;
...
Query query = entityManager.createNamedQuery("findForumByIdFetchTopics");
query.setParameter("forumId", 2);
List<Forum> forumList = query.getResultList();
```

The named query since JPA 2.1 can be programmatic. At runtime, you can create a named query and execute it. Here's a sample of creation:

```
Query query = entityManager.createQuery("select f from Forum f left outer
join fetch f.topics where f.id = :forumId");
entityManager.getEntityManagerFactory().addNamedQuery("my_runtime_named_que
ry");
```

Then it can be called as any named query:

```
query = entityManager.createNamedQuery("my_runtime_named_query");
query.setParameter("forumId", 1);
forumList = query.getResultList();
```

Relationships

See now how to add a relation to the two entities. The category will get the field:

```
@OneToMany(mappedBy = "category", cascade = REMOVE)
private List<Forum> forums;
```

The forum can get this other field:

```
@ManyToOne
@JoinColumn(name = "JBP_CATEGORY_ID")
private Category category;
```

As you can see, to establish a many-to-one relationship simply put the "category" name on the list of forums annotated with @OneToMany. Optionally, you can establish the @ManyToOne relationship inside the forum entity too.

The mappedBy field assigns the relation to the field category of the forum entity.

The cascade field indicates the strategy of how to apply the action to the relationship. REMOVE indicates that if you remove a category, automatically it is refreshed by both objects.

`@JoinColumn` indicates the join key. In this case, the forum table will have a field, `JBP_CATEGORY_ID`, that will be put in join with the primary key of the category table. If the category field is not in the forum entity, you need to annotate the list of forums and specify the table join:

```
@ManyToMany
@JoinTable(name = "JBP_FORUMS_FORUMS", joinColumns = @JoinColumn(name =
"JBP_CATEGORY_ID"), inverseJoinColumns = @JoinColumn(name = "JBP_ID"))
private List<Forum> forum;
```

Where name is the table of the forum entity, `JBP_CATEGORY_ID` is the foreign key in the forum table in relation with the category, and `JBP_ID` is the ID of the category table.

Another important thing in the relations is the fetch type. It works inside the `@ManyToOne`, `@OneToMany`, and `@OneToOne` annotations. It can be of two types:

- EAGER: If set, all dependencies will be valued at the first query and you will get all objects in memory. It's the default for the `@ManyToOne` annotation.
- LAZY: The dependencies will be not valued, so to get the list of forums of a category for example, you will need a second specified query. With this option, you will have a lighter memory. It's the default for the `@OneToMany` annotation.

Here is an example to force the fetch type in a `@OneToMany` annotation:

```
@OneToMany(mappedBy = "poll", fetch = EAGER, cascade = REMOVE)
private List<PollOption> options;
```

Add this property in the forum entity:

```
private Collection<Watch> watch;
```

Note that each property inside a class annotated by `@Entity` is part of a table also if you don't specify the `@Column`. In this case, Hibernate will create a relationship using default values. Because the table of the relationship is not specified, Hibernate will create a new field valued with the serialized list of watches.

If you don't want this field to be in the database, simply use this annotation:

```
@Transient
private Collection<Watch> watch;
```

See now some details about the CASCADE type.

Cascading is used for parent-child associations. It means that the parent entity state transition will be cascaded to its child entities. Cascading from child to parent is not very important and usually it's not a good mapping.

In the next paragraphs, we will analyze all JPA parent-child associations.

Cascade on one-to-one and one-to-many

Achieving cascade in the one-to-one and one-to-many relationships is very similar. In this paragraph, we consider the most common one-to-one bidirectional association:

```
@Entity
public class Info {
...
    @OneToOne(mappedBy = "info",
        cascade = CascadeType.ALL, orphanRemoval = true)
    private InfoDetails details;
...
}
@Entity
public class InfoDetails {
    @OneToOne
    @JoinColumn(name = "id")
    @MapsId
    private Info info;
...
}
```

In this sample, the Info entity has the parent role while the InfoDetails has the child role.

It's important the bidirectional associations always be made on both sides. The parent has the addChild and removeChild methods to work with the children. These methods allows synchronization of both the sides of the association to avoid data corruption issues of the related objects.

In this sample, the CascadeType.ALL and orphan removal are important because the InfoDetails life cycle is strictly tied to that of its Info parent entity.

Cascading the one-to-one persist operation

The `CascadeType.PERSIST` comes along with the `CascadeType.ALL` configuration, so we only have to persist the Info entity, and the associated `InfoDetails` entity is persisted as well:

```
Info info = new Info();
info.setName("Wildfly Book Info");
InfoDetails details = new InfoDetails();
info.addDetails(details);
...
entityManager.persist(info);
...
```

Generating the following output:

```
INSERT INTO info(id, NAME)
VALUES (DEFAULT,'Wildfly Book Info')
insert into InfoDetails (id, created_on, visible)
values (1, '2016-01-03 16:17:19.14', false)
```

Cascading the one-to-one merge operation

The `CascadeType.MERGE` is inherited from the `CascadeType.ALL` setting, so we only have to merge the Info entity and the associated `InfoDetails` is merged as well:

```
Info info = entityManager.find(Info.class, 1L);
info.getDetails().setVisible(true);
entityManager.merge(info);
```

The merge operation generates the following output:

```
UPDATE infodetails SET
    created_on = '2016-01-03 16:20:53.874', visible = true
WHERE   id = 1
UPDATE info SET
    NAME = 'Wildfly Book Info'
WHERE   id = 1
```

Cascading the one-to-one delete operation

The `CascadeType.REMOVE` is also inherited from the `CascadeType.ALL` configuration, so the Post entity deletion triggers a `PostDetails` entity removal too:

```
Info info = entityManager.find(Info.class, 1L);
entityManager.remove(info);
```

The remove generates the following operations:

```
delete from InfoDetails where id = 1
delete from Info where id = 1
```

The one-to-one delete orphan cascading operation

If a child entity is separated from its parent, the child foreign key will take the NULL value. If we really want to remove the child row, we must use the orphan removal support:

```
Info info = (Info)entityManager.get(Info.class, 1L);
info.removeDetails();
```

Using the orphan removal, this operation will be generated:

```
delete from InfoDetails where id = 1
```

Cascade on Many To Many

The many to many relationship is complex because both sides of this association have roles of parent and child. Moreover, only one side can be identified from where we'd like to propagate the state changes of the entity.

We shouldn't default to `CascadeType.ALL`, because the `CascadeTpe.REMOVE` could delete more than we're expecting (as you'll soon find out):

```
@Entity
public class Author {
    ...
    @ManyToMany(mappedBy = "authors",
        cascade = {CascadeType.PERSIST, CascadeType.MERGE})
    private List<Book> books = new ArrayList<>();
            ...
}
@Entity
public class Book {
    ...
    @ManyToMany(cascade =
```

```
            {CascadeType.PERSIST, CascadeType.MERGE})
    @JoinTable(name = "Book_Author",
        joinColumns = {
            @JoinColumn(
                name = "book_id",
                referencedColumnName = "id"
            )
        },
        inverseJoinColumns = {
            @JoinColumn(
                name = "author_id",
                referencedColumnName = "id"
            )
        }
    )
    private List<Author> authors = new ArrayList<>();
    ...
}
```

Cascade of the persist many to many operation

Now see what happens persisting the Author entities of the books:

```
Author luca_stancapiano = new Author("Luca Stancapiano");
Author davide_barillari = new Author("Davide Barillari");
Author davide_scala = new Author("Davide Scala");
Book wildfly_book = new Book("Mastering Java EE Development with WildFly
10");
Book maledetti_grillini = new Book("Maledetti grillini");
luca_stancapiano.addBook(wildfly_book);
davide_barillari.addBook(wildfly_book);
luca_stancapiano.addBook(maledetti_grillini);
davide_barillari.addBook(maledetti_grillini);
davide_scala.addBook(maledetti_grillini);
entityManager.persist(luca_stancapiano);
entityManager.persist(davide_barillari);
entityManager.persist(davide_scala);
```

The Book and the Book_Author rows will be inserted automatically together with the Authors:

```
insert into Author (id, full_name) values (default, 'Luca Stancapiano')
insert into Book (id, title) values (default, 'Mastering Java EE
Development with WildFly 10')
insert into Author (id, full_name) values (default, 'Davide Barillari')
insert into Book (id, title) values (default, 'Maledetti grillini')
insert into Author (id, full_name) values (default, 'Davide Scala')
insert into Book_Author (book_id, author_id) values (1, 1)
```

```
insert into Book_Author (book_id, author_id) values (1, 2)
insert into Book_Author (book_id, author_id) values (2, 1)
insert into Book_Author (book_id, author_id) values (2, 2)
insert into Book_Author (book_id, author_id) values (2, 3)
```

Dissociation of one side in the many to many association

To delete an `Author`, we must dissociate all `Book_Author` relations together with the entity to remove:

```
Author davide_scala = (Author) entityManager.createQuery("from Author where
fullName = :fullName").setParameter("fullName", "Davide
Scala").getSingleResult();
davide_scala.remove();
entityManager.remove(davide_scala);
```

Here we can see the generated output:

```
delete from Book_Author where book_id = 2
insert into Book_Author (book_id, author_id) values (2, 1)
insert into Book_Author (book_id, author_id) values (2, 2)
delete from Author where id = 3
```

The many-to-many association generates way too many redundant SQL statements and often, they are very difficult to tune. Next, I'm going to demonstrate the many-to-many `CascadeType.REMOVE` hidden dangers.

Tricks for many to many CascadeType.REMOVE

The `CascadeType.ALL` in the many to many is really dangerous in the code. `CascadeType.REMOVE` is automatically inherited when using `CascadeType.ALL`, but the deleting of the entity doesn't work only on the annotated table; it will work on the other side of the association too.

Now put `CascadeType.ALL` in the Author entity books with the many to many association instead:

```
@ManyToMany(mappedBy = "authors",
    cascade = CascadeType.ALL)
private List<Book> books = new ArrayList<>();
```

Delete the author:

```
Author davide_scala = getByName(entityManager, "Davide Scala");
entityManager.delete(davide_scala);
Author luca_stancapiano = getByName(entityManager, "Luca Stancapiano");
assertEquals(1, luca_stancapiano.books.size());
```

All books together with the deleted Author will be deleted, even if other Authors were still associated with the deleted Books:

```
delete from Book_Author where book_id=2
delete from Book where id=2
delete from Author where id=3
```

Usually, this behavior is not what the developer expects, so at the first deletion they will be surprised.

The same problem we can get when setting the `CascadeType.ALL` to the Book entity side. Here is a sample:

```
@ManyToMany(cascade = CascadeType.ALL)
@JoinTable(name = "Book_Author",
    joinColumns = {
        @JoinColumn(
            name = "book_id",
            referencedColumnName = "id"
        )
    },
    inverseJoinColumns = {
        @JoinColumn(
            name = "author_id",
            referencedColumnName = "id"
        )
    }
)
```

This time, not only Books but also Authors are deleted:

```
Author davide_scala = getByName(entityManager, "Davide Scala");
entityManager.delete(davide_scala);
Author luca_stancapiano = getByName(entityManager, "Luca Stancapiano");
assertNull(luca_stancapiano);
```

The deleting of the `Author` causes the deletion of all associated Books, which in the same time removes all associated Authors. This is a dangerous operation because it results in a massive deletion of all entities that's rarely is the behavior that the users expect:

```
delete from Book_Author where book_id=2
delete from Book_Author where book_id=1
delete from Author where id=2
delete from Book where id=1
delete from Author where id=1
delete from Book where id=2
delete from Author where id=3
```

This use case is wrong in so many cases. There are a series of unnecessary `SELECT` statements and a dangerous complete deletion. Take care when you use `CascadeType.ALL` in a many-to-many association.

Practical test cases for real many-to-many associations are rare. Often you need additional information stored in a secondary link table. In this case, it is much better to use two one-to-many associations instead of an intermediate link class. In fact, most associations are one-to-many and many-to-one. For this reason, when you use other association styles, that should work.

Conclusion

Cascading is a good **Object Relational Mapping (ORM)** feature, but it could generate issues. The better thing to avoid problems with deletion is to use the cascade only from parent entities to children and not vice versa. Always use with attention to the cascade operations and use them only when your business logic requires. Another important thing, never put `CascadeType.ALL` inside a default parent-child association entity state propagation configuration.

News from Java EE 7

In this section, we analyze the new common Java EE annotations implemented by Hibernate.

Result set

The `@SqlResultSetMapping` annotation lets you declare a result set and invoke it next time through a native query so that you don't need to implement.

Now you can map the results through simple **Plain Old Java Objects (POJO)** too thanks to the `@ConstructorResult` annotation. Here's a sample of an entity that declares a result set through simple POJO:

```
@SqlResultSetMapping(name = "CustomerDetailsResult", classes = {
    @ConstructorResult(targetClass = ResultDetails.class, columns = {
        @ColumnResult(name = "id", type = Integer.class),
        @ColumnResult(name = "title"),
        @ColumnResult(name = "orderCount", type = Integer.class),
        @ColumnResult(name = "postCount", type = Integer.class)
    })
})
@Entity
public class ResultEntity {...}
```

The `@ConstructorResult` annotation declares the class POJO that will represent the result set. Here is the constructor of the `ResultDetails` class:

```
public ResultDetails(Integer id, String title, Integer orderCount, Integer
postCount) {
    this.id = id;
    this.title = title;
    this.orderCount = orderCount;
t a result set after the query. In the previous API, you can map the result
set only to entities or columns.

Now you can map the results through simple Plain Old Java Objects (POJO)
too thanks to the @ConstructorResult annotation. Here's a sample of an
entity that declares a result set through simple POJO:

@SqlResultSetMapping(name = "CustomerDetailsResult", classes = {
    @ConstructorResult(targetClass = ResultDetails.class, columns = {
        @ColumnResult(name = "id", type = Integer.class),
        @ColumnResult(name = "title"),
        @ColumnResult(name = "orderCount", type = Integer.class),
        @ColumnResult(name = "postCount", type = Integer.class)
    })
})
@Entity
public class ResultEntity {...}
The @ConstructorResult annotation declares the class POJO that will
represent the result set. Here is the constructor of the ResultDetails
```

```
class:

public ResultDetails(Integer id, String title, Integer orderCount, Integer
postCount) {
        this.id = id;
        this.title = title;
        this.orderCount = orderCount;
        this.postCount = postCount;
  }
```

The native query that we execute to generate the result set:

```
Query query = entityManager.createNativeQuery(
        "SELECT c.JBP_ID as id, c.JBP_TITLE as title, f.JBP_POST_COUNT as
orderCount, f.JBP_POST_COUNT AS postCount "
            + "FROM JBP_FORUMS_CATEGORIES c, JBP_FORUMS_FORUMS f "
            + "WHERE f.JBP_CATEGORY_ID = c.JBP_ID " + "GROUP BY c.JBP_ID,
c.JBP_TITLE", "CustomerDetailsResult");
List<ResultDetails> resultDetails = query.getResultList();
```

The query will automatically generate a list of `ResultDetail` specifying the name of the
result set `CustomerDetailsResult` inside.

Stored procedures

WildFly JPA subsystem implements the JPA 2.1 container-managed requirements. JPA 2.1
introduces the support for the stored procedures. Now you can manage a stored procedure
from your database directly in your Java code. In this sample, we will see how to execute a
stored procedure in JPA.

Suppose we have this simple function; it returns a sum of two numbers in our H2 database:

```
CREATE ALIAS my_sum AS $$
      int my_sum(int x, int y) {
          return x+y;
      }
} $$;
```

As the first thing, we need to create a stored procedure query through our Entity Manager
specifying the name of the function:

```
StoredProcedureQuery query =
entityManager.createStoredProcedureQuery("my_sum");
```

Now we can register and pass two values as input:

```
query.registerStoredProcedureParameter("x", Integer.class, IN);
query.registerStoredProcedureParameter("y", Integer.class, IN);
query.setParameter("x",5);
query.setParameter("y",5);
```

Execute the query:

```
query.execute();
```

And take the result:

```
Integer sum = (Integer) query.getSingleResult();
```

The result will be 9.

Converters

A nice feature is the `AttributeConverter`. When you persist an object, it can be useful as an interceptor that catches a particular attribute to do some conversion during the serialization versus the database.

For example, we can create a converter to manage the password of a user. The password could be secured through a Base64 algorithm before the persist and after a query.

The converter could be a good pattern to decouple this operation. See now how to do it.

Here is a Citizen entity:

```
@Entity(name = "citizen")
public class Citizen {
    ...
    private string password;
    ...
}
```

This entity has a password. Here's the code to persist the entity:

```
Citizen citizen = new Citizen();
citizen.setPassword("prova");
entityManager.persist(citizen);
```

In this case, the password will be put clean into the database. We now register it as encrypted. Here's a converter that ensures the password:

```
@Converter
public class PasswordConverter implements AttributeConverter<String,
String> {
    public static String NEVER_DO_IT;

    @Override
    public String convertToDatabaseColumn(String password) {
        if (password != null) {
            String newPassword =
getEncoder().encodeToString(password.getBytes());
            NEVER_DO_IT = newPassword;
            return newPassword;
        else return null;
    }

    @Override
    public String convertToEntityAttribute(String password) {
        if (password != null) {
            return new String(getDecoder().decode(password));
        } else return null;
    }
}
```

The converter is declared by the `@Converter` annotation and implements the JPA interface `AttributeConverter` so it can override the main two methods.

`convertToDatabaseColumn` is used when the field is put in the database. So we will encrypt our password, when `convertToEntityAttribute` is the result from a query from the database. In this case, we decrypt the password and provide it.

Because we want the password field to be intercepted by the converter, we can annotate the password field of the Citizen specifying the converter class:

```
@Convert(converter = PasswordConverter.class)
private String password;
```

In the end during the query or persist operation, we will always work with the clean password, but the real registered password in the database can be seen in the `NEVER_DO_IT` field. It will be something like `cHJvdmE=`.

Named entity graphs

Lazy loading had some issues in JPA 2.0. There are two modes to load the relations. FetchType.LAZY (default) and FetchType.EAGER. FetchType.EAGER is used if we want to always load the relation during the fetch of the root entity. FetchType.LAZY is used to receive the relation a second time only when requested.

But this has drawbacks. If you must access a LAZY property, you must be sure that the transaction is started and the persistence context is open before to get the property. This can be done by using a specific query from the database that reads both the entity and the relations. But this approach is dependent on the queries. Otherwise you can navigate the relation within your code which will result in an additional query executed for each LAZY relation. Both approaches are intricate.

JPA 2.1 entity graphs are a better solution for it. The definition of an entity graph is not dependent on the query and defines the attributes to fetch in the database. An entity graph can be used as a fetch or a load graph, giving additional possibility to get queries.

JPQL improvements

There are several improvements that can be useful. In the Criteria you can now use the ON keyword to add multiple JOIN clauses and call database functions through the clause FUNCTION.

API Criteria bulk operations

Now the Criteria API provides support for delete and update bulk operations. Prior to JPA 2.1, it could be done only to perform this operations updating an entity or to write a native query to update multiple data at once.

Unsynchronized persistence context

Usually, JPA works on a synchronized persistence context to propagate all the changes to the database. As for the main Java EE 7 components, JPA is also adapted to use the asynchronous functions. Now we can configure the persistence context in an asynchronous mode. To do it, simply add the parameter *synchronization* to your injected Persistence context so:

```
@PersistenceContext(synchronization=SynchronizationType.UNSYNCHRONIZED).
```

When you must synchronize all the calls to the database, simply call the method `EntityManager.joinTransaction()` to manually synchronize the changes.

Indexes

JPA 2.1 introduces the `@Index` annotation. It lets you automatically create indexes on the database. Here is a sample for the Book entity:

```
@Table(name = "book",
    indexes = {
        @Index(name = "index_title", columnList = "title", unique = true),
        @Index(name = "index_publisher", columnList = "publisher", unique =
false) })
public class Book {
    private String title;
    private String publisher;...}
```

In your database, in the table book, you will see the two indexes called `index_title` and `index_publisher` tied respectively to the fields title and publisher of the Book entity. The unique field of the annotation indicates that the index enforces the constraint that you cannot have two equal values in that column in two different rows. Here are the indexes created in the database:

```
CREATE UNIQUE INDEX index_title ON book(title);
CREATE INDEX index_publisher ON book(publisher);
```

Another type of index is application side. An application server or any simple Java application can work with the database and decide to manage indexes on its own instead of on the database. The advantages are portability, decoupling, and scalability.

The decoupling because of the application is not dependent on the database so it can get more control over the indexes and choose the most appropriate configuration.

The application side indexes can be propagated in a cluster. It's a joke for a Java EE application server to manage the scalability of its components.

Lucene is the major open source index engine. Hibernate Search supports a set of annotation to manage the Lucene indexes. See now a sample of an entity indexed with Hibernate Search:

```
@Indexed(index = "indexes/topics")
public class Topic implements Serializable, Comparable<Topic> {

@Id
```

```
    private Integer id;
     @IndexedEmbedded(includeEmbeddedObjectId = true, targetElement =
    Forum.class)
    private Forum forum;

    @Field(index = true)
    private String subject;

    private List<Post> posts;
     ...
    }
```

The @Indexed annotation establishes the Topic class to be indexed. All indexes will be installed in the directory indexes | topics.

@IndexedEmbedded is very similar to the JPA @Embedded annotation. It specifies that an association is to be indexed in the root entity index. This allows queries involving associated objects properties. IncludeEmbeddedObjectId returns true if the ID of the embedded object should be included into the index, and false otherwise. targetElement overrides the target type of an association in case a collection overrides the type of the collection generics.

By default, the primary key marked as @Id is always indexed. See a sample of Post entity too:

```
@Indexed(index = "indexes/posts")
public class Post implements Serializable {
    @IndexedEmbedded(targetElement = Message.class)
    @Embedded
    private Message message;
    ...
}
```

And the embedded message:

```
@Embeddable
public class Message implements Serializable,Cloneable {
    @Field(index=YES)
    ...
    private String text = "";
...}
```

If you want a different indexed property from the primary key, you need to add the @Field annotation with index to YES so that it will be in the index repositories and it will be possible to search it.

See now how to execute a search through the indexes in Hibernate Search.

As the first thing, we need a search session called `FullTextSession`. It can be taken thanks to the current Entity Manager:

```
FullTextSession fullTextSession = getFullTextSession((Session)
entityManager.getDelegate());
```

The `getDelegate` method of the Entity Manager returns the Hibernate session important to start the session of Hibernate search. Then we need a builder:

```
Builder builder = new Builder();
```

The builder builds the query programmatically. It can include more than a query, so it can elaborate them all together. See how to add the queries:

```
String[] fields = new String[]{"message.text","topic.subject"};
MultiFieldQueryParser parser = new MultiFieldQueryParser(fields,new
StandardAnalyzer());
builder.add(parser.parse("my_text"),MUST);
```

This query lets you search by a string keyword, in this case `my_text`. The text will be searched in the indexed fields `message.text` and `topic.subject` of the Topic entity seen before. Here another set of queries that will be added in AND. The MUST key implies that the set of queries will be executed in AND. Other options are:

- **SHOULD**: The set of queries will be executed in OR
- **MUST_NOT**: The negation of MUST
- **FILTER**: As with MUST, except that these clauses do not participate in scoring:

```
builder.add(new TermQuery(new Term("topic.forum.id","0")),MUST);
builder.add(new TermQuery(new Term("topic.forum.category.id","0")),MUST);
builder.add(new WildcardQuery(new Term("poster.userId","*root")),MUST);
```

The first is a query by topic `id = 0`, the second by category `id=0`. The third by `userId = "*root"`. The WildcardQuery is an extension of the TermQuery where you can search by wildcards. In our example the * lets you find all `userId` that end with root and not only the fixed key. Once we have configured the builder we can create our query:

```
FullTextQuery fullTextQuery =
fullTextSession.createFullTextQuery(builder.build(),Post.class);
fullTextQuery.setSort(getSort()); fullTextQuery.setProjection("topic.id");
```

And execute the results:

```
List topics = fullTextQuery.list();
```

Packages and entities

See now what we need to use JPA in our applications. Entities can be used in all applications such as web, EJB, or simply **Contexts and Dependency Injection (CDI)**. Because CDI is included in web and EJB application, we can deduce that the minimum configuration for a JPA applications is CDI. Here is a sample of a JAR--deployable package:

```
common-test.jar
        Entity classes....
        META-INF
                beans.xml
                persistence.xml
```

The `beans.xml` in our case is mandatory but it can be empty. The important configuration file in the persistence is the `persistence.xml`. It contains all information about connections and transactions useful to establish the connection with the database. In WildFly you can add the Hibernate properties too useful for getting major performances to the application. Here is a sample of a persistence file:

```
<persistence...
    <persistence-unit name="mainPu">
            <jta-data-source>
                java:jboss/datasources/ExampleDS</jta-data-source>
            <properties>
                <property name="javax.persistence.schema-
generation.database.action"
                    value="drop-and-create" />
                <property name="hibernate.format_sql" value="false" />
                <property name="hibernate.show_sql" value="false" />
            </properties>
    </persistence-unit>
</persistence>
```

The `persistence-unit` establishes a name for the Entity Manager callable by the `@PersistenceContext` annotation. If there is only one persistence unit, the annotation will take that one as default.

The DataSource represents the connection to the database. A serious application server should always work with the DataSources to increment security and high performances. **Java Connector Architecture (JCA)** is the technology that manages DataSources and connectors in the Java EE compliant application servers. We will analyze this specification in the following paragraph.

`javax.persistence.schema-generation.database.action` establishes the strategy for the creation of the database tables represented by the entities. There are four types:

- **create**: If there are no tables in the database, the tables will be created at deployment time.
- **drop-and-create**: It creates or recreates the tables of the database at deployment time and drops all the tables during the `undeploy` of the application. Used for tests so we can always have a clean database.
- **drop**: Validate that the schema matches, makes no changes to the schema of the database, you probably want this for production. It's the default.
- **none**: It expects the database tables to be created and no operations for it do.

The property `hibernate.show_sql` is very useful to enable the log of the queries executed in the application. The `hibernate.format_sql` exposes a well-formatted log of the queries.

In this sample, we have specified a JTA DataSource. It works only inside a transaction. As an alternative you can choose the `non-jta-data-source`. It is never recommended in a serious application server because you will lose all transactional properties in your container. Major details of the transactions will be seen in `Chapter 5`, *Working with Distributed Transactions*.

In `persistence.xml` thanks to Hibernate, you can declare an SQL script to populate the entities. Here is an example of `persistence.xml`:

```
<property name="javax.persistence.sql-load-script-source"
value="forums.import.sql" />
```

The `forums.import.sql` file will be read in the root of the JAR package. Here is an example of the file to populate categories and forums:

```
insert into JBP_FORUMS_CATEGORIES (jbp_id, jbp_order, jbp_title) values
('0', '10', 'Dummy demo category');

insert into JBP_FORUMS_FORUMS (jbp_id, jbp_category_id,
jbp_description, jbp_name, jbp_order, jbp_topic_count, jbp_post_count,
jbp_status) values ('0', '0', 'First description', 'First forum', '10',
```

```
'0', '0', '0');

insert into JBP_FORUMS_FORUMS (jbp_id, jbp_category_id,
jbp_description, jbp_name, jbp_order, jbp_topic_count, jbp_post_count,
jbp_status) values ('1', '0', 'Second description', 'Second forum',
'20', '0', '0', '0');
```

This script will start at deploy time during the creation of the session factory.

Add now the main properties for Hibernate Search:

```
<property name="hibernate.search.lucene_version" value="LUCENE_CURRENT" />
<property name="hibernate.search.default.indexBase" value="forums-indexes"
```

The first property indicates the Lucene version to use. LUCENE_CURRENT is the last version of Lucene currently supported by Hibernate Search. If you need an older version, simply put the number of the version in the value.

The second property indicates the root folder where it put the indexes. This folder is created in the directory where you start the application server or your Maven test. For example, if you start WildFly:

$JBOSS_HOME/bin/standalone.sh

You will find this folder:

$JBOSS_HOME/bin/forum-indexes

Inside forum-indexes, you will find the indexes grouped by the name you have specified with the @Indexed annotation. Here is a sample of our forum:

```
- forum-indexes
  - indexes
        - topics
        - forums
        - posts
        - categories
```

DataSources and connectors

JCA 1.7 is the specification implemented by WildFly 10. This technology lets us specify DataSources or external connectors to connect to external systems such as databases or enterprise technologies such as SAP or messaging systems.

JCA allows through an interface to connect to an external system importing the following contracts:

- **Connection management**: The contract that allows the application server to manage the resource connections. It must follow the JCA specifications. It's important the connections to be managed by a pool. The pool allows to optimize the connections according to the requests of the clients.
- **Security Management**: The contract that guarantees secured access to the DataSources and resource managers.
- **Transaction Management**: The contract that allows the application server to manage transactions through the DataSources and resource managers.

IronJacamar 1.3 is the product implementing JCA. A DataSource is an adapter used exclusively to connect to the relational databases. It has all the properties needed for the connection to the database including the security and the transaction type. In the next paragraph we will show exclusively the DataSource management.

Deployment of the DataSource

A DataSource can be deployed in three modes.

DS file

This file can be put inside the application or deployed with the default instruments provided by WildFly. It is recognized by the extension that it must end with -ds.xml. Here's a sample of jpa-ds.xml:

```
<datasources xmlns="http://www.jboss.org/ironjacamar/schema">
    <xa-datasource
        jndi-name="java:/jboss/datasources/forums_mdefault" pool-
name="forums_mdefault">
        <xa-datasource-class>org.h2.jdbcx.JdbcDataSource
        </xa-datasource-class>
        <xa-datasource-property name="URL">jdbc:h2:mem:test
        </xa-datasource-property>
        <driver>h2</driver>
        <security>
            <user-name>sa</user-name>
        </security>
    </xa-datasource>
</datasources>
```

Each DataSource provides a JNDI name to be called simply. The persistence unit calls the DataSource through it. In this sample we can see the JDBC driver, used to distinguish the database, the connection URL, and the username where to access it. A real DataSource will get a password field too. For simplicity we use H2, an in-memory database used for tests. By default it doesn't need the password.

XA and non XA

You have two choices about the type of DataSource, XADataSource or non-XADataSource. See the following differences.

An XA transaction can be defined as a global transaction because it can work on multiple resources. Unlike the XA transaction, a non-XA transaction always works on one resource. An XA transaction works on a transaction manager that coordinates one or more databases (or different resources, such as JMS) all inside one global transaction. Non-XA transactions often called local transactions also don't need a transaction coordinator because a single resource makes all transaction work itself.

The X/Open group specification defines the XA transactions on distributed and global transactions. **Java Transaction API (JTA)** supports this specification, in a form adapted to Java and DataSources.
XA transactions are not often used but they are very important when you must coordinate more resources in the same time. You could need to coordinate two or more databases more than just one connection or other JCA resources all together. If one of these resources fails by some accident, all the operations come back with a rollback, otherwise the commit will update all resources.

The protocol used by the Transaction Manager coordinator that we have described is called Two Phase Commit or 2PC. It's important this protocol also is supported by the individual resources as the databases and other external resources, else the 2PC doesn't work.

An XA DataSource is a particular DataSource that participates in an XA global transaction. WildFly supports it through Ironjacamar, the official JCA resource adapter implementation and Narayana, the transaction manager implementation in WildFly. A non-XA DataSource can't participate in a global transaction because it will not be read by the transaction manager coordinator.

Activating the deployer

To work correctly with the DataSources, always ensure that the library of the driver is installed in your application server.

A default DataSource is present in WildFly. It can be called through the JNDI name `java:/jboss/datasources/ExampleDS`

This file can be integrated in our application by putting in the META-INF directory and adding a `META-INF | MANIFEST.MF file` including this property:

`Dependencies: org.jboss.as.controller-client,org.jboss.dmr`

It will let you activate the WildFly deployer, so automatically the DataSource will be deployed in the application server.

XML configuration

Another way to install a DataSource in WildFly is through the configuration file. Supposing we are starting WildFly through the `standalone.sh` script command, we can open the relative configuration file situated at:

$JBOSS_HOME/standalone/configuration/standalone.xml

Here is how we configure the ExampleDS:

```
<datasources>
    <datasource jndi-name="java:jboss/datasources/ExampleDS" pool-
name="ExampleDS" enabled="true" use-java-context="true">
        <connection-url>
        jdbc:h2:mem:test;DB_CLOSE_DELAY=-1;DB_CLOSE_ON_EXIT=FALSE
        </connection-url>
        <driver>h2</driver>
        <security>
            <user-name>sa</user-name>
            <password>sa</password>
        </security>
    </datasource>
    <drivers>
        <driver name="h2" module="com.h2database.h2">
            <xa-datasource-class>org.h2.jdbcx.JdbcDataSource
            </xa-datasource-class>
        </driver>
    </drivers>
</datasources>
```

To add a new DataSource, simply encode the new DataSource properties and relative driver inside the DataSources and drivers voices.

Web console

WildFly provides a very useful web console to monitor and install all its components. Here we will see how to configure a new DataSource. In your WildFly instance, connect to `http://localhost:9990/console` with admin/admin as configured in *Chapter 1, Introducing Java EE and Configuring the Development Environment* and go to **Configuration** | **Subsystems** | **Datasources** | **Non-XA** | **Add**. Follow the wizard adding all properties such as the database type that you see in the ds file:

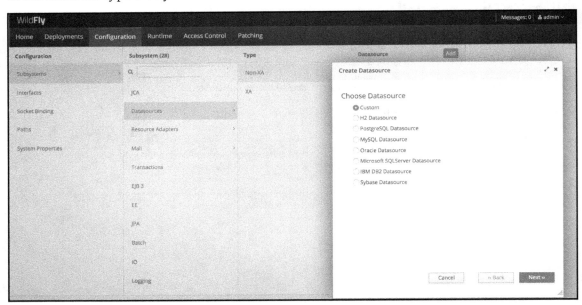

You will see at the end of the wizard the following installed DataSources:

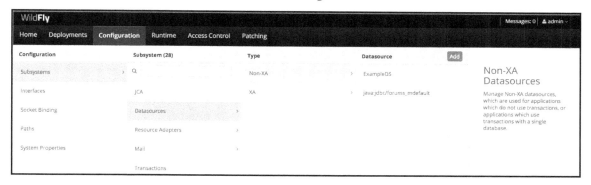

As you can see, there is the default **ExampleDS** Datasource and the **forum_mdefault** just installed.

Summary

In this chapter we have shown all available EE instruments to make persistent a Java object. Now we know the better method to manage the persistent objects in WildFly through the JPA annotations. The persistence is strictly tied to the transactions that we will see deeply in *Chapter 5, Working with Distributed Transactions*. In the next chapter, we will the business logic and the containers that host the persistence objects. Have a good read!

4
Implementing Business Logic

In Chapter 2, *Working with Dependency Injection* and Chapter 3, *Persistence*, we covered beans and entities. These components represent data models, the first is very flexible and the second is driven by the persistence model. Both must be driven by an application layer. An application layer provides operations that manipulate beans, receive requests, and, in the end, return the result requested by a client.

The application layer can receive information from different systems but not all is requested by the client. The art of manipulating beans is called **business logic**. A set of operations tied by a single goal is called a **domain**. Models, APIs, and services are the instruments used to represent a domain.

Java Enterprise provides much of its background to give components that are able to write the business logic. Through the same CDI we saw in Chapter 2, *Working with Dependency Injection*, we can share operations of business that a client can use simply through the injection. The @Provides annotation is made for this purpose. We can write business logic in a method, manipulate injected beans, and then provide a result shared through the @Provides annotation.

Enterprise Java Beans (EJBs) are a more complex instrument for writing business logic. They work inside the CDI context but add a very competitive set of instruments to share data, have a high configurable management of the scopes, and include authentication and authorization. With them, we can choose the type of transaction to use. Unlike the simple CDI, they can be invoked remotely too through protocols such as JNDI, RMI, or IIOP.

EJBs join in a clustering environment. In a simple manner, we decide what data or operations are shared in our cluster. All these properties will be seen in detail in this chapter according to the following points:

- **EJB types and scopes**: You will see when to use an EJB and what scope is preferred according to the situation.
- **EJB synchronous annotations**: All the available annotations for the synchronous EJB. The asynchronous EJB will be seen deeply in `Chapter 11`, *Asynchronous EJB*.
- **Security in the EJB**: We will configure a domain and we will test the authentication and authorization through the EJB.
- **EJB local and remote clients**: We will test EJB calls with custom Java clients.

Scopes in EJB

We will now start analyzing a simple EJB. Here we have a module that provides read and write operations for posts inside a forum. Here is the first sample:

```
@Stateless
public class MyPosts {
    public List<Post> getLastPosts() {...}
    public List<Post> getPostsByDay() {...}
    public void addPost(String topicName, String message) {...}
}
```

`@Stateless` converts a simple class in a stateless session bean, the first EJB type that we are analyzing next.

Stateless means an EJB without state. Each operation done inside this service is missed when the call ends. Suppose this class wants to register the list of requested posts calling the `getPostsByDay` operation:

```
@Stateless
public class MyPosts {
    private List<Post> lastRequestedPosts;

    public List<Post> getPostsByDay() {
        lastRequestedPosts = asList(new Post[]{new Post("first message"),
new Post("second message")})
        ...
    }
    public List<Posts> getLastRequestedPosts() {
        return lastRequestedPosts;
    }
```

```
    . . .
}
```

A local client can call the operation:

```
@Inject
private MyPosts myPosts
. . .
myPosts.getPostsByDay(0);
List<Post> posts = myPosts.getLastRequestedPosts
```

The `getPostsByDay` operation includes caching of the last posts requested by the client; so when we call this operation, we expect two posts registered inside the bean. But when we call the `getLastRequestPosts`, we notice that the size of posts will be 0.

This is because the EJB is without any state. Now try to transform the EJB with this new annotation:

```
@Stateful
public class MyPosts {...}
```

And retry executing the two operations seen before. We will get two posts from the `getLastRequestedPosts` operation.

This EJB now has a state. Stateful Session Beans are declared with the annotation `@Stateful` and they must be used when you need a state for the component. Classic uses of `@Stateful` are a marketplace, where the user needs a temporary list of purchases during navigation in a website.

Singleton

Another type of EJB introduced in Java EE 6 EJB 3.1 is the singleton.

Unlike stateful, when there is not more trace of the client associated with the instance of the EJB, the singleton continues to maintain the state. Whereas a stateful would release the state and reset the instance in the pools of EJB.

There is one Stateful Session Bean per user in a application and only one singleton bean per application for every user.

The singleton has the same role as the `@ApplicationScope` and `@Singleton` seen in `Chapter 2`, *Working with Dependency Injection*. The difference is that by using the EJB singleton, we can use all of the baggage imported by the EJB container as the security information and the transaction management.

To set the singleton, simply annotate your POJO:

```
@Singleton
public class MyHarderPosts {...}
```

The singleton is created when it is executed for the first time. If we need to create the singleton at startup of the EJB container, we simply add the `@Startup` annotation at the class level:

```
@Singleton
@Startup
public class MyHarderPosts {...}
```

A new configuration by EJB 3.1 for the EJB singletons is concurrency.

By default, a singleton has a lock at write. Two components can read the singleton at concurrency and get a lock at write. The lock can be global or for a single method.

The concurrency can be of two types: BEAN or CONTAINER. When using the CONTAINER configuration, the concurrency is managed by the container, so you don't need to implement the concurrency. If set to BEAN, you should implement the thread concurrency using threads or third-party libraries. CONTAINER is the default setting.

Here is a sample configuration of concurrency for a singleton managed by the EJB container and locked at read:

```
@Singleton
@ConcurrencyManagement(CONTAINER)
@Lock(READ)
public class MyHarderPosts {...}
```

Another important feature is dependency management. We can configure the dependencies of a singleton. For example, we would want `MyHarderPosts` to be created only after the creation of other singletons, so it can get important information before being created.

We can add to `MyHarderPosts` the following annotation:

```
...
@DependsOn("messages", "notifications")
public class MyHarderPosts {...}
```

Messages and notifications are two other singletons that insert posts during their creation:

```
@Singleton(name = "messages")
public class Messages {
    @PersistenceContext
    private EntityManager entityManager;

    @PostConstruct
    public void init() {
        entityManager.persist(new Post("messages"));
    }
}

@Singleton(name = "notifications")
public class Notifications {
    @PersistenceContext
    private EntityManager entityManager;

    @PostConstruct
    public void init() {
        entityManager.persist(new Post("notifications"));
    }
}
```

They persist two posts that can be read later by `MyHarderPosts`:

```
...
public class MyHarderPosts ... {
    @PersistenceContext
    private EntityManager entityManager;
    private List<Post> posts;

    @PostConstruct
    public void init() {
        posts = entityManager.createQuery("from Post").getResultList();
    }
...}
```

Local and remote interfaces

By default, an EJB is always local. A local EJB can be invoked only inside the same deployment package. A good coupling for the local EJB is the CDI injection. In previous paragraphs, we used the `@Inject` annotation to inject the EJB. It is only possible if the EJBs are local.

The annotation that represents a local EJB is `@Local`. Our EJB, by default, can be seen as annotated with it:

```
@Singleton
@Local
public class MyPosts {...}
```

The remote EJB can be invoked by a different deployment package through JNDI. Here is an implementation of remote EJB:

```
@Singleton
@Remote
public class MyHarderPosts {...}
```

When we deploy a remote EJB, WildFly automatically creates three RMI stubs named through a JNDI name. Here is a sample of JNDI names created for the singleton `MyHarderPosts`:

```
java:global/business-
logic/MyHarderPosts!it.vige.businesscomponents.businesslogic.MyHarderPosts
java:app/business-
logic/MyHarderPosts!it.vige.businesscomponents.businesslogic.MyHarderPosts
java:module/MyHarderPosts!it.vige.businesscomponents.businesslogic.MyHarder
Posts
java:global/business-logic/MyHarderPosts
java:app/business-logic/MyHarderPosts
java:module/MyHarderPosts
```

Now analyze the first name of the list. It can be divided into four parts.

`java:global` is the root folder where our EJB is located. Global means that the EJB inside of it can be invoked by an external deployment package. Other options are `app`, where access is restricted to the deployment package (in our case, it is called business-logic), and `module`, where access is restricted to the module, or the same EJB.

Business-logic is the name of the application or deployment package. This EJB is deployed inside a `business-logic.jar`; the extension is the default for Java archives or EJB archives.

The application name is by default the file name of the enterprise archive. Often the archive file name contains other info such as the version number. The application name is also used as context path, so it could be useful to change the application name in the `application.xml` deployment descriptor in a simpler mode, as shown here:

```
<application xmlns="http://xmlns.jcp.org/xml/ns/javaee"
    xmlns:xsi="http://www.w3.org/2001/XMLSchema-instance"
    xsi:schemaLocation="http://xmlns.jcp.org/xml/ns/javaee
http://xmlns.jcp.org/xml/ns/javaee/application_7.xsd" version="7">
    <application-name>myapplication</application-name>
    ...
</application>
```

`MyHarderPosts` is the name of the EJB or module. To resolve the problem seen before it is useful to configure the name of the EJB module. The module name can be configured in the `ejb-jar.xml` deployment descriptor shown as follows:

```
<ejb-jar xmlns="http://xmlns.jcp.org/xml/ns/javaee"
xmlns:xsi="http://www.w3.org/2001/XMLSchema-instance"
xsi:schemaLocation="http://xmlns.jcp.org/xml/ns/javaee
http://xmlns.jcp.org/xml/ns/javaee/ejb-jar_3_2.xsd" version="3.2">
    <module-name>remote</module-name>
</ejb-jar>
```

`!it.vige.businesscomponents.businesslogic.MyHarderPosts` is the interface of the EJB. In our case we don't use interfaces, so it takes the name of the implemented EJB class.

 The same JNDI names are created on the local EJB. The difference is that an external client cannot use the global folder of a local bean.

An alternative manner to call an EJB is the `@EJB` annotation:

```
@EJB
private MyHarderPosts;
```

Unlike `@Inject`, the `@EJB` annotation provides a capable set of properties to satisfy all the configurations of the EJB. As an example, we create a new EJB using the interfaces. It's a good practice to use interfaces for EJBs and separate them in a JAR to make them easy to distribute for other systems or applications clients. Here is a local interface:

```
@Local
public interface Topics {...}
```

And its stateless implementation:

```
@Stateless
public class MyTopics implements Topics
```

Now the EJB must be called through interface. If we try to inject it through CDI:

```
@Inject
private Topics topics;
```

We will get an error because internally the EJB container has assigned a different EJB name by default. Also through this annotation we get the same problem:

```
@EJB
private Topics topics;
```

With the EJB annotation we can choose the correct EJB name. So the correct injection will be:

```
@EJB(mappedName="java:module/MyTopics")
private Topics topics;
```

We are using one of the JNDI names created by the container. Here's the complete set for an interfaced EJB:

```
java:global/business-
logic/MyTopics!it.vige.businesscomponents.businesslogic.interfaces.Topics
java:app/business-
logic/MyTopics!it.vige.businesscomponents.businesslogic.interfaces.Topics
java:module/MyTopics!it.vige.businesscomponents.businesslogic.interfaces.To
pics
java:global/business-logic/MyTopics
java:app/business-logic/MyTopics
java:module/MyTopics
```

The scope of the standard JNDI paths as `java:global`, `java:app`, and `java:module` namespaces is reserved for the container and the application client container. All components accessible outside the container through the naming service must be registered with the namespace `java:jboss/exported/`. Only components that are registered in this namespace can be accessed remotely through the naming service.

The last three JNDI names shown in the log message are short forms of the same names. These JNDI names are available only if the EJB implements an applicable interface.

It's a good practice to annotate a bean implementing no interfaces with the `@LocalBean` annotation. It marks the bean as local:

```
@LocalBean
@Stateless
public class RequiredBean {
}
```

Remote clients

WildFly provides an EJB client library to invoke remote EJB components. Your client needs to get it in the class path. Each application server provides its proprietary libraries. There are no real standards for a client implementation because each application server is free to implement its connection protocols but we can use JNDI specifying the implementation classes to use. Here are the common JBoss JNDI properties:

```
prop.put(INITIAL_CONTEXT_FACTORY,
"org.jboss.naming.remote.client.InitialContextFactory");
prop.put(PROVIDER_URL, "http-remoting://127.0.0.1:8080");
```

`INITIAL_CONTEXT_FACTORY` is the interface that communicates with the remoting client implementation and `PROVIDER_URL` represents the connection properties.

A client can be used internally and externally. If externally the `PROVIDER_URL` is mandatory.

The client library is `jboss-ejb-client 2.1.4 Final`. It can be downloaded through Maven. A complete JAR for the clients is inside the client directory of WildFly called `jboss-client.jar`. It includes all clients not only for EJB but also for example JMS, JMX, and connection pools.

We will see in the next paragraphs different types of remote clients, how to create them, configure, and connection samples.

EJB client library

Remote EJB components can be invoked through the EJB client library. This library works inside the `InitialContext`. The library provides a JNDI context factory to invoke the EJBs. You must only configure the value `org.jboss.ejb.client.naming` for the `java.naming.factory.url.pkgs` key in your `InitialContext` instance:

```
Properties prop = new Properties();
prop.put(Context.URL_PKG_PREFIXES, "org.jboss.ejb.client.naming");
Context context = new InitialContext(prop);
```

With this environment property the `IntitalContext` has the URL context factory implementation of the EJB client library to handle the JBoss-specific namespaces for the EJB. Other configuration properties to invoke the EJB must be put in a specific file, the `jboss-ejb-client.properties`. It's important for this file to be inside the class path. Usually, it is put in the root package of your classes. Following is an example:

```
remote.connections=default
remote.connection.default.host=127.0.0.1
remote.connection.default.port=8080
remote.connection.default.connect.options.org.xnio.Options.SASL_POLICY_NOAN
ONYMOUS=false
remote.connection.default.connect.options.org.xnio.Options.SASL_POLICY_NOPL
AINTEXT=false
remote.connection.default.connect.options.org.xnio.Options.SASL_DISALLOWED_
MECHANISMS=${host.auth:JBOSS-LOCAL-USER}
remote.connection.default.username=${username}
remote.connection.default.password=${password}
```

Following is an example to call the EJB through JNDI:

```
context.lookup("ejb:/myapp/remoting/machine!it.vige.businesscomponents.busi
nesslogic.remote.Machine");
```

When you invoke the stateless EJB through JNDI, a proxy is created for the client. There is no server connection until you invoke a method of the EJB. This invocation avoids network problems at the start of the client.

A different achievement is when you must invoke a stateful EJB. The stateful needs a session created server-side, so the invocation will be more sophisticated and a network server connection is mandatory. To invoke a stateful EJB you need to add the extension *stateful* to your JNDI URL.

The EJB client library supports the clustering too. Load balancing and failover are automatically managed by the lookup according to the chosen configuration.

Remote naming project

Another way to invoke the EJB is through the remote naming project. It implements a factory class used to create initial contexts. To configure it you must add the following properties to your initial context creation:

```
Properties prop = new Properties();
prop.put(Context.INITIAL_CONTEXT_FACTORY,
"org.jboss.naming.remote.client.InitialContextFactory");
prop.put(Context.PROVIDER_URL, "http-remoting://127.0.0.1:8080");
prop.put(Context.SECURITY_PRINCIPAL, "username");
prop.put(Context.SECURITY_CREDENTIALS, "password");
prop.put("jboss.naming.client.ejb.context", true);
Context context = new InitialContext(prop);
```

The environment property `jboss.naming.client.ejb.context` indicates that the `InitialContext` implementation created by the remote naming project will create an internal EJB client context too through the EJB client library. It is mandatory to invoke EJB components through the remote naming project:

```
context.lookup("/app/remoting/machine!it.vige.businesscomponents.businesslo
gic.remote.Machine");
```

Unlike the EJB client library, the remote naming project doesn't use the EJB proxy, so the invocation will be entirely remote starting with the lookup. The remote naming project works only for the remote namespace `java:jboss/exported/`. All invoked EJB outside this namespace will end with a `RemoteException`.

In this case use `InitialContext` to handle the lookup of EJB proxies and other objects from the naming service.

Against, the remote naming implementation cannot create an EJB proxy on the client-side so a fine-grained configuration of the EJB client context is not supported. As for the EJB client library it includes configuration for load balancing and session failover.

This client works outside the container, so you need to add the EJB client library to your client. A comfortable manner to install the client library is through pom import so you must not care attention to the sub-dependencies of the library. This pom comprehends the JBoss EJB client library seen in the previous paragraph:

```
<dependency>
    <groupId>org.wildfly</groupId>
    <artifactId>wildfly-ejb-client-bom</artifactId>
    <version>10.1.0.Final</version>
    <type>pom</type>
    <scope>import</scope>
</dependency>
```

Combining the remote naming project and EJB client library

To get the benefits of both approaches it is possible to combine the EJB client library and the remote naming implementation without any restrictions. This approach requires that the environment property jboss.naming.client.ejb.context is set to false. Then, the remote naming project creates no internal EJB client context.

To invoke remote EJB components, this approach requires in addition to add the URL package prefix org.jboss.ejb.client.naming. With this environment property, the InitialContext creates the necessary EJB client context to handle the ejb:namespace via the URL context factory implementation of the EJB client library. The EJB client context can now be configured separately with the jboss-ejb-client.properties file.

The only disadvantage is that this approach requires a configuration of the EJB client context and the remote naming project. The benefit is that only one InitialContext is required to invoke EJB components with all optimizations and configuration capabilities of the EJB client library, and the possibility to lookup other objects with the same InitialContext:

```
Properties prop = new Properties();
prop.put(Context.INITIAL_CONTEXT_FACTORY,
"org.jboss.naming.remote.client.InitialContextFactory");
prop.put(Context.PROVIDER_URL, "http-remoting://127.0.0.1:8080");
prop.put(Context.SECURITY_PRINCIPAL, "username");
prop.put(Context.SECURITY_CREDENTIALS, "password");
prop.put("jboss.naming.client.ejb.context", false);
prop.put(Context.URL_PKG_PREFIXES, "org.jboss.ejb.client.naming");
Context context = new InitialContext(prop);
```

Local and remote homes

EJB 3.x gives a new smart approach to building business logic in respect to the old 2.x. For now the home interfaces are excluded but still guarantees the retro compatibility with EJB 2.x. Once you need the home interface to call an EJB.

The home interface provides the functions to instantiate and destroy the bean. These interfaces are now as annotations and interfaces. The annotations can be used to inject the homes in our components.

The home interface is actually a factory object. When you write an EJB home interface, you must extend the interface `EJBHome`, and provide override methods for all the desired methods `create()` and `find()`. An object implementing the home interface can be automatically generated by the tools of the EJBs. Here is a sample for a remote home of a stateful:

```
public interface Ejb21StateRemoteHome extends EJBHome {
    public Ejb21StateRemote create() throws CreateException,
RemoteException;
    public Ejb21StateRemote create(String message) throws CreateException,
RemoteException;
    public Ejb21StateRemote create(Collection<?> messages) throws
CreateException, RemoteException;
}
```

The EJB object also called a remote object, is a wrapper. It is used in the container between the client and the business logic. It manages the setup and the shutdown tasks (such as restoring data state, opening transactions, or saving the data store) immediately before and after the enterprise bean is called.

The EJB object is generated by the container, so nothing must be written on it. Only your EJB has to implement an interface called remote interface or `EJBObject` interface that extends the interface `javax.ejb.EJBObject` and provides method signatures for all the business methods. The server automatically generates a Java class that implements the remote interface. This object is registered through RMI. You can use the home interface to get a reference to it. So the home interface can be defined as a factory object.

It is important your EJB implements the `ejbCreate()` method too for each `create()` method in the home interface. The same thing applies to the `ejbFind()`/`find()` methods.

`Ejb21StateRemote` is the mandatory remote interface if you want use an EJB 2.x style. Here is how it is written:

```
public interface Ejb21StateRemote extends EJBObject {
int int go(int speed) throws RemoteException;
    // other methods.....
}
```

Here is a bean implementation built with the remote home and the remote interface:

```
@Stateful(name = "ejb21StateEngineRemote")
@RemoteHome(value = Ejb21StateRemoteHome.class)
@Remote(value = Ejb21StateRemote.class)
public class Ejb21StateEngineRemoteBean implements Ejb21StateRemote {
    @Init
 public void init() {
        ...
    }
    @Init
 public void init(String message) {
        ...
    }
    @Init
    public void init(Collection<?> messages) {
        ...
    }
}
```

The remote interface forces the bean to implement all the methods defined in the remote interface. If we use only the annotation as seen before we have to pay attention to not forget the implementations.

The home interface can be injected as a common EJB. To instantiate the bean you can use the `create()` methods. Here is a sample of an injection of a home interface and create:

```
@EJB
private Ejb21RemoteHome ejb21EngineRemoteHome;
...
Ejb21StateRemote ejb21StateEngineRemote2 =
ejb21StateEngineRemoteHome.create();
Ejb21StateRemote ejb21StateEngineRemote3 =
ejb21StateEngineRemoteHome.create("input data");
Ejb21StateRemote ejb21StateEngineRemote4 =
ejb21StateEngineRemoteHome.create(new ArrayList<String>());
...
```

Because the bean implementation is marked as `@Stateful`, the `create()` methods will create different instances of the bean.

The `@Init` annotation works together with the `create()` method of the home interface. In our example, executing, for example, the `create("input data")` method, automatically will be used by the constructor:

```
@Init
public void init(String message) {
    ...
}
```

The `@EJBs` annotation introduced in EJB 3.0 lets you configure a set of EJB 2.x in a bean and inject them through JNDI. Here is a sample of EJB 3.x that provides two EJB 2.x:

```
@Stateless
@EJBs({
@EJB(name = "injected1", beanInterface = Ejb21Local.class),
@EJB(name = "injected2", beanInterface = Ejb21StateLocal.class)
})
public class BeanCallingOtherBeans {
    public Ejb21Local getEjb21Local() {
        try {
            InitialContext jndiContext = new InitialContext();
            Ejb21LocalHome sessionHome = (Ejb21LocalHome)
            jndiContext.lookup("java:comp/env/injected1");
            return sessionHome.create();
        } catch (Exception e) {
            throw new RuntimeException(e);
    }
    }
    public Ejb21StateLocal getEjb21StateLocal() {
        try {
            InitialContext jndiContext = new InitialContext();
            Ejb21StateLocalHome sessionHome = (Ejb21StateLocalHome)
jndiContext.lookup("java:comp/env/injected2");
            return sessionHome.create();
        } catch (Exception e) {
            throw new RuntimeException(e);
    }
    }
}
```

The names declared in @EJBs let the beans be invoked locally from a bean inside the same environment. Note how the beans need the home interface to be invoked.

The session context

Our EJB have with them a context containing all the memory information of the current bean. The state of the bean is propagated thanks to this context and we can manipulate it inside our EJB container. The session context can be injected in our bean as a resource:

```
@Resource
private SessionContext context;
```

From it we can receive the following objects:

- **Principal**: The object containing the user logged information if the authentication is present
- **Homes**: We can estrapolate the implemented home interfaces if they are present
- **Remote and local interfaces**: We can estrapolate the local and remote interfaces if they are present
- **Context data**: The map where we register the variables of our bean. If the bean is a stateful they will be persisted in all the lifecycles of the bean

We have the isCallerInRole() function too. In our EJB we can query a role and see if our EJB has the correct permissions.

The session context can be manipulated implementing the SessionBean interface too:

```
@Stateless(name = "ejb21EngineLocal")
@LocalHome(value = Ejb21LocalHome.class)
@Local(value = Ejb21Local.class)
public class Ejb21EngineLocalBean implements Ejb21Local, SessionBean {
    ...
    @Override
    public void setSessionContext(SessionContext ctx) throws EJBException,
RemoteException {... }
    @Override
    public void ejbRemove() throws EJBException, RemoteException {... }
    @Override
    public void ejbActivate() throws EJBException, RemoteException {... }
    @Override
    public void ejbPassivate() throws EJBException, RemoteException {... }
    ...}
```

Through this interface we can:

- Set a custom session context. It will be set during the first operation of a bean.
- Define new operations after the removal of the bean.
- Define new operations after the activation or passivation of the bean. These operations work when the bean exits the pool or enter again depending on the invocations of the clients. They are useful only for the statefuls.

 This class is a very old feature deriving from EJB 1.1. The RemoteException has no sense in a local bean. So it will be ignored by the local beans.

A modern and better mode to manage the activation and the passivation is provided since EJB 3.0. Simply add these annotations to your methods:

```
@Remove
public void remove() {
  logger.info("the bean is removing");
}
@PostActivate
public void activate() {
    logger.info("the bean is active");
}
@PrePassivate
public void passivate() {
    logger.info("the bean is passivating");
}
```

EJB 3.x provides the EntityBean interface to create an old style Entity 2.x. Here's a sample:

```
public class Topic implements EntityBean {
    @Override
    public void setEntityContext(EntityContext ctx) throws EJBException,
RemoteException {...}
    @Override
    public void unsetEntityContext() throws EJBException, RemoteException
{...}
    @Override
    public void ejbRemove() throws RemoveException, EJBException,
RemoteException {...}
    @Override
    public void ejbActivate() throws EJBException, RemoteException {...}
    @Override
    public void ejbPassivate() throws EJBException, RemoteException {...}
    @Override
```

```
public void ejbLoad() throws EJBException, RemoteException {...}
@Override
public void ejbStore() throws EJBException, RemoteException {...}
```

This monumental class finds its sense during a migration from the Entity 2.x to the JPA API. Since Java EE 6, they decided to remove the retro compatibility and leave only the essentials for the migrations. This class as the `SessionBean` is one of them.

Implementing the remote interface as `EJBObject`, we find other old methods useful to manipulate the session context:

```
@Override
public EJBHome getEJBHome() throws RemoteException {...}
@Override
public Object getPrimaryKey() throws RemoteException {...}
@Override
public void remove() throws RemoteException, RemoveException {...}
@Override
public Handle getHandle() throws RemoteException {...}
@Override
public boolean isIdentical(EJBObject ejbo) throws RemoteException {...}
```

They can be considered as utilities. They are an alternative mode to get the order of the methods:

- The remote home interface
- An identifier of the bean as primary key
- An additional remove operations
- An handler that returns the remote interface of the bean
- An utility to compare the remote interfaces of the bean

All these utilities don't work in the container. They can be used only programmatically. It's a similar thing for the `EJBLocalObject`:

```
@Override
public EJBLocalHome getEJBLocalHome() throws EJBException {...}
@Override
public Object getPrimaryKey() throws EJBException {...}
@Override
public void remove() throws RemoveException, EJBException {... }
@Override
public boolean isIdentical(EJBLocalObject obj) throws EJBException {... }
```

It's a local interface so the RemoteException is excluded.

Transactions

All EJB are transactional. If they start in a transaction they automatically are configured inside the transaction. A simple way to manage the transactions is through the SessionSynchronization interface. Here's a stateful sample implementing it:

```
@Stateful(name = "stateEngineRemote")
public class StateEngineRemoteBean implements SessionSynchronization {
    ...
    @Override
    public void afterBegin() throws EJBException, RemoteException {
        logger.info("the bean is begun");
    }
    @Override
    public void beforeCompletion() throws EJBException, RemoteException {
        logger.info("the bean is completing");
    }
    @Override
    public void afterCompletion(boolean committed) throws EJBException,
RemoteException {
        logger.info("the bean is completed");
    }
...}
```

Here's a transactional client that invokes the EJB:

```
@Inject
private UserTransaction userTransaction;
@EJB
private StateEngineLocal stateEngineLocal
...
try {
    userTransaction.begin();
    stateEngineLocal.go(1);
    userTransaction.commit();
catch(Exception ex) {
    try {
        userTransaction.rollback();
    catch(Exception e) {...}
}
```

After the beginning the transaction, the `afterBegin` method of the bean will start. During the commit two methods will start, the `beforeCompletion` before the end and the `afterCompletion` after the commit.

Since EJB 3.1, the same thing can be done through annotations:

```
@Stateful(name = "stateEngineLocal")
public class StateEngineLocalBean... {
   @AfterBegin
   public void afterBegin() {
      logger.info("the bean is begun");
   }
   @BeforeCompletion
   public void beforeCompletion() {
      logger.info("the bean is completing");
   }
   @AfterCompletion
   public void afterCompletion() {
      logger.info("the bean is completed");
   }
...}
```

If the bean is stateless and the client doesn't use the transactions, it will execute the `afterBegin`, `beforeCompletion`, and `afterCompletion` at each invocation of the operations.

A stateful never will work if it's declared as `SessionSynchronization` and the client doesn't use the transactions because after the first operation invocation it will be removed once executing the `afterCompletion` method, so at the second operation invocation the client will lose the ID of the bean and a `javax.ejb.NoSuchEJBException` will be thrown.

Exceptions

A more elegant manner to manage the rollback for a transaction is through the `@ApplicationException` annotation. This annotation is added in an exception to ensure the rollback when it's thrown so you don't need to write it in your code. Here's a sample of a rollback managed with an exception:

```
@ApplicationException(rollback = true)
public class SimpleAppException extends Exception {...
}
```

The `rollback` attribute establishes that the exception if thrown, will start the rollback. The other attribute is the inheritance. It's true by default. With it we could write an exception child to throw instead of it:

```
public class RequiredException extends SimpleAppException {
...}
```

In this case either the `RequiredException` is thrown or the `SimpleAppException`, the rollback will be thrown because `RequiredException` inherits the `SimpleAppException`.

Here's how the transaction code will become:

```
@Inject
private UserTransaction userTransaction;
@EJB
private StateEngineLocal stateEngineLocal
...
userTransaction.begin();
stateEngineLocal.go(1);
userTransaction.commit();
```

Transaction management annotation

The `@TransactionManagement` annotation establishes whether the transactions of a bean will be managed by bean or container. If there are not specified values or the annotation is not declared, `CONTAINER` is the default. Here is a sample of a `BEAN` transaction:

```
@TransactionManagement(BEAN)
public class StateEngineLocalBean... {...}
```

Here are the differences:

- `BEAN`: The EJB must implement the conditions of the commit, must inject the `UserTransaction` and decide when to start and end the transaction.
- `CONTAINER`: All of this is automatic. The EJB doesn't need to inject the `UserTransaction`, and it must not decide when to begin or commit the transaction. All this is done by the container.

Transaction attributes

The transaction attribute annotation establishes the achievement of the bean inside a transaction. The attribute can be of five types:

- MANDATORY: If a client calls the method of an enterprise bean while the client is associated with a transaction context, the container calls the enterprise bean's method in the same client's transaction context.
- NOT_SUPPORTED: In this case, the container calls an enterprise bean method whose NOT_SUPPORTED transaction attribute with a non specified transaction context.
- NEVER: The client must call without a transaction context, otherwise an error is generated.
- SUPPORTS: If the client calls an enterprise bean with a transaction context, the container will execute the same steps as shown in the REQUIRED case.
- REQUIRED: If a client calls the method of an enterprise bean while the client is associated with a transaction context, the container calls the method in the same client's transaction context. If not declared it's the default.
- REQUIRED_NEW: The container must call a method of an enterprise bean whose transaction attribute is set with a new transaction context.

The TransactionAttribute annotation can be declared globally at class level or in a single method. Each method could be declared with a different transaction attribute. Here is a sample of a method of declaration of a bean:

```
@Override
@TransactionAttribute(MANDATORY)
public int retry(int speed) {
    return this.speed -= speed;
}
```

Security

Provided by the CDI javax.annotation.security package, it contains all we need to ensure an enterprise component as an EJB or a servlet. With these annotations, each bean can be authorized with default or custom roles by simply adding them in the bean that you want authorized. See now how to use these annotations. We need an EJB container because at difference of Weld it already works under an authentication and authorization system.

Start with an interface:

```
public interface Caller {
      <V> V call(Callable<V> callable) throws Exception;
}
```

And two actors, the manager and the employee representing with implementations of the `Caller` interface. The manager runs with a role called `Manager`:

```
@RunAs("Manager")
public class ManagerBean implements Caller {
   @PermitAll
   public <V> V call(Callable<V> callable) throws Exception {
      return callable.call();
   }
}
```

And the employee with a role called `Employee`:

```
@RunAs("Employee")
public class EmployeeBean implements Caller {
   @PermitAll
   public <V> V call(Callable<V> callable) throws Exception {
     return callable.call();
   }
}
```

Add a third bean that represents actions to do:

```
public class Movies {
    private List<Movie> movies = new ArrayList<Movie>();
    @RolesAllowed({ "Employee", "Manager" })
    public void addMovie(Movie movie) throws Exception {
        movies.add(movie);
    }
    @RolesAllowed({ "Manager" })
    public void deleteMovie(Movie movie) throws Exception {
        movies.remove(movie);
    }
    @PermitAll
    public List<Movie> getMovies() throws Exception {
        return movies;
    }
}
```

Our annotations permits you to assign roles to the operations. In this case, the manager can add a movie and delete it. The employee can add a movie but they cannot delete it. Both can read the list of movies.

Now execute the injection:

```
@EJB(mappedName = "java:module/Movies")
private Movies movies;
@EJB(mappedName = "java:module/ManagerBean")
private Caller manager;
@EJB(mappedName = "java:module/EmployeeBean")
private Caller employee;
```

And execute the addition of movies through the `manager` role:

```
manager.call(new Callable<Object>() {
        public Object call() throws Exception {
                Movie movie1 = new Movie("Sabina Guzzanti", "La trattativa",
2014);
                movies.addMovie(movie1);
                List<Movie> list = movies.getMovies();
                movies.deleteMovie(movie1);
                        return null;
                }
        });
}
```

It normally works.

Now execute the operation using the `employee` role:

```
employee.call(new Callable<Object>() {
        public Object call() throws Exception {
                Movie movie1 = new Movie("Sabina Guzzanti", "La trattativa",
2014);
                movies.addMovie(movie1);
                List<Movie> list = movies.getMovies();
                movies.deleteMovie(movie1);
                return null;
        }
});
```

It will fail to delete the movie, throwing an `EJBAccessException`!

We can try to execute an operation of the `Movie` class through an unauthorized user too:

```
movies.addMovie(new Movie("Sabina Guzzanti", "La trattativa", 2014));
```

It again will fail throwing the `EJBAccessException` exception.

EJB container configuration

The EJB container is highly configurable by web console and XML file. For example, if we start WildFly through the command `standalone.sh` we will have a configuration as:

```xml
<subsystem xmlns="urn:jboss:domain:ejb3:1.2">
  <session-bean>
    <stateless>
      <bean-instance-pool-ref pool-name="slsb-strict-max-pool"/>
    </stateless>
    <stateful default-access-timeout="5000" cache-ref="simple" clustered-cache-ref="clustered"/>
    <singleton default-access-timeout="5000"/>
  </session-bean>
  <entity-bean>
    <bean-instance-pool-ref pool-name="entity-strict-max-pool"/>
  </entity-bean>
  <pools>
    <bean-instance-pools>
      <strict-max-pool name="slsb-strict-max-pool" max-pool-size="20"
instance-acquisition-timeout="5" instance-acquisition-timeout-
unit="MINUTES"/>
      <strict-max-pool name="entity-strict-max-pool" max-pool-size="100"
instance-acquisition-timeout="5" instance-acquisition-timeout-
unit="MINUTES"/>
    </bean-instance-pools>
  </pools>
  <caches>
    <cache name="simple" aliases="NoPassivationCache"/>
    <cache name="passivating" passivation-store-ref="file"
aliases="SimpleStatefulCache"/>
    <cache name="clustered" passivation-store-ref="infinispan"
aliases="StatefulTreeCache"/>
  </caches>
  <passivation-stores>
    <file-passivation-store name="file"/>
    <cluster-passivation-store name="infinispan" cache-container="ejb"/>
  </passivation-stores>
  <remote connector-ref="remoting-connector" thread-pool-name="default"/>
  <thread-pools>
```

```
      <thread-pool name="default">
         <max-threads count="10"/>
         <keepalive-time time="100" unit="milliseconds"/>
      </thread-pool>
   </thread-pools>
   <iiop enable-by-default="false" use-qualified-name="false"/>
   <in-vm-remote-interface-invocation pass-by-value="false"/>
</subsystem>
```

Session beans

In this section we will show the main synchronous EJB configurations: Stateless, Stateful and Singleton analyzing the configuration file shown over.

Stateless

This element is used to configure the instance pool that is used by default for stateless session beans. If it is not present, stateless session beans are not pooled but are instead created on demand for every invocation. The instance pool can be overridden on a per deployment or per bean level using jboss-ejb3.xml or the org.jboss.ejb3.annotation.Pool annotation. The instance pools themselves are configured in the <pools> element.

Stateful

This element is used to configure Stateful Session Beans:

- default-access-timeout: This attribute specifies the default time concurrent invocations on the same bean instance and will wait to acquire the instance lock. It can be overridden via the deployment descriptor or via the javax.ejb.AccessTimeout annotation.

- cache-ref: This attribute is used to set the default cache for non-clustered beans. It can be overridden by jboss-ejb3.xml, or via the org.jboss.ejb3.annotation.Cache annotation.

- clustered-cache-ref: This attribute is used to set the default cache for clustered beans.

Singleton

This element is used to configure **Singleton Session Beans**:

- `default-access-timeout`: This attribute specifies the default time concurrent invocations will wait to acquire the instance lock. It can be overridden via the deployment descriptor or via the `javax.ejb.AccessTimeout` annotation.

Entity beans

As for the Session beans section we will analyse the configuration for the entity beans. This element is used to configure the behavior for EJB2 entity beans:

`<bean-instance-pool-ref>` : This element is used to configure the instance pool that is used by default for entity beans. If it is not present, they are not pooled but are instead created on demand for every invocation. The instance pool can be overridden on a per deployment or per bean level using `jboss-ejb3.xml` or the `org.jboss.ejb3.annotation.Pool` annotation. The instance pools themselves are configured in the `<pools>` element.

Remote

This is used to enable remote EJB invocations. It specifies the remoting connector to use (as defined in the remoting subsystem configuration), and the thread pool to use for remote invocations.

Thread pools

This is used to configure the thread pools used by async, timer, and remote invocations.

IIOP

This is used to enable IIOP (that is, CORBA) invocations of EJBs. If this element is present then the JacORB subsystem must also be installed. It supports the following two attributes:

- `enable-by-default`: If this is true then all EJBs with EJB2.x home interfaces are exposed via IIOP, otherwise they must be explicitly enabled via `jboss-ejb3.xml`

- `use-qualified-name`: If this is true then EJBs are bound to the CORBA naming context with a binding name that contains the application and modules name of the deployment (for example, `myear/myejbjar/MyBean`), if this is false the default binding name is simply the bean name

In VM remote interface invocations

By default remote interface invocations use pass by value, as required by the EJB specification. This element can be used to enable pass by reference, which can give you a performance boost. Note that WildFly will do a shallow check to see if the caller and the EJB have access to the same class definitions, which means if you are passing something such as a `List<MyObject>`, WildFly only checks the list to see if it is the same class definition on the call and EJB side. If the top-level class definition is the same, JBoss will make the call using pass by reference, which means that if `MyObject` or any objects beneath it are loaded from different class loaders, you would get a `ClassCastException`. If the top-level class definitions are loaded from different class loaders, JBoss will use pass by value. JBoss cannot do a deep check of all of the classes to ensure no `ClassCastExceptions` will occur because doing a deep check would eliminate any performance boost you would have received by using call by reference. It is recommended that you configure pass by reference only on callers that you are sure will use the same class definitions and not globally. This can be done via a configuration in the `jboss-ejb-client.xml` as shown as follows.

To configure a caller/client use pass by reference, you configure your top-level deployment with a `META-INF/jboss-ejb-client.xml` containing:

```
<jboss-ejb-client xmlns="urn:jboss:ejb-client:1.0">
    <client-context>
        <ejb-receivers local-receiver-pass-by-value="false"/>
    </client-context>
</jboss-ejb-client>
```

Summary

In this chapter we have shown deeply how to write the business logic for our beans and how the synchronous EJB works in WildFly 10. Now we can write an EJB, share it to the other enterprise components or call them through remote clients. We have shown how the EJBs work together with the transactions, that they are the main goal when you use a Java Enterprise compliant application server but we have not shown deeply the transactions. This will be the goal of the next chapter.

5
Working with Distributed Transactions

Transactions and transactional support are crucial for many Java EE applications. Java EE provides thorough and solid support for transactions on WildFly 10 in the form of JTA 1.2.

Java Transaction Architecture (**JTA**) is the delegate architecture implemented in WildFly to manage transactions.

This chapter begins with a brief overview of transaction terminology, including **ACID** (**Atomic, Consistent, Isolated**, and **Durable**) properties and transaction isolation levels as well as the concepts of local and distributed transactions. It then describes various distributed transaction scenarios, such as reading a data from a business component and updating information in a database table within a single transaction. The chapter covers the programmatic transaction model provided by JTA and also describes the declarative transaction model used with Java EE components.

Transaction support is an essential part of many Java and EE APIs such as JDBC and EJB. Since JPA, described in `Chapter 3`, *Persistence*, represents the standard persistence model for Java EE, JPA 2.1 have extensive support for JTA-based transactions. Hibernate, the open source persistence API discussed in `Chapter 3`, *Persistence*, also provides support for JTA-based transactions.

Narayana 5.3 is the transaction manager implementation used by WildFly 10. It is based on Arjuna core, a historical transaction manager used since JBoss AS 5.x and now included in Narayana. Narayana includes the engine used to process standard and custom transactional annotations. It works inside WildFly containers; however, it can be used as a standalone transaction manager as well.

In this chapter, we will analyze the following focal points:

- Overview of the transactions. Why and when to use them.
- Transaction types in Java EE and supported transactions in WildFly 10.
- How to configure the transactions in EJB and DataSources.

Transaction overview

Before starting with the details, we need to understand the basic terminologies. A transaction is a working unit, a set of operations that can succeed or fail in a single atomic unit. Transactions ensure that a unit is either completely executed or completely rolled back. Transactions are important for a secure and solid working of critical operations in enterprise applications. Several resources work in a transaction, for example, business components, databases, and services.

The next image shows a simple concept of a transaction. A transaction consists of three main operations: **begin**, **commit**, and **rollback**. The transaction is started by the `begin` operation. A series of steps is performed, and if all succeeds in the end, the `commit` operation is executed. The transaction must be rolled back through the `rollback` operation if some error occurs.

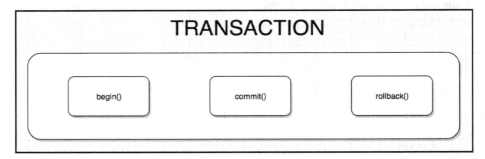

For example, we want to move money from our checking account to our savings account. Consider two operations: an operation to put off the money from the checking account and another operation to add the money to the savings account. Both the operations have to either fail together or succeed together. Credit and debit operations must work together in the same transaction. So for this transaction, the following operations must be executed:

- Begin
- Debit the checking account

- Credit the savings account
- Commit if successful and roll back in case of failure

Therefore, it's important that the entire transaction either succeeds or fails as a single piece. Without the transaction, the success or failure of just one operation in this transaction based on two operations will leave the system and the accounts in a very inconsistent state. The application cannot be used if the transactions are not correctly implemented.

Transactions have evolved over the years, always becoming simpler to use. JTA 1.2 introduces a very innovative annotation to make beans transactional. In Java EE 7, JTA 1.2 and JCA 1.7 are a very good couple for managing transactions. JTA lets us start a transaction; it provides us the begin, commit and rollback methods. JCA lets us propagate them inside the resources. For example, when an error is thrown in a database or some other external system, it must advice the JTA transaction to throw rollback. This is done through the resource adapter implementing the JCA specifications. Now, let's look at some examples of transactions working together in a H2 database. On returning to the banking transaction, we will obtain an account entity:

```
@Entity
public class Account {
    @Id
    private int number;
    private double credit;

    public int getNumber() {
        return number;
    }
    public void setNumber(int number) {
        this.number = number;
    }
    public double getCredit() {
        return credit;
    }
    public void setCredit(double credit) {
        this.credit = credit;
    }
    public void add(double credit) {
        this.credit += credit;
    }
    public void less(double credit) throws Exception {
        if (credit > this.credit)
            throw new Exception();
        this.credit -= credit;
    }
}
```

We will also obtain the `Bank` bean that manages the accounts:

```
public class Bank {
    @PersistenceContext
    private EntityManager entityManager;

    public void move(int accountToTake, int accountToPut, double amount)
throws Exception {
        Account from = entityManager.find(Account.class, accountToTake);
        Account to = entityManager.find(Account.class, accountToPut);
        from.less(amount);
        to.add(amount);
        entityManager.merge(from);
        entityManager.merge(to);
    }
}
```

This lets you move an amount between the two accounts. The first example represents the `Bank` as a stateless EJB:

```
@Stateless
public class PoorBank extends Bank {
}
```

In our database, let us assume that we have these two accounts:

```
INSERT INTO ACCOUNT(NUMBER, CREDIT) VALUES (123, 5555.87);
INSERT INTO ACCOUNT(NUMBER, CREDIT) VALUES (345, 2555.87);
```

Now, let us execute the move of the amount. Inject the stateless, as follows:

```
@EJB
private PoorBank poorBank;
```

Now, let's execute the move operation of 566.9 $ between the accounts 123 and 345:

```
poorBank.move(123, 345, 566.9);
```

Everything is okay. The amount from account 123 is reduced by 566.9 $ to 4988.97 $ and the amount in account 345 is increased to 3122.77 $. Now, use these two new accounts:

```
INSERT INTO ACCOUNT(NUMBER, CREDIT) VALUES (1231, 5555.87);
INSERT INTO ACCOUNT(NUMBER, CREDIT) VALUES (3451, 2555.87);
```

Now, try to execute a wrong operation; for example, try to move an amount greater than the current amount:

```
poorBank.move(1231, 3451, 20000);
```

As a result, we will see that the amount in the account 1231 is not reduced by 20000 $ and will remain 5555.87 $; however, the account 3451 is increased by 20000 $ to 22555.87 $. This is a bug for the bank and it risks the default!

BMT and CMT

This transaction succeeded because the EJB by default is not transactional. To resolve this error, we can make two changes:

- **Manage BMT**: A bean managed transaction. Here, we have to manually manage the transaction through the `UserTransaction` object. This object is an interface that provides the operations of begin, rollback, and commit as seen earlier. We should write the move operation as follows:

```
@Inject
private UserTransaction userTransaction;
...
try {
    userTransaction.begin();
    poorBank.move(2231, 4451, 20000);
    userTransaction.commit();
} catch (Exception ex) {
    try {
        userTransaction.rollback();
    } catch (IllegalStateException | SecurityException |
            SystemException e) {
    }
}
```

- **Manage CMT**: A container managed transaction. Here, we don't need to write the transactional logic because we can use the container that automatically manages the commits and rollbacks. To do this, Java EE 7 introduces a new annotation transaction to insert in EJB or any other bean:

```
@Stateless
@Transactional(rollbackOn = Exception.class)
public class PoorBank extends Bank {
}
```

If we execute one of these two examples, the result we will obtain is that the amount in the account 1231 is not reduced, thus remaining 5555.87 $ and amount in the account 3451 does not increase, thus remaining 2555.87 $. The bank is safe! The @Transactional annotation by default is a REQUIRED type, but we configure it with the type REQUIRED_NEW, MANDATORY, NEVER ,SUPPORTS or NOT_SUPPORTED transaction as seen in Chapter 4, *Implementing Business Logic*. Here is an example of a MANDATORY transaction type:

```
@Transactional(value=TxType.MANDATORY, rollbackOn = Exception.class)
```

The rollbackOn property is very important as it establishes the exceptions list that can start the rollback. Our case is a generic exception because it maps the following method of accounts that generates an error:

```
public void less(double credit) throws Exception {
    if (credit > this.credit)
        throw new Exception();
    this.credit -= credit;
}
```

By default, an unchecked exception will generate a rollback, so we will get a bad transaction unless we define it. The other good parameter is the dontRollbackOn property. It establishes the exceptions list that should not be a part of the rollback. So, the exceptions defined in the dontRollbackOn property will not start the rollback.

 The @Transactional annotation can be used not only for EJB, but also for simple beans. It's a big innovation in Java EE 7, pointing to the simplicity.

Descriptor configuration

If you want use an XML configuration instead of annotations, you need the `ejb-jar.xml` file in the META-INF directory of your jar package. Let us look at an example of transaction configured by a descriptor file. Consider the remote interface:

```
@Remote
public interface XMLRemote {
    int transactionStatus();
}
```

Now, consider the bean implementation:

```
@Stateless(name = "bank")
public class XMLBank implements XMLRemote {

    @Resource(lookup="java:jboss/TransactionManager")
    private TransactionManager transactionManager;

    @Override
    public int transactionStatus() {
        try {
            return transactionManager.getStatus();
        } catch (SystemException e) {
            throw new RuntimeException(e);
        }
    }
}
```

In this bean, we can see how to inject the transaction manager. This object is very similar to the user transaction but it exposes more functions. Here, the new functions of the transaction manager are as follows:

- **Suspend**: When launched, the thread is out of the transaction
- **Resume**: When launched, the thread takes again the transaction

These are very powerful methods, so it's better to use the transaction manager inside the beans and expose only to the user transaction. In this example of EJB, we received the status of the transaction to test the configuration.

The configuration of the transaction for EJB is as follows:

```
<enterprise-beans>
    <session>
        <ejb-name>bank</ejb-name>
        <session-type>Stateless</session-type>
        <transaction-type>Container</transaction-type>
    </session>
</enterprise-beans>
<assembly-descriptor>
    <container-transaction>
        <method>
            <ejb-name>bank</ejb-name>
            <method-intf>Remote</method-intf>
            <method-name>transactionStatus</method-name>
        </method>
        <trans-attribute>Never</trans-attribute>
    </container-transaction>
</assembly-descriptor>
```

The transaction type is a container by default. We show it only to expose the configuration. As for the @Transactional annotation that can be configured at class and method level, the same action can be performed with a descriptor. We can see an example of method configuration. We configured the transaction attribute to never for the transactionStatus method of the bank EJB. Now, let's see a remote client that tests the bean.

Remote transaction

WildFly has an interesting tool to call remote objects from a client, the EJBClient class provided by the jboss-ejb-client 2.0.2 library. Here is an example to take a user transaction from a remote client:

```
String hostname = InetAddress.getLocalHost().getHostName().toLowerCase();
final UserTransaction userTransaction =
EJBClient.getUserTransaction(hostname);
```

The client needs to know the name of the instance initiated by WildFly. By default, WildFly starts an instance called with a lower case hostname of the machine. Once you acquire the hostname, you can take the user transaction.

If we do the lookup of the bank EJB and execute the `transactionStatus` method, we will get 6 as the status number responding to the `STATUS_NO_TRANSACTION` field of the `javax.transaction.Status` interface. This is never configured in XML.

If we execute this method after beginning the transaction, we will get `EJBException` because the bean is not transactional:

```
try {
    userTransaction.begin();
    bean.transactionStatus();
} catch (EJBException e) {
    logger.info("the transaction is not supported");
}
```

Transactions make the development of applications simple because developers do not need to manage all the errors and exceptions that can occur while working with resources inside a shared network. When these error and exception conditions occur, transactions resolve the failure through the recovery operations, for example, by restoring the shared resources to a consistent state. The application must only receive an exception generated from the underlying transactional service; everything else is done by the transaction manager. This simplified model frees the developers from writing complex concurrency issues along multiple users and along multiple and potentially distributed applications that do access at the same time to the same resource.

Transactions and resource managers

Transactions are performed to work together with one or more resources, as we've already mentioned before. Usually, the resources are managed by a database. The most used databases are Oracle, H2, MySQL, IBM DB2, and Sybase. The other type of resources, for example, message-oriented middleware destinations can be transactional. A transaction does not directly know the resources. The resources are managed by the resource manager; the resource manager is built into the product that manages the resources (database or MOM). A transaction works with the resource managers through the transaction manager, also known as **Transaction Processing Monitor** (**TP**). The transaction manager can also be found embedded inside the resource manager itself, such as some relational databases and messaging services and within Java EE containers and application servers. The following figure shows the relationship among resources, TP monitors, and resource managers.

The transaction manager passes the same transaction context to all the resource managers joined in the transaction. The transaction manager has a very important role of keeping track of the all transactions that work in the resource manager.

Here is a figure that shows how a Transaction Processing Monitor works:

Database resource managers in WildFly and all Java application servers compliant with the EE specifications are configured through DataSources. A DataSource can join a transaction unless we configure them in a different way. In JPA, for example, we can establish DataSource as a part of the transaction or independent. If the DataSource is not a part of a transaction, we cannot use the transaction tools, and all operations will be done one for one without a final commit.

The `persistence.xml` file is the official descriptor file in JPA. It declares the persistence unit and configures different properties (e.g. DataSource name). It must be inside a jar file or directory in the META-INF directory.

In the `persistence.xml` file, we can choose from among two types of approaches:

- `<jta-data-source>java:/jboss/datasources/transactions_mdefault</jta-data-source>`
- `<non-jta-data-source>java:/jboss/datasources/transactions_mdefault</non-jta-data-source>`

JTA use is not mandatory in database connections but it is definitely recommended. Do not use JTA means that the application throws away a ready-to-use and well-tested feature set preferring custom solutions, which in turn makes it more vulnerable to bugs.

ACID properties

A transaction must cover four important properties, called ACID properties. They must be Atomic, Consistent, Isolated, and Durable. Here, we will see the details of these properties:

- **Atomic**: This means that a transaction is a unit of work collecting many operations that succeed or fail as a single unit of work. In our previous example, the credit operation and the debit operation were one atomic unit.
- **Consistent**: This implies that the result of a transaction must leave the system and managed resources in a stable state. The state of the system must be consistent regardless of whether the transaction succeeds or fails. In our example, the bank accounts must be in a consistent state, so if the operation succeeds, the accounts will be moved by the same amount of money, one less and one more.
- **Isolated**: This means that the updates of a transaction cannot be executed immediately if it works with other transactions; else, the consistency is not guaranteed. The updates will always be executed in the end through the final commit.
- **Durable**: This means that all the operations will be permanent. The result of a commit will always register something in the external resource manager, database, or other system.

Enterprise concurrent API

In this section, we introduce the concurrent API ready in Java EE 7 under the `javax.enterprise.concurrent` package. This is a new set of utilities represented by the **Java Specification Request (JSR)** 236 specifications that guides the developer to a correct use of the threads inside the enterprise components. Using threads directly in the container is dangerous and it often generates out-of-control situations.

A standard management of threads is useful to let a major control. With a specification, it is easy to get instruments of monitoring and more robust processes. In the next section, we will analyze the threads together with the distributed transactions.

Java 5 SE introduces the standard concurrent API. The EE concurrent API works together with them.

Managed executor service

The main interface is the `ManagedExecutorService.` interface. This service can be easily injected in our code, and it can start or shutdown the processes. Here is an example of managing a `Callable` class:

```
public class MyCallableTask implements Callable<Product> {
    private int id;
    public MyCallableTask(int id) {
  this.id = id;
 }
    @Override
    public Product call() {
     return new Product(id);
    }
}
```

This class implements the `call` method of the `Callable` interface. This is very similar to the `Runnable` interface. Both run inside a thread but the `Runnable` interface doesn't return results. Here is an example of a simple `Product` class:

```
public class Product {
    . . .
}
```

Here is an example of the manager executor service:

```
@Resource(name = "DefaultManagedExecutorService")
private ManagedExecutorService defaultExecutor;
private Callable<Product> callableTask = new MyCallableTask(1);
. . .
Future<Product> future = defaultExecutor.submit(callableTask);
Product product = future.get();
```

The `submit` method of the executor starts the `MyCallableTask` as a thread. Through the `get` method of the `Future` class ready in the concurrent SE API, can be called the call method of `MyCallableTask`.

Set of threads

We can invoke easy in the same time a set of threads. Here's a sample:

```
Collection<Callable<Product>> callableTasks = new ArrayList<>();
for (int i = 0; i < 5; i++)
    callableTasks.add(new MyCallableTask(i));
List<Future<Product>> results = defaultExecutor.invokeAll(callableTasks);
for (Future<Product> f : results)
    f.get();
```

The `invokeAll` method of the managed executor service starts at the same time as all objects in the list as multiple threads. Then, each thread will expire once the `get` method starts returning a result; in this case, a `Product` object.

Transactional tasks

Now, in the following code, we can see a managed executor service that works with a transactional runnable object:

```
public class MyTaskWithTransaction implements Runnable {
    private int id;
    @Inject
 private MyTransactionScopedBean bean;
...
    @Override
    @Transactional
 public void run() {
  try {
        foundTransactionScopedBean = bean.isInTx();
      } catch (Exception e) {
    e.printStackTrace();
  }
    }
}
```

As seen in the previous sections, we can use a `@Transactional` annotation to define a transactional method. This can be done on the threads as well. This class injects the following managed bean:

```
@TransactionScoped
public class MyTransactionScopedBean implements Serializable {
    public boolean isInTx() {
        return true;
    }
}
```

The `@TransactionScoped` annotation is a new normal scope class introduced in JTA 1.2 and indicates the annotated object to work only inside a transaction. Now, you can try to execute this code:

```
@Inject
private MyTaskWithTransaction taskWithTransaction;
...
defaultExecutor.submit(taskWithTransaction);
```

After we use the `submit` method, we will get the `foundTransactionScopedBean` field to true.

Levels and transaction isolation problems

When you work on different isolation levels in ACID, you can find different cases of isolation in the transactions. Transaction isolation levels represent the level to which isolation violations are prevented or allowed. The following section shows all types of transaction isolation violations and isolation levels defining the allowed violations in a transaction context.

Isolation violations

In this section, we look at all the possible problems you can face not using the isolation levels to protect the transactions. Here is the list of violations:

Dirty read

Dirty read happens when a transaction reads the data that another transaction has updated but still not committed. For example, two runnable objects can work with the same account entity on two different transactions. The runnable object reads the account object as follows:

```
@Transactional(value = REQUIRES_NEW)
public class ReadAccount implements Runnable {
    @PersistenceContext
  private EntityManager entityManager;
    ...
    @Override
  public void run() {
      ...
      CountDownLatch latch = new CountDownLatch(1);
      latch.await(firstWaitTime, MILLISECONDS);
      Account account = entityManager.find(Account.class,
```

```
        accountNumber);
    firstResult = account.getCredit();
        latch.await(secondWaitTime, MILLISECONDS);
        account = entityManager.find(Account.class, accountNumber);
        secondResult = account.getCredit();
        ...
    }
}
```

Through the REQUIRED_NEW transaction type, we force the thread to start a new transaction during the read operation. We will read the credit of the same account twice. The CountDownLatch provided by the SE concurrent API allows us to wait for an established time, so in the meantime we can start another transaction. This new transaction can execute the write operations provided by the second runnable object:

```
@Transactional(value = REQUIRES_NEW)
public class WriteAccount implements Runnable {
    @PersistenceContext
    private EntityManager entityManager;
    ...
    @Override
    public void run() {
        ...
        CountdownLatch latch = new CountDownLatch(1);
    Account account = entityManager.find(Account.class,
        accountNumber);
    account.add(amount);
        entityManager.merge(account);
        latch.await(waitTime, MILLISECONDS);
        result = account.getCredit();
        ...
    }
}
```

In this object, we will increase the credit of the account. Now, execute the two transactions through the managed executor service:

```
@Inject
private ReadAccount readAccount;
@Inject
private WriteAccount writeAccount;
...
readAccount.setAccountNumber(123);
readAccount.setFirstWaitTime(1000);
readAccount.setSecondWaitTime(0);
writeAccount.setAccountNumber(123);
writeAccount.setAmount(456.77);
writeAccount.setWaitTime(2000);
```

```
defaultExecutor.submit(writeAccount);
defaultExecutor.submit(readAccount);
```

The operations can be simplified so:

- The first transaction starts and we have a first read of account 123
- The second transaction starts and an update of credit of 456.77 is done in account 123
- The second transaction ends
- The first transaction ends

Non-repeatable read

Non-repeatable read happens when a transaction reads the same data twice with different results. For example, in transaction A, consider reading data item C. Before transaction A completes, transaction B changes and commits data item C. A later operation within transaction A reads the same data again and sees a new value of data C. The first data read in transaction A can be considered *non-repeatable* because transaction B's change has been allowed to work into the context of the transaction A. To simulate this read, we can execute these operations:

```
...
readAccount.setAccountNumber(345);
readAccount.setFirstWaitTime(0);
readAccount.setSecondWaitTime(2000);
writeAccount.setAccountNumber(345);
writeAccount.setAmount(456.77);
writeAccount.setWaitTime(1000);
defaultExecutor.submit(writeAccount);
defaultExecutor.submit(readAccount);
```

The operations can be simplified so:

- The first transaction starts and we have a first read of account 345
- The second transaction starts and an update of the credit of 456.77 is done in account 345
- The second transaction ends
- A second read of account 345 is done in the first transaction
- The first transaction ends

Phantom read

Phantom read happens when data is read more times and unexpectedly goes away or when data is read more times and unexpectedly a different value is shown. For example, in transaction A, through a query you get a set result. Before transaction A is completed, transaction B adds a row that matches the query executed in transaction A, and this row is committed before the completion of transaction A. If transaction A executes the same query again, it will get a different data. This situation is called phantom read because new data not created by transaction A has appeared in the resource. To simulate this read, we must execute a query. Consider the named query of the account entity:

```
@Entity
@NamedQueries({ @NamedQuery(name = "SelectAll", query = "SELECT e FROM
Account e") })
public class Account {...}
```

Here is a runnable to execute the query in the first transaction:

```
@Transactional(value = REQUIRES_NEW)
public class QueryReadAccount implements Runnable {
    @Override
    public void run() {
        ...
        CountDownLatch latch = new CountDownLatch(1);
        latch.await(firstWaitTime, MILLISECONDS);
        firstResult =
entityManager.createNamedQuery("SelectAll").getResultList().size();
latch.await(secondWaitTime, MILLISECONDS);
        secondResult =
entityManager.createNamedQuery("SelectAll").getResultList().size();
        ...
    }
}
```

Here is a runnable that inserts a new account in the second transaction:

```
@Transactional(value = REQUIRES_NEW)
public class QueryWriteAccount implements Runnable {
    @Override
    public void run() {
        ...
        CountDownLatch latch = new CountDownLatch(1);
        Account account = new Account();
        account.setNumber(accountNumber);
        account.add(amount);
        entityManager.persist(account);
        latch.await(waitTime, MILLISECONDS);
        result = account.getCredit();
```

```
        . . .
    }
}
```

Now, start the two transactions with the managed executor service:

```
@Inject
private QueryReadAccount queryReadAccount;
@Inject
private QueryWriteAccount queryWriteAccount;
. . .
queryReadAccount.setFirstWaitTime(0);
queryReadAccount.setSecondWaitTime(2000);
queryWriteAccount.setAccountNumber(953);
queryWriteAccount.setAmount(456.77);
queryWriteAccount.setWaitTime(1000);
defaultExecutor.submit(queryWriteAccount);
defaultExecutor.submit(queryReadAccount);
```

The operations can be simplified so:

- The first transaction starts and we have a first query of all accounts
- The second transaction starts and an insert of a new account is done
- The second transaction ends
- A second read of all accounts is done in the first transaction
- The first transaction ends

The results of these operations change according the configured transaction isolation level that we will introduce in the next section.

Isolation levels

An isolation level describes the level of a transaction to which the access to a resource manager by a transaction is isolated compared to other transactions executed concurrently . This section shows all the transaction isolation levels that prevent or allow the isolation violations seen in the previous section.

 Because our examples use the database as the resource manager, we will show how to configure the DataSource to obtain the desired isolation level. The configuration of other resource managers is not threat in this book

Read committed

With this isolation level, a transaction can never read uncommitted data so dirty reads do not happen. Unlike the dirty reads, phantom reads and non-repeatable reads can occur. This level is default in many popular databases such as MySQL and Oracle.

To set the read uncommitted, simply add this row in your DataSource:

```
<transaction-isolation>TRANSACTION_READ_COMMITTED</transaction-isolation>
```

Read uncommitted

There is no isolation when a transaction can read an uncommitted data. This level is few useful in most business applications that need the ACID transaction properties. However, some applications of data warehouse find this thing useful, in particular those which principally read rather than update data. This isolation level allows dirty read, phantom read, and non-repeatable read.

To set the read uncommitted, simply add this row in your DataSource:

```
<transaction-isolation>TRANSACTION_READ_UNCOMMITTED</transaction-isolation>
```

Repeatable read

With this isolation level, non-repeatable reads and dirty reads do not occur but phantom reads can still occur.

To set the read uncommitted, simply add this row to your datasource:

```
<transaction-isolation>TRANSACTION_REPEATABLE_READ</transaction-isolation>
```

Serializable

No isolation violations are allowed using this isolation level. Non-repeatable reads, phantom reads and dirty reads do not occur.

To set the read uncommitted, simply add this row to your DataSource:

```
<transaction-isolation>TRANSACTION_SERIALIZABLE</transaction-isolation>
```

We can see the relationship between transaction isolation violations and transaction isolation levels as follows:

Isolation level	Dirty read	Nonrepeatable read	Phantom read
Read uncommitted	Can happen	Can happen	Can happen
Read committed		Can happen	Can happen
Repeatable read			Can happen
Serializable			

We have seen that the serializable isolation is stronger than the others, so someone could ask himself if it is always the correct isolation to configure. The answer is no because concurrency and transaction isolation level are inversely related. The higher the isolation level, the lower the concurrency you have. With low concurrency, the system performances go bad so that the system can support fewer users. Therefore, we need to find a balance between greater performance possible at lower isolation levels and safety of higher isolation levels. Also this choice has an impact on the complexity of the code we write. With higher isolation levels, we must worry less about concurrency issues in our code because the transaction manager is dealing with them for us. With lower isolation levels, we must worry about the isolation violations that we're letting through, consider whether they might actually occur or not, and potentially deal with them ourself in our application code.

In many cases, the isolation level has been chosen for us. For example, if our application works with a single relational database, its transaction manager will have a default isolation configuration optimized by the vendor for typical uses.

Transaction models

There are different transaction models available in enterprise contexts. We will expose them in the further sections.

Flat transactions

The **Flat Transaction Model** (**FTM**) is the most common and simplest transaction model. It establishes that only one transaction at any given time is active among other transactions. A lawful question is if we can start another transaction at the same time. There are two ways to do this:

- We can disallow starting another transaction until the first transaction ends. It's very rigid but it guarantees a solid state.
- We can suspend the current transaction and start a new transaction. Once the new transaction finishes, the original transaction is resumed. In this case, the second transaction can commit while the first transaction executes a rollback. The data of the second transaction remains committed anyway.

Savepoints

Savepoints are a quite common type of flat transaction model. Through the savepoints, the resource saves the work done within a transaction, periodically. It's important to use them correctly because they allow an entire commit of data during a transactional work. The transaction will be partially rolled back to a specific savepoint. The savepoint works directly through JDBC, so it is not supported by JTA, but it can be managed by the resource manager. Here is an example of savepoint:

```
@Resource(lookup = "java:jboss/datasources/ExampleDS")
private DataSource myData;
...
String insert = "INSERT INTO ACCOUNT(NUMBER, CREDIT) VALUES (";
try (Connection conn = myData.getConnection()) {
    conn.setAutoCommit(false);
    Statement insertAccount = null;
    Statement getAccount = null;
    Savepoint savepoint = null;
    Savepoint mySavepoint = null;
    try {
        savepoint = conn.setSavepoint();
        insertAccount = conn.createStatement();
        insertAccount.executeUpdate(insert + "48112, 436564.87)");
    } catch (SQLException e) {
        ...
    }
    try {
        mySavepoint = conn.setSavepoint("mySavepoint");
        insertAccount.executeUpdate(insert + "48113, 436564.87)");
    } catch (SQLException e) {
```

```
    . . .
  }
  try {
    insertAccount.executeUpdate(insert + "48114, 436564.87)");
    conn.rollback(mySavepoint);
  } catch (SQLException e) {
    . . .
  }
  conn.releaseSavepoint(savepoint);
} catch (SQLException e) {
  . . .
}
```

Because savepoints are not supported by JTA, as first thing, we have to exclude the autocommit imported by the default JTA DataSource, ExampleDS, configured as JTA transaction using the `setAutoCommit` method. In this code, we created two savepoints, one by default without name and one called `mySavePoint`. After the creation of first savePoints, we inserted a new account `48112`. After the second savepoint, we inserted `48113` and `48114`. Then, we performed a rollback pointing the transaction to savepoint `mySavePoint`. As a result, we found `48112` inserted in our database and `48113` and `48114` missing.

Nested transactions

Other useful transaction model is the **Nested Transaction Model** (**NTM**), created to fix some problems of the flat transaction model. The nested transactions, as the name says are nested, so they can form a tree of transactions with multiple transactions active at the same time. Nested transactions can be emulated through the savepoints.

Saga

A saga is a set of flat transactions that work as one unit. In the case of a rollback, the partial work is undone thanks to a compensation work between the transactions, so the rollback must be executed in a sequence according to the number of current transactions. The transactions of a saga don't work isolated from the others. If we try to do a saga through the user transaction, we will get `javax.transaction.NotSupportedException`. So, we will never perform the following action:

```
@Inject
private UserTransaction userTransaction;
...
userTransaction.begin();
userTransaction.begin();
```

A `NotSupportedException` will be thrown at the second beginning.

Chained transactions

Another interesting variation of transactions model is represented by chained transactions. When a transaction ends could be useful for the resource managers to automatically start a new transaction. This thing allows the client to work automatically inside a transaction without worrying about the environment where it runs. JDBC, JCA, and JMS can work with chained transactions by default just for the fact of support, commits, and rollbacks. The start of the transaction, in this case, should be done at the connection level. JMS or JDBC clients can make a connection, start a session from the connection and after start the transaction. In the section on transaction isolation, we just saw a nested exception through concurrent beans. The same representation can be done with no concurrent beans as well. Here is a new bean that starts a new transaction automatically through the `@Transactional` annotation:

```
@Transactional(value = REQUIRES_NEW)
public class NoConcurrentWriteAccount {
    @PersistenceContext
    private EntityManager entityManager;
    private int accountNumber;
    private double amount;

    public void run() {
        ...
        Account account = new Account(accountNumber, amount);
        entityManager.persist(account);
        ...
    }
    public double getAmount() {
        return amount;
    }
    public void setAmount(double amount) {
        this.amount = amount;
    }
    public int getAccountNumber() {
        return accountNumber;
    }
    public void setAccountNumber(int accountNumber) {
        this.accountNumber = accountNumber;
    }
}
```

Now, execute the checked transaction:

```
@PersistenceContext
private EntityManager entityManager;
@Inject
private NoConcurrentWriteAccount writeAccount;
@Inject
private UserTransaction userTransaction;
...
userTransaction.begin();
Account account = new Account(28111, 436564.87);
entityManager.persist(account);
writeAccount.setAccountNumber(45699);
writeAccount.setAmount(2224.988);
writeAccount.run();
userTransaction.rollback();
```

In this example, we executed the following operations:

- We started a transaction through the begin method of the user transaction
- We created a new account 28111
- We created a new account 45699 through a new bean, starting a new transaction automatically
- We executed the rollback

As a result, we will get the account 45699 inserted successfully but miss the account 28111 because we have executed the rollback only in the first transaction.

Most JTA implementations such as Narayana support only the flat transaction model. This model is considered complete for most cases. If we try to use this inside a JTA transaction and other models in WildFly, an exception will be thrown.

Distributed transactions and the JTA

A local transaction is a transaction that communicates with just one resource, so a transaction monitor doesn't occur. The resource manager works with the local transactions at the connection level. Applications working with a single relational database are good candidates to use the local transactions. Otherwise, distributed applications working with several resource managers as messaging systems or databases need a transaction monitor to manage all the resources and connections, so a global or distributed transaction will be more appropriate.

The number of distribution of clients is not important to determine the need for a distributed transaction. When more different components in an application ask the application server to coordinate a transaction working with the same resource manager, a local transaction will be candidate.

Here, `ExampleDS` is a local DataSource:

```
<datasource jndi-name="java:jboss/datasources/ExampleDS" pool-
name="ExampleDS">
    <connection-url>jdbc:h2:mem:test;DB_CLOSE_DELAY=-1</connection-url>
    <driver>h2</driver>
    <pool>
        <min-pool-size>10</min-pool-size>
        <max-pool-size>20</max-pool-size>
        <prefill>true</prefill>
    </pool>
    <security>
        <user-name>sa</user-name>
        <password>sa</password>
    </security>
</datasource>
```

There are different protocols and specifications written to support and coordinate the distributed transactions. The most popular specification for distributed transactions is the **X/Open XA** (**Open Group's XA Protocol**). Other important specifications are the **Open Systems Interconnect** (**OSI**) transaction processing protocol defined by the **ISO** (**International Organization for Standards**), and the LU 6.2 **SNA** (**Systems Network Architecture**) defined by IBM.

Both the applications and application work with JTA API programmatically or declaratively to manage distributed transactions through **service provider interfaces** (**SPI**) API that an application server must support and the API provided by Java EE for the application to join and move in a transaction in the `javax.transaction` package . Also, the X/Open XA protocol can be used through a special java package `javax.transaction.xa`. This packages contain the interfaces to work with both distributed X/Open XA and local transactions.

Here is an example of XA DataSource configuration:

```
<xa-datasource jndi-name="java:/jboss/datasources/readcommitted" pool-
name="readcommitted">
    <xa-datasource-class>org.h2.jdbcx.JdbcDataSource</xa-datasource-class>
    <xa-datasource-property name="URL">jdbc:h2:mem:readcommitted</xa-
datasource-property>
    <driver>h2</driver>
    <security>
        <user-name>sa</user-name>
    </security>
    <transaction-isolation>TRANSACTION_READ_COMMITTED</transaction-
isolation>
</xa-datasource>
```

Most implementations of JTA such as Narayana use the **Java Transaction Service (JTS)**. JTS usage is an optional service providing Java bindings for the CORBA **OTS (Object Transaction Service)**. This chapter doesn't cover this service, but it is important to know this if you need to work with legacy systems such as CORBA.

Distributed transaction scenarios

There are different common distributed transaction scenarios. An example of this scenario is a distributed transaction that uses two or more databases. We discussed other scenarios which include those that span a database and message queue together or only multiple message servers. In the end, we will see a scenario with a distributed transaction started by a Java EE client invoking different Java EE components.

Multiple databases

In the following scenario, a transaction spans two databases. An example of this scenario is a transaction that spans updates to a database maintaining the data of the customers and updates to another database managing data for the online orders of products. Both the operations, on the customer database and on the database of the orders, are a part of the same transaction.

Here is an example of a distributed transaction--multiple databases:

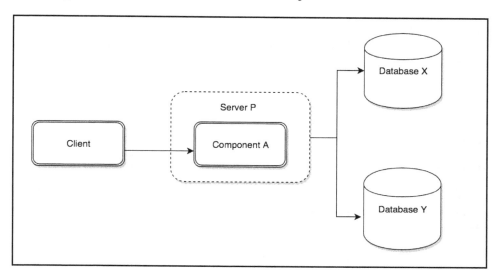

Now, we will see a simple test for distributed transactions with multiple databases. Here, we will take two DataSources:

```
    <xa-datasource jndi-name="java:/jboss/datasources/texts" pool-
name="texts">
    <xa-datasource-class>org.h2.jdbcx.JdbcDataSource</xa-datasource-class>
    <xa-datasource-property name="URL">jdbc:h2:mem:texts</xa-datasource-
property>
    ...
```

We will also use the popular ExampleDS. It has a XA configuration by default. Now, take two persistent units that point to the two DataSources:

```
<persistence-unit name="mainTexts">
    <jta-data-source>
        java:jboss/datasources/texts
    </jta-data-source>
    ...
<persistence-unit name="mainImages">
    <jta-data-source>
        java:jboss/datasources/ExampleDS
    </jta-data-source>
    ...
```

Now, create an entity for the `mainTexts` persistent unit:

```
@PersistenceUnit(unitName="mainTexts")
@Entity
public class Text {
   private Format format;
   private String value;
   ...
   public Text(Format format, String value) {
      this.format = format;
      this.value = value;
   }
   ...
```

Also, create an entity for the `mainImages` persistent unit:

```
@PersistenceUnit(unitName="mainImages")
@Entity
public class Image {
   ...
   private String name;
   private byte[] file;
   public Image(String name, byte[] file) {
      this.name = name;
      this.file = file;
   }
   ...
```

These entities can be managed by two stateless:

```
@Stateless
public class Images implements Magazine<Image> {
    @PersistenceContext(unitName="mainImages")
    private EntityManager images;
    @Override
    public void write(Image element) {
       images.persist(element);
    }
    @Override
    public List<Image> read() {
       return images.createQuery("from Image").getResultList();
    }
}
```

And:

```
@Stateless
public class Texts implements Magazine<Text> {
    @PersistenceContext(unitName="mainTexts")
    private EntityManager texts;
    @Override
    public void write(Text element) {
        texts.persist(element);
    }
    @Override
    public List<Text> read() {
        return texts.createQuery("from Text").getResultList();
    }
}
```

Here is the common interface:

```
public interface Magazine<T> {
    void write(T element);
    List<T> read();
}
```

Now, we can execute some inserts from the two databases:

```
@Inject
private UserTransaction userTransaction;
@EJB(mappedName = "java:module/Images")
private Magazine<Image> images;
@EJB(mappedName = "java:module/Texts")
private Magazine<Text> texts;
...
userTransaction.begin();
images.write(new Image("image_title_1.jpg", "First title".getBytes()));
texts.write(new Text(BOLD, "starting first chapter"));
texts.write(new Text(ITALIC, "starting first paragraph"));
images.write(new Image("image_title_2.jpg", "Second title".getBytes()));
texts.write(new Text(BOLD, "starting second chapter"));
texts.write(new Text(ITALIC, "starting first paragraph"));
images.write(new Image("image_title_1.jpg", "Third title".getBytes()));
texts.write(new Text(BOLD, "starting third chapter"));
```

Now, we end with `rollback`:

```
userTransaction.rollback();
```

We can also start some query from the two databases:

```
images.read().size();
texts.read().size();
```

You will note that nothing is the database. The rollback was executed automatically in both databases!

Message queue and database

In the following distributed transaction scenario, a transaction spans a message queue and a database. In Java EE, application is a very common scenario. For example, an application receives a message on a queue and wants to process it. After processing, the application will save the result of the process to the database. Both the operations on the database and topic must be a part of the same distributed transaction. If the save on the database fails, we would have all the transactions rolled back, also the operations on the queue.

Here is an example of a distributed transaction--message queue and database:

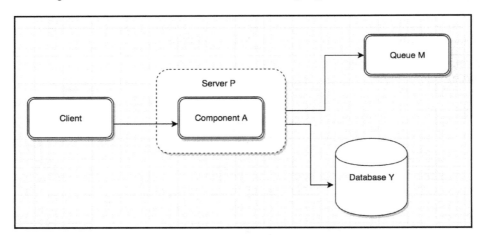

This will be seen in detail in Chapter 8, *Working with Messaging*.

Multiple application servers

In the following scenario, a transaction spans two different application server instances. Here is an example of a distributed transaction--multiple application servers

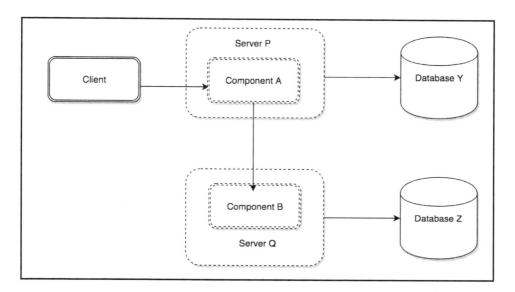

The example in this scenario is a change of bank account. The customer would close the actual account of the bank to pass to another bank. Each bank has its application but the transaction must be one. The JTA specifications allow to do this if the application servers are from different vendors thanks to the SPI.

Transaction started by the client

In the following scenario, the client begins a transaction. After this, the client invokes some components; for example, EJB, CDI beans, or web components running on more application servers. The transaction of the client container is propagated to various components that the client calls. This scenario is like the multiple application server example seen in the previous section, with a difference that an external client starts the transaction context, instead of starting this inside the component container of the application servers.

Here is a figure explaining a distributed transaction--client demarcation:

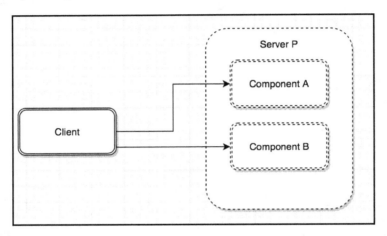

These distributed transaction scenarios illustrate the necessity of distributed transaction support in Java EE. The Java EE application server becomes the coordinator of distributed transactions. It coordinates the transaction across different resources, servers, and components. But how does a distributed transaction work under the covers? What is the protocol that a transaction coordinator uses to coordinate disparate resources? The protocol that a transaction coordinator uses is known as a two-phase commit, which we will discuss next.

These transactions cannot work without a coordinator that keeps trace of the transactions and the state of the resources. Only an application server can do it. In the following section, we will see how the application server coordinates these distributed transactions using the two-phase commit protocol mentioned in the previous *Distributed transactions and the JTA* section.

Two-phase commit

The two-phase commit protocol is used to implement and coordinate distributed transactions between more resource managers. This protocol guarantees the durability and consistency of distributed transactions by managing the state of all resource managers that work in a transaction. The two-phase commit acts when a rollback or commit is started on a distributed transaction. Rollbacks and commits can be requested by either the application or the current transaction manager behind the application.

As the name says, two phases are involved in the two-phase commit protocol. The first phase is addressed to prepare phase, while the second phase is addressed to execute commits or rollbacks according to what happens in the transaction. In the prepare phase, the transaction manager sends a start message to all the resources joined in the transaction. Each resource sends back a ready or abort response according to the state. In the second phase, if any resource responds with abort, the transaction manager executes the rollback in the entire transaction, as shown next. Only if all the resources respond with a ready message, the transaction manager commits the whole transaction.

Here is an example of rollback in the first phase of a two-phase commit represented in **Unified Modeling Language (UML)** sequence figure:

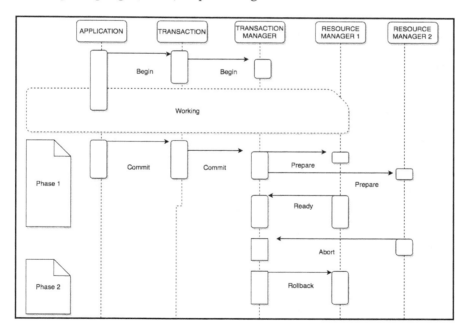

Here is a UML figure representing a successful commit in the two-phase commit protocol:

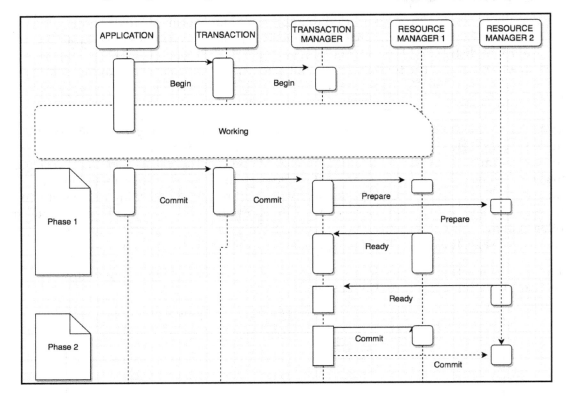

Here is a transaction rollback in a two-phase commit:

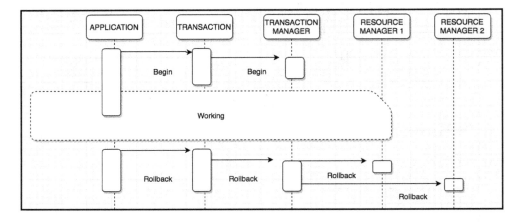

Now, see what happens if no response returns from the resource manager to the transaction manager for a long time. JTA provides the timeout configurable through the `transactionManager.setTransactionTimeout( )` method of the `TransactionManager` interface. Simply put, the transaction manager will wait the timeout time and then it will start the rollback.

Transactions can get unrecoverable issues. The programming cannot prevent accidental errors made by the current network problems or by the crash of a machine. The transaction manager has the power to decide when to start the rollback in these cases. This decision can be made by the resource manager as well by sending an abort message to the transaction manager. This operation is called heuristic decision.

In other cases, the transaction manager cannot execute the rollback; for example, it crashes before it can do it. This is a very dangerous case that can be resolved only by administrator care and attention to read all the log files and tempting to restore the state by executing the correct operations provided by the resource manager.

Emulating two-phase commit

All the resources joined to a two-phase commit transaction must be a XA compliant resource, so they must support the X/Open XA distributed transaction protocol shown in the previous section *Distributed transactions and JTA*. But there are cases where the resources don't support the XA protocol. How does it do it in these cases? There are workarounds for it.

Some databases don't support a XA connection so could happen to have a non-XA resource in its own distributed XA transaction. In these cases, the resource could work anyway because the transaction manager could emulate the XA operation passing them as successful. The problem is when the non-XA resource throws an error. In this case, the XA transaction manager is not unable to understand the error, so an inconsistent state could happen. Always take extra care about these cases. An important thing is to establish a priority to the used resources. For example, when you project the application, a non-XA database has no sense to manage important data.

Some emulating transaction managers could add restrictions on their support for this, such as allowing only one non-XA resource to join in a distributed XA transaction.

Summary

With this chapter, we have concluded our deep dive into transactions, but we will continue to see transactions in the next chapter because they are the cornerstones of enterprise applications. So, do return often to read this chapter if you want to revise transactions.

6
Creating REST Services

Representational State Transfer (**REST**) is an architecture for software distributed hypertext systems such as the World Wide Web. The term REST was introduced in 2000 in the doctoral dissertation by one of the principal authors of Hypertext Transfer Protocol (HTTP), Roy Fielding, and was quickly adopted by the developer community on the Internet. The term REST is often used in the sense of describing any simple interface that transmits data over HTTP without an optional layer, such as **SOAP** or session management via cookies. These two concepts may conflict as well as overlap. You can design any complex software system in accordance with the REST architecture fielding without using HTTP and not interact with the World Wide Web. You can also design a simple XML + HTTP interface that does not conform to the REST principles and instead, follow a Remote Procedure Call model. The difference between the different uses of the word "REST" then cause some confusion in the debates.

JAX-RS Java API for RESTful web services is the Java specification implementing REST actually arrived to the version 2.0 in the Java EE 7. The main targets are (among others) a common client API and support for Hypermedia following the HATEOAS principle of REST. Through HATEOAS, we have a simpler manner to configure the media types, and it establishes that each call is only a change of resources. In May 2013, it reached the final release stage.

RESTEasy 3.0.19.Final is the JAX-RS implementation in WildFly 10. This product is born in the JBoss community, and it was integrated for the first time in JBoss AS 7 with the 2.x version.

Java EE 7 includes the JSON specifications.

JSON (JavaScript Object Notation), is a scripting specification based on JavaScript used mainly as an interface for messages through the HTTP protocol. A good combination is of JSON and REST--a very simple manner to communicate through a single and simple protocol, HTTP. Used for several years, it is now a standard in Java EE 7.

JSON is a simple data format processed on the web.

The Java JSON specification includes an API to work with the JSON format and SPI to build the JSON provider. The official JSON engine in WildFly 10 is Jackson 2.7.4 by FasterXML, a famous open source community expert in XML products.

In this chapter, we will analyze the REST API, including some JSON samples. This is what you will see in this chapter:

- Implementation of REST services
- How to use the REST annotations
- Writing REST clients
- REST components
- REST interceptors
- Test cases with Selenium and Drone

Services

The application is a class extending the `Application` class, and it declares the root HTTP path that a client will use through the `@ApplicationPath` annotation. Here's a sample of the application:

```
@ApplicationPath("/services")
public class CalculatorApplication extends Application {
    @Override
    public Set<Class<?>> getClasses() {
        final Set<Class<?>> classes = new HashSet<>();
        ...
        classes.add(Calculator.class);
        return classes;
    }
    ...
}
```

The `getClasses()` method contains all the components and services used in the application.

The REST services are beans annotated with the JAX-RS annotations. These services can be declared along with the other enterprise components, such as servlets or EJB. The REST services must be contained in an application. In this sample, we see a stateless REST service:

```
@Path("/calculator")
@Stateless
public class Calculator {
    @GET
    @Path("/sum")
    @Produces(MediaType.TEXT_PLAIN)
    public double sum(@QueryParam("value") double... values) {
        return execute(SUM, values);
    }
    @GET
    @Path("/sub")
    @Produces(MediaType.TEXT_PLAIN)
    public double sub(@QueryParam("value") double... values) {
        return execute(SUB, values);
    }
    @POST
    @Path("/multi")
    @Consumes(MediaType.APPLICATION_JSON)
    @Produces(MediaType.TEXT_PLAIN)
    public double multi(double... values) {
        return execute(MULTI, values);
    }
    @PUT
    @Path("/div")
    @Produces(MediaType.APPLICATION_JSON)
    public double divide(double... values) {
        return execute(DIV, values);
    }
    ...
}
```

This class implements a calculator available on the web. The `@Path` annotation is used to construct the URL that a client will call. For example, the URL built to do an addiction becomes `http://$SERVER_NAME:$SERVER_PORT/$WEB_CONTEXT/services/calculator/sum`.

Here, service is the name of the REST application, calculator the name of the service, and sum the name of the method.

The `@Produces` annotation declares the media type of the method. Each media type provides its own formatted message that will be sent or received over the internet after an HTTP call. JAX-RS provides several media types. Here are the most popular ones:

- `APPLICATION_XML`: An XML format, as follows:

```
<home>
   <room>bathroom<room>
</home>
```

- `APPLICATION_ATOM_XML`: It is very similar to XML and is used for the RSS feeds.
- `APPLICATION_JSON`: The famous JSON format. Here's a sample:

```
{"menu": {
  "id": "file",
  "value": "File",
  "popup": {
    "menuitem": [
      {"value": "New", "onclick": "CreateNewDoc()"},
      {"value": "Open", "onclick": "OpenDoc()"},
      {"value": "Close", "onclick": "CloseDoc()"}
    ]
  }
}}
```

- `APPLICATION_FORM_URLENCODED`: The bytes set sent by a default HTML form.
- `TEXT_PLAIN`: The simpler format--a text without tree information.

In the end, we specify the HTTP methods in our methods in the cases we have a GET, a POST, and a PUT annotated. Take a look at the methods in the next paragraph.

REST and HTTP

JAX-RS provides API to work with the six HTTP methods. These methods are used to interact with the web servers through a browser or some other client; look at the details.

GET methods

GET is the most used. It lets you accommodate the address data of the requested page, followed by the name of the page, a question mark, and the name/value pairs of data that interest us. Name and value are separated by an equals sign. The different name/value pairs are separated by &. So, imagine having the `product.html` page that shows the characteristics of a product passing the code and the category of the product itself. To show the A7 product data category 2, we will have to call up the page like this:

```
<a href="product.html?cod=a7&cat=2">
```

The string that is after the question mark, containing the names and values of the parameters, is called a **query string**. When the `product.html` page is called up in this way, it will be elaborated by a web server. So, to return to the example of the catalog, we can imagine having a page where we show a table with the name of each product on one line, and, next, the link that allows us to see the features of that product. In each row, then, this link always recalls the `product.html` page, valuing the different values of cod and cat each time.

Here's a sample of a client that calls a REST service through the GET method:

```
@ArquillianResource
private URL url;
...
Client client = ClientBuilder.newClient();
WebTarget target = client.target(url +
"services/calculator/sum?value=4&value=6");
Response response = target.request().get();
double value = response.readEntity(Double.class);
response.close();
```

The `ClientBuilder` is new in JAX-RS 2.0. Earlier, you were forced to write a client through implementation classes. The `newClient` method automatically finds the RESTEasy builder and returns a client to elaborate calls. You can see how the REST builder is declared in RESTEasy here:

```
public class ResteasyClientBuilder extends ClientBuilder
{ ...}
```

The REST builder extends the `javax.ws.rs.client.ClientBuilder` abstract class. As good practice in Java, JAX-RS 2.0 finds the builder searching inside the JAR libraries the file `META-INF/services/javax.ws.rs.client.ClientBuilder`. In the content RESTEasy, put the name of the implementation class:

```
org.jboss.resteasy.client.jaxrs.ResteasyClientBuilder
```

In the target method, you specify the GET URL with the parameters. Then the `get()` method returns the result as the `Response` class. The result can be cast according to the declared class of the service. In this case, the sum returns a double value:

```
public double sum(@QueryParam("value") double... values)
```

In the URL, we send the parameters `value` declared through the `@QueryParam` annotation. In this case, we can send a chain of value parameters. They will be managed by the server as an array or a vararg.

 Arquillian provides a function to obtain the current URL of the deployment package, simply injecting a URL field through the `@ArquillianResource` annotation.

POST methods

The POST method sends a set of parameters as a unique encoded block respect to the GET that sends them declaring them in the URL. The preferred media types used are the `APPLICATION_FORM_URLENCODED` very similar to a string, `MULTIPART_FORM_DATA` used to send entire files to the server, and `TEXT_PLAIN`. Usually, the POST method is used together with an HTML form. See how call the multiplication of the calculator declared as POST method and media type `APPLICATION_JSON`:

```
...
Entity<List<Double>> valuesAsList = Entity.entity(asList(new Double[] {
4.5, 6.7 }), MediaType.APPLICATION_JSON);
response = target.request().post(valuesAsList);
value = response.readEntity(Double.class);
...
```

The client needs to send data as entities. The `javax.ws.rs.client.Entity` class resolves this problem. The entity lets you declare the media type too. An important thing in this case is to set the data as list. The array is not permitted as it's not permitted to declare a media type different by the declaration of the service:

```
@Consumes(MediaType.APPLICATION_JSON)
@Produces(MediaType.TEXT_PLAIN)
public double multi(double... values) {
    ...
```

The `@Consumes` annotation establishes that only a JSON can be sent to the service.

PUT methods

The PUT method is very similar to the POST method with little differences.

PUT is used to put files or resources in a specific URI. If that URI already has files or resources, PUT replaces them. If there is no file or resource there, PUT creates it. PUT is idempotent, but PUT responses are not cacheable.

Unlike PUT, POST is not idempotent, but its response is cacheable so long as the server sets the specific expires headers and cache-control.

To call a PUT method through JAX-RS, simply move the POST method to put:

```
WebTarget target = client.target(url + "services/calculator/div");
Entity<List<Double>> valuesAsList = entity(asList(new Double[] { 4.5, 6.7
}), MediaType.APPLICATION_JSON);
Response response =
target.request(APPLICATION_JSON_TYPE).put(valuesAsList);
double value = response.readEntity(Double.class);
```

HEAD methods

The HEAD method is used to send headers to the server. As the name says, they are the headers of the message. A header provides additional information about the message, and it is managed by the browser and the server. A browser can automatically send headers to the server without the application knowing. We can send headers through the application, and we can also modify the default headers sent by the browser or by the server; simply call the same names of headers. Here's a sample of delivery of a header through JAX-RS:

```
target = client.target(url + "services/receiver/header");
Builder builder = target.request().header("my_new_header", "Hi all");
response = builder.get();
```

In this sample, we send a header--my_new_header--with value Hi all to the server calling through GET the header service. Here's the header service declaration:

```
...
@GET
@Path("/header")
public String header(@HeaderParam("my_new_header") String my_new_header) {
    return my_new_header;
}
...
```

The header is received thanks to the @HeaderParam annotation declared in the service. There is an alternative mode to declare the service:

```
...
@GET
@Path("/header")
public String headerWithContext(@Context HttpHeaders headers) {
    return headers.getRequestHeader("my_new_header").get(0);
}
...
```

Thanks to the @Context annotation along with the javax.ws.rs.core.HttpHeaders interface, we can import all the headers actually sent and elaborate them, inserting new headers or choosing one.

OPTIONS method

This method allows the client to receive the options or/and requirements associated with an uploaded resource or the technical information of a server, executing no actions on a resource and no restore of the resource. It is a privileged channel to receive information of a service. The client is very similar to the other methods:

```
WebTarget target = client.target(url + "services/receiver/options");
Response response = target.request().options();
double value = response.readEntity(Double.class);
```

This is the service declaration:

```
@OPTIONS
@Path("/options")
@Produces(MediaType.TEXT_PLAIN)
public double options() {
    return 88.99;
}
```

DELETE method

The DELETE method is used to send a deletion message to the server to remove the resource specified in the request-URI. This method can be overridden on the origin server. The client can receive a status from the server indicating the successful operation, but it cannot be guaranteed. It will be the job of the developer to guarantee the correct operation in the service. The developer must operate to delete the resource or move it to an unaccessible location.

The client will receive a status response: 200 (OK) if the operation results successfully, 202 (accepted) if the action was accepted but not yet been executed, or 204 (no content) if the response does not return the deleted entity, and also if the action has been successfully executed.

If the request runs in a cache and the URI of the request identifies cached entities, those entries must be considered as stale. Responses for this method must not be cacheable.

This is a simple override of the DELETE method through JAX-RS:

```
@DELETE
@Path("/delete")
@Produces(MediaType.TEXT_PLAIN)
public double delete() {
    return 99.66;
}
```

Using RESTEasy directly

Here's a sample client using RESTEasy direcly instead of the standard JAX-RS 2.0:

```
ResteasyClient client = new ResteasyClientBuilder().build();
target = client.target(url + "services/receiver/delete");
response = target.request().delete();
value = response.readEntity(Double.class);
```

To implement a client, the only library you need is the RESTEasy client. If you work with maven, you can simply add this library in your pom.xml:

```
<dependency>
    <groupId>org.jboss.resteasy</groupId>
    <artifactId>resteasy-client</artifactId>
    <version>3.0.19.Final</version>
</dependency>
```

REST application and components

In this paragraph, we will analyze the JAX-RS application interface.

This interface is mandatory when sharing the services. If you must only write simple services, and you don't want to write this class, there is a valid and nice alternative to it. Simply add this piece to your web.xml:

```
<servlet-mapping>
  <servlet-name>javax.ws.rs.core.Application</servlet-name>
  <url-pattern>/myjaxrs/*</url-pattern>
</servlet-mapping>
```

Automatically, the next services you will write will be callable using the myjaxrs context together with the name of the service declared with the @Path annotation. The URL-pattern in this case is used instead of the @PathApplication annotation.

However, the application is not only used to host the services. Many other components are provided by JAX-RS. In this paragraph, we will see the main components and how to register them.

Container components

The component works on two different channels--*CLIENT* and *SERVER*--specified in the `javax.ws.rs.RuntimeType` enumeration. The container components are configured in the `javax.ws.rs.core.Application` interface. Here's an example of configuration:

```
@ApplicationPath("/services")
public class HttpApplication extends Application {
    @Override
    public Set<Class<?>> getClasses() {
        final Set<Class<?>> classes = new HashSet<>();
        classes.add(RegisterCall.class);
        classes.add(RegisterResponse.class);
        classes.add(HttpReceiver.class);
        return classes;
    }
}
```

The container components work on the server side. There are two interfaces to implement a container component.

Container request filter

It manages the requests through the `ContainerRequestContext`. This context manages different informations as the used language, the input stream, the headers and the security contexts. Here a sample:

```
public class RegisterCall implements ContainerRequestFilter
{
    @Override
    public void filter(ContainerRequestContext requestContext) throws
IOException {
        String calledMethod = requestContext.getMethod();
        requestContext.setProperty("calledMethod", calledMethod);
    }
}
```

This filter adds a property to the request setting the actual method used by the client against the service.

Container Response Filter

It manages the responses through the `ContainerRequestContext` and the `ContainerResponseContext`. This context manages different information as the used language, the output stream, the headers, the security contexts, and the status of the response. Here's an example:

```
public class RegisterResponse implements ContainerResponseFilter {
    @Override
    public void filter(ContainerRequestContext requestContext,
ContainerResponseContext responseContext) throws IOException {
            responseContext.getHeaders().add("calledMethod",
requestContext.getProperty("calledMethod"));
    }
}
```

This filter takes the property inserted previously by the Container Request Filter and adds it to the response headers. To see the result, take as example this REST service:

```
@Path("/receiver")
@Stateless
public class HttpReceiver {
    @OPTIONS
    @Path("/options")
    @Produces(MediaType.TEXT_PLAIN)
    public double options() {
        return 88.99;
    }
    ...
}
```

Also, the client calling the `options` method:

```
...
WebTarget target = client.target(url + "services/receiver/options");
Response response = target.request().options();
String calledMethod = response.getHeaderString("calledMethod");
...
```

In the `calledMethod` variable, we will find the value `OPTIONS`.

Name binding

Name binding container filters are called for each call sent to a service in the application. JAX-RS 2.0 provides a new feature to restrict the container components only to a service or a method of the service. See how to do it. The first thing we need is an annotation marked with the new annotation @NameBinding:

```
@Target({ TYPE, METHOD })
@Retention(value = RUNTIME)
@NameBinding
public @interface Logged {
}
```

Now, add this annotation to the filter:

```
@Logged
public class RegisterResponse implements ContainerResponseFilter
```

Also, add it to a method of the service:

```
@Path("/receiver")
@Stateless
public class HttpReceiver {
    @OPTIONS
    @Path("/options")
    @Produces(TEXT_PLAIN)
    @Logged
    public double options() {
        return 88.99;
    }
    ...
}
```

At this point, the annotated filter will be executed only when the client will call the option method of the service.

Providers

A REST provider is a class marked with the @Provider annotation. This annotation makes a class discoverable by JAX-RS runtime during a provider scanning phase. This phase usually starts after the start of the JAX RS application or the client builder so that the provider is reachable at runtime.

Client components

The client components work in the CLIENT runtime. They are registered by the client, so they must not be configured in the `getClasses()` of the application. If we use a remote client to connect to the REST service, we need this component to be inside the remote client package. They will not interact with the container. Here's how to register client components:

```
Client client = newClient();
client.register(ClientFirstReaderInterceptor.class);
```

As for the container component, we have two types of client components; we will discuss these further now.

Client Request Filter

Client Request Filter is very similar to the Container Request Filter. A `ClientRequestContext` is used to manage the information. Here are some operations you can do with a Client Request Context:

- Read and write headers.
- Read and write properties. The properties are very similar to the headers with the difference that they work only inside the context.
- Manipulate the stream entity of the POST and PUT methods.
- Change the Entity class type.
- Read and write cookies.
- Configure the client.

This is a sample of Client Request Filter:

```
@Provider
@Priority(Priorities.ENTITY_CODER)
public class MyClientRequestFilter implements ClientRequestFilter {
    private static final Logger logger =
getLogger(MyClientRequestFilter.class.getName());
    @Override
    public void filter(ClientRequestContext requestContext) throws
IOException {
        logger.info("getClient : " + requestContext.getClient());
        logger.info("getConfiguration : " +
requestContext.getConfiguration());
        logger.info("getCookies : " + requestContext.getCookies());
        logger.info("getEntityClass : " + requestContext.getEntityClass());
        logger.info("getEntityStream : " + requestContext.getEntityStream());
```

```
        logger.info("getEntityType : " + requestContext.getEntityType());
        logger.info("getHeaders : " + requestContext.getHeaders());
        logger.info("getPropertyNames : " +
requestContext.getPropertyNames());
        ...
    }
}
```

As you can see, the Client Request Context has several methods of working:

The new `javax.ws.rs.Priorities` class provides new priority numbers for REST services:

- `AUTHENTICATION`: Security authentication filter/interceptor priority; the value is 1000
- `AUTHORIZATION`: Security authorization filter/interceptor priority; the value is 2000
- `HEADER_DECORATOR`: Header decorator filter/interceptor priority; the value is 3000
- `ENTITY_CODER`: Message encoder or decoder filter/interceptor priority; the value is 4000
- `USER`: User-level filter/interceptor priority; the value is 5000

> For more details, you can find the priorities in `Chapter 2`, *Working with Dependency Injection* on the voice observer methods.

Client components need to be marked with the `@Provider` annotation, seen in the preceding paragraph.

Client Response Filter

The Client Response Filter work in the phase next to the request filters phase and elaborate the response to give it to the client. In this example, we will see a collaborative work between the client request and response filters. Here's a sample of client request filter that set a header content-type to text/HTML:

```
@Provider
@Priority(ENTITY_CODER)
public class MyClientRequestFilter implements ClientRequestFilter {
    ...
    @Override
```

```
    public void filter(ClientRequestContext requestContext) throws
IOException {
        ...
        requestContext.getHeaders().add(CONTENT_TYPE_STRING, TEXT_HTML);
    }
}
```

This is a Client Response Filter that takes the created header and sets it to the response:

```
@Provider
@Priority(ENTITY_CODER + 2)
public class MyClientResponseFilter implements ClientResponseFilter {
    ...
    @Override
    public void filter(ClientRequestContext requestContext,
ClientResponseContext responseContext) throws IOException {
        ...
        responseContext.getHeaders().putSingle(CONTENT_TYPE_STRING,
requestContext.getHeaderString(CONTENT_TYPE_STRING));
    }
}
```

The client will be something like this:

```
Client client = newClient();
client.register(new MyClientResponseFilter());
client.register(new MyClientRequestFilter());
WebTarget target = client.target(url + "myjaxrs/simple/");
WebTarget resourceTarget = target.path("/valuesget");
resourceTarget = resourceTarget.queryParam("OrderID",
"111").queryParam("UserName", "Luke");
Invocation invocation = resourceTarget.request().buildGet();
Response response = invocation.invoke();
```

As for the container components, the filters are executed in a chain of components in a mode very similar to the interceptors seen in Chapter 2, *Working with Dependency Injection*. If you want to break the chain, there is a very useful method in the ClientRequestContext interface:

```
@Provider
@Priority(ENTITY_CODER - 1)
public class BlockChainFilter implements ClientRequestFilter {
    @Override
    public void filter(ClientRequestContext requestContext) throws
IOException {
        ResponseBuilder responseBuilder = serverError();
        Response response = responseBuilder.status(BAD_REQUEST).build();
        requestContext.abortWith(response);
```

```
    }
}
```

This filter creates an HTTP response through the `javax.ws.rs.core` tools and then executes the `abortWith` method. This method blocks the request chain, directly passing a response to give to the client. To test the chain, we can register this new filter to our client:

```
Client client = newClient();
client.register(new MyClientResponseFilter());
client.register(new MyClientRequestFilter());
client.register(new BlockChainFilter());
```

`BlockChainFilter` has a priority lower than `MyClientRequestFilter`, so it will be started for the first time, and it will block the chain, and the `MyClientRequestFilter` never will be executed.

During the execution, `MyClientResponseFilter` will not find the header created by the request, so the content-type header will not be created in the response.

We can register components either as classes or instances. The difference is that if we have the ready instance, the same instance will be used always. Using the class, the instance will be created and managed by the container.

Interceptors

Like CDI, JAX-RS also has its interceptor chain. JAX-RS has two types of interceptors: the readers and the writers.

Reader interceptors

The reader interceptors manage the reader interceptor context. This context lets you manage the following things:

- Headers
- Input stream

See an example of interceptor that manipulates the input stream of a POST method call:

```
@Provider
@ConstrainedTo(SERVER)
@Priority(ENTITY_CODER + 30)
public class ServerReaderInterceptor implements ReaderInterceptor {
```

```
    @Override
    public Object aroundReadFrom(ReaderInterceptorContext
interceptorContext) throws IOException, WebApplicationException {
        InputStream inputStream = interceptorContext.getInputStream();
        byte[] bytes = new byte[inputStream.available()];
        inputStream.read(bytes);
        String requestContent = new String(bytes);
        requestContent = requestContent + ".Request changed in
ServerReaderInterceptor.";
        interceptorContext.setInputStream(new
ByteArrayInputStream(requestContent.getBytes()));
        return interceptorContext.proceed();
    }
}
```

This interceptor catches the input stream and appends a text. At difference of the filters that work for a particular runtime scope, the interceptors are configurable through the @ConstrainedTo annotation, where you can specify the runtime scope CLIENT or SERVER through the enum javax.ws.rs.RuntimeType. If the @ConstrainedTo is not declared, the component will work both as a client and server.

The registration of the interceptor follows the same specifications seen in the filter according to the declared runtime scope. A server interceptor marked as @Provider doesn't need to be registered to work.

The proceed method lets us go to the next interceptor of the chain.

Writer interceptors

The writer interceptors manage the writer interceptor context. This context lets you manage the following things:

- Headers
- Output stream
- Entities

The entity and the output streams represent the result of a REST call. The entity is the serialized object declared in the service methods. Here's a sample of writer interceptor that adds an encrypted MD5 string in the output stream:

```
@Provider
public class ContentMD5Writer implements WriterInterceptor {
    @Override
    public void aroundWriteTo(WriterInterceptorContext context) throws
```

```
IOException, WebApplicationException {
    MessageDigest digest = null;
    try {
        digest = getInstance("MD5");
    } catch (NoSuchAlgorithmException e) {
        throw new IllegalArgumentException(e);
    }
    ByteArrayOutputStream buffer = new ByteArrayOutputStream();
    DigestOutputStream digestStream = new DigestOutputStream(buffer,
digest);
    OutputStream old = context.getOutputStream();
    context.setOutputStream(digestStream);
    try {
      context.proceed();
      byte[] hash = digest.digest();
      String encodedHash = getEncoder().encodeToString(hash);
      context.getHeaders().putSingle(CONTENT_MD5_STRING, encodedHash);
      byte[] content = buffer.toByteArray();
      old.write(content);
    } finally {
      context.setOutputStream(old);
    }
  }
}
```

The result can be seen in the client:

```
Client client = newClient();
client.register(ContentMD5Writer.class);
String md5 = response.getHeaderString(CONTENT_MD5_STRING);
```

The variable MD5 will return the hcEzFGyuhOARcfBb4bM1sw== encrypted value.

Features

A feature is a configurable component. It is enabled during a registration through the register methods of the clients or getClasses of the application. It adds new aspects to the applications or clients. It can update the current JAX-RS configuration or add other subcomponents. The feature context lets you modify the current configuration. The following is a sample of the feature that adds a property in the feature context, updating the configuration:

```
public class AddProperties implements Feature {
    @Override
    public boolean configure(FeatureContext context) {
        context.property("configured_add_property", true);
```

```
        return true;
    }
}
```

This is a client that registers the feature and receives the new property from the feature:

```
Client client = newClient();
Configuration configuration = client.getConfiguration();
AddProperties addProperties = new AddProperties();
client.register(addProperties);
Map<String, Object> properties = configuration.getProperties();
boolean property = (Boolean) properties.get("configured_add_property");
```

The value of the property variable will be true.

The `Configuration` class can do the following things:

- Read and write class components
- Read and write instance components
- Read and write properties
- Read and write contracts

Contracts

The contracts are the interfaces implemented by the class components. A contract can be declared in the `register` method along with the component class. Let's look at a sample of client configuration:

```
Map<Class<?>, Integer> myContracts = new HashMap<Class<?>, Integer>();
myContracts.put(Feature.class, 1200);
client.register(AddProperties.class, myContracts);
```

Here's how to register contracts through the feature:

```
public boolean configure(FeatureContext context) {
    ...
    Map<Class<?>, Integer> myContracts = new HashMap<Class<?>, Integer>();
    myContracts.put(Feature.class, 1200);
    context.register(MyComponent.class, myContracts);
}
```

It's a good practice to add only the contracts implemented by the class. Other classes will be ignored by the containers. In this method, you can specify the priority number for each contract. This priority establishes the order to execute the implemented methods by the component that implements the contract.

Dynamic features

A dynamic feature, if registered, interacts automatically with each REST call to the service. It allows you to elaborate the call and add operations to it. Here's an example of dynamic feature declared as singleton through the `@Singleton` interface seen in `Chapter 2, Working with Dependency Injection`:

```
@Singleton
public class MyResourceSingleton implements DynamicFeature {
    ...
    @Override
    public void configure(ResourceInfo resourceInfo, FeatureContext context)
{
        Class<?> resourceClass = resourceInfo.getResourceClass();
        Method method = resourceInfo.getResourceMethod();
        context.property("new_dynamic_feature", resourceClass + "|" +
method);
    }
}
```

This component catches the class of the called JAX-RS service and its called method through the `javax.ws.rs.container.ResourceInfo` interface and adds a property with the called service information. The service can be the `calculator` called by the client:

```
WebTarget target = client.target(url +
"services/calculator/sum?value=4&value=6");
Response response = target.request().get();
...
WebTarget target = client.target(url + "services/calculator/div");
Entity<List<Double>> valuesAsList = entity(asList(new Double[] { 4.5, 6.7
}), APPLICATION_JSON);
Response response =
target.request(APPLICATION_JSON_TYPE).put(valuesAsList);
```

In this case, the dynamic feature will be called twice for each method. This is how we register the `MyResourceSingleton` feature as singleton in the `Application` class:

```
@ApplicationPath("/services")
public class CalculatorApplication extends Application {
    @Inject
```

```
        private MyResourceSingleton myResourceSingleton;
        @Override
        public Set<Class<?>> getClasses() {
          final Set<Class<?>> classes = new HashSet<>();
          ...
          classes.add(Calculator.class);
          return classes;
        }
        @Override
        public Set<Object> getSingletons() {
          Set<Object> objects = new HashSet<Object>();
          objects.add(myResourceSingleton);
          return objects;
        }
        ...
    }
```

The `getSingletons()` method is very similar to `getClasses()` with the difference that it doesn't instantiate the components. So, only singletons can be registered there.

Forms and beans

A nice feature of JAX-RS is the interactions with the web forms. The parameters of a form that point to a REST service can be automatically imported in the service without too much code to write. Take a look at this simple HTML form code:

```
<html>
  <body>
      <h1>JAX-RS @FormParam Example</h1>
        <form action="myjaxrs/simple/form" method="post">
          <label for="data">Data: </label>
          <input id="data" type="text" name="data" />
          <input type="submit" value="Submit" />
        </form>
  </body>
</html>
```

This form points to the `myjaxrs/simple/form` REST service represented by the service:

```
@Path("/simple")
@Stateless
public class SimpleService {
    ...
    @POST
    @Path("form")
    @Produces(TEXT_HTML)
```

```
        public String values(@FormParam("data") String data) {
           return data;
        }
    }
```

The @FormParam lets you automatically take the input fields of the form and serialize them in the service as input parameters.

A more complete annotation introduced in JAX-RS 2.0 is the @BeanParam. With it, you can serialize a set of parameters through one bean. For example, we can move the values method of the service as follows:

```
@POST
@Path("{id}")
@Produces(TEXT_HTML)
public String values(@BeanParam Param param) {
    return param.getResourceId() + "|" + param.getData() + "|" +
param.getHeader();
}
```

This can be done using a form such as the following:

```
<html>
  <body>
    <h1>JAX-RS @BeanParam Example</h1>
      <form action="myjaxrs/simple/6" method="post">
         <label for="data">Data: </label>
         <input id="data" type="text" name="data" />
         <input type="submit" value="Submit" />
      </form>
  </body>
</html>
```

With the @BeanParam annotation, you can use a bean to represent the parameters of the forms. Let's look at the bean parameter declaration in detail:

```
public class Param {
    private String resourceId;

    @FormParam("data")
    private String data;

    @HeaderParam(CONTENT_TYPE_STRING)
    private String header;

    @PathParam("id")
    public void setResourceId(String id) {
       resourceId = id;
```

```
    }

    public String getResourceId() {
        return resourceId;
    }
    public String getData() {
        return data;
    }
    public void setData(String data) {
        this.data = data;
    }

    public String getHeader() {
        return header;
    }

    public void setHeader(String header) {
        this.header = header;
    }
}
```

The bean includes the field data declared as `FormParam`, as seen in the preceding sample, a `PathParam`, and a `HeaderParam`. As you can see in the preceding service sample, we have parameterized the `@Path` with an EL annotation `{id}`.

The `@PathParam` lets you value it with the value 6 passed to the path of the form.

The `@HeaderParam` configured with the value `CONTENT_TYPE_STRING` catches the header content-type always present in the streams. The following is the last form interpreted by the browser:

If we pass a value to the **Data** field and click on **Submit** we will get as result the string calculated in the method values of the service:

Selenium and Drone

The test cases of the forms are realized with Selenium and Drone. Selenium lets you test web applications, simulating navigation with the browser. To start a Selenium test, you simply need a web driver configured with the name of the browser that you want to use, and then you can put the Java commands to navigate in the web. Here's an example of injection of the web driver through Drone, a sophisticated inject engine by Arquillian, the filling of the data field and, in the end, a click on the **Submit** button:

```
@Drone
private WebDriver driver;
...
driver.get(url);
driver.findElement(id("data")).sendKeys("my_data");
driver.findElement(xpath("html/body/form/input[2]")).click();
```

Summary

Now we are able to write services for our enterprise applications. REST Services are the starting point to write more complex architectures, such as SOA and microservices, not covered in WildFly because it limits its tools to the Java enterprise edition. With this chapter, we end the second part of the book covering the business logic and the main enterprise components. REST is now asynchronous too. This part of REST will be analyzed in the next part of the book about the asynchronous and real time, in the Chapter 10, *Asynchronous REST* to be precise.

7
Implementing WebSockets

WebSockets are a private channel from the web browser and the servers or vice versa only using the HTTP protocol with HTML 5. Your web page can receive events, so you can keep listening for a message without click buttons. Finally, you can receive real-time messages from your web page. A chat system is a simpler example that illustrates WebSockets. In this chapter, we will start by a chat, going forward to more complex examples. Here are the focal points we will go over:

- History of WebSockets
- How write a chat with WebSockets
- Notes on the implemented WebSocket in WildFly 10
- How secure a WebSocket
- All available annotations for our enterprise components

History of the web

The internet has been developed in a way to allow you to share information efficiently and without delays. Information on the internet is transported through a suite of protocols called TCP/IP, which defines the method of sharing information between computers with a decentralized network with reasonable certainty of their arrival in destination.

TCP/IP links the message like origin and destination. The message contains a summary calculated from the origin message that can be used by the receiver to verify that all state information is successfully received.

After the network has spread increasingly and we passed through the HTTP protocol. HTTP provides a level of abstraction bundling TCP/IP connections in a wrapper and contains information on the request and the required data for the application, for example, the form fields or the cookies' values. HTTP requests provide a simple response interface that works well for actions such as receiving a web page, moving and loading data or images, or sending data to a server to make it persistent.

After 2004, there was a high evolution on the development of web applications thanks to Ajax. Web became a more extremely useful and friendly method by which to retrieve and send data server and client side. Ajax is an interface where using JavaScript you can create HTTP requests and handle the response in a asynchronous mode through callback functions.

Before Ajax, you had to wait for the complete loading of the page to receive a little bit of results. With Ajax and a little JavaScript, you have to wait only for the loading of the part of the page you are interested in. So, it became a good practice to provide a single page containing all data. Examples of this are Gmail, Facebook, and Twitter, which give the user a smoother workflow collecting data through the server calls working in background. HTTP was the same since 1999, supporting the transmission of these packets through disposable connections.

Next, the need for real-time communication in the web applications has grown. Online games, reporting systems and chat applications are based on a forced use of the HTTP protocol through polling systems. Examples of polling are Ajax and Comet-persistent HTTP connections. Flash too can open iFrames to poll for new data from the server. Although evolved and spread, these systems had problems as complexity or inefficiencies. TCP already provides a two-way links system and direct connections through client and server. So why don't take advantage of these features and do a direct connections through browser and server so we can work with asynchronous messages? The idea of WebSocket stems from here.

The WebSocket specification was completed in a good moment in the era of the development of web applications thanks the spread of HTML5 and a large set of related web open technologies. Now this specification is stable and it is supported by many browsers like Firefox, Chrome, Internet Explorer 10 and Safari.

With WebSockets, ends the era of the system polling to receive asynchronous messages and start the direct channel between browser and server, all described in the TCP protocol. Online games for example take advantages becoming more stable and more efficient and performant in the real time. Cooperative online games are now a reality.

With WebSockets, many users at the same time can cooperate inside the browser with immediate responses and requests. All this can be built with WildFly through its open web technologies.

Implementation engine

Undertow implements WebSockets in WildFly. It's the new web server of WildFly moving from the historical Tomcat servlet engine in all JBoss AS. The main reason of this substitution is done by WebSocket. Undertow is the first web server implementing WebSockets together with the other Java web specifications as JSF, servlet and JSP.

A first basic example

In this paragraph, we will start a sample and will show all basic annotations and classes for WebSockets. See at the first an HTML page:

This page is represented by a link that sends a message through a WebSocket. Here is the code of the page:

```
<!DOCTYPE html>
<html>
    <head>
        <meta charset="UTF-8">
        <title>WebSocket Client</title>
        <script type="text/javascript">
            var ws = new WebSocket("ws://127.0.0.1:8080/web-sockets/chat");
            ws.onopen = function() {
                alert("Web Socket is connected!!");
            };
            ws.onmessage = function(evt) {
                var msg = evt.data;
                alert("Message received:" + msg);
            };
            ws.onclose = function() {
                alert("Connection is closed...");
            };
```

```
        function sendMessage() {
            ws.send("Message to server from client");
        }
    </script>
</head>
<body>
    <a href="javascript:sendMessage()">Send message</a>
</body>
</html>
```

The WebSockets specifications introduced in HTML 5 provide a JavaScript client implemented by the class WebSocket. Implementations of WebSocket can be written in JavaScript, Java, or languages that work on the web. All implementations have the following four functions:

- onopen: The event working when the WebSocket is opened
- onmessage: The event working when a message is received
- onclose: The event working when the WebSocket is closed
- send: The function to send the message to the channel of the WebSocket

A WebSocket is a real direct channel through the client and server via the web. Before WebSockets, there were only tricks to simulate this functionality, for example, Ajax. In the next paragraph, we will analyze the differences with Ajax.

When we start this page or we receive a message, an alert will automatically appear on the page:

We could change the alert with a dynamic build of the page as HTML 5 pages usually do. The important thing to understand is that this is done without too much code to write.

As as example, now see the server side of the socket. Of course, we will use the WebSockets API for Java 1.0 implemented by WildFly:

```java
@ServerEndpoint(value = "/chat")
public class WebSocketServer {
@OnOpen
public void onOpen(Session session) throws NamingException {
    ManagedExecutorService mes =
        doLookup("java:comp/DefaultManagedExecutorService");
    final Session s = session;
    mes.execute(new Runnable() {
    @Override
    public void run() {
        try {
            for (int i = 0; i < 3; i++) {
                sleep(10000);
                s.getBasicRemote().sendText("Message from server");
            }
        } catch (InterruptedException | IOException e) {
            ...
        }
    }
    });
}
@OnMessage
public String onMessage(String message, Session session) {
    return "Server received [" + message + "]";
}
@OnClose
public void onClose(Session session) {
    ...
}
@OnError
public void onError(Throwable exception, Session session) {
    ...
}
```

As you can note, the server has the same functions of the client implemented in this case by the methods annotated by the annotations @OnClose, @OnMessage, and @OnOpen. If you have an error during the transport or the connection of the WebSocket, the @OnError annotation interacts, allowing you to manage the error in the annotated method.

The `@ServerEndpoint` annotation declares the annotated class in a server endpoint callable with the URL declared in the value of the annotation. For example, if the web application has the name web-sockets, the URL of the endpoint could be `ws://127.0.0.1:8080/web-sockets/chat`.

In the `onOpen` method, we send the same message three times to client and it will receive them through the JavaScript `onMessage` function as alerts.

WebSocket container

In more complex scenarios, WebSockets can be called by other enterprise components, for example, to intercept messages, filter, or decorate them. An enterprise component can connect directly to the WebSocket statically through `javax.websocket.ContainerProvider`. Here is an example:

```
final WebSocketContainer serverContainer =
ContainerProvider.getWebSocketContainer();
serverContainer.connectToServer(WebSocketClient.class,
Uri.parse("ws://127.0.0.1:8080/web-sockets/chat"));
```

Through `ContainerProvider`, the client obtains `javax.websocket.WebSocketContainer`, and then it can connect through an annotated client class to the WebSocket URL shown before. Here is a sample client Java class:

```
@ClientEndpoint
public class WebSocketClient {
    ...
    private static final BlockingDeque<String> queue = new
LinkedBlockingDeque<>();

    ...
    @OnOpen
    public void open(final Session session) throws IOException {
       session.getBasicRemote().sendText("Hello");
    }

    @OnMessage
    public void message(final String message) {
       queue.add(message);
    }

    public static String getMessage() throws InterruptedException {
       return queue.poll(5, SECONDS);
    }
```

```
    . . .
}
```

The `@ClientEndpoint` annotation signals a class as a client WebSocket. Once connected to the WebSocket, the `WebClientSocket` instance is free to receive messages through the `message(...)` method because it is registered to the WebSocket channel with the URL `ws://127.0.0.1:8080/web-sockets/chat` seen before.

WebSocket session

The client can send or receive messages thanks to the session. The session is represented by the `javax.websocket.Session` interface.

The session is generated at runtime. Two sessions start when you connect to a WebSocket-- one for the client and one for the server. See the details of these functions in the next paragraphs.

Security

The session preserves security information for the connection:

- Negotiated sub protocol
- User principal
- User properties
- Negotiated extensions
- Function verifying if a connection is secure

The security configuration in the WebSockets depends on the used protocol. Setting the socket server with the HTTPS protocol, we get a good level of security.

HTTPS

HTTPS (HyperText Transfer Protocol over Secure Socket Layer), also known as HTTP over SSL, HTTP over TLS and Secure HTTP) is a secure communication protocol working through a network of computers, widely used on the internet.

HTTPS is communication via **HTTP (HyperText Transfer Protocol)** inside an encrypted connection through **Transport Layer Security (TLS)** or its parent, **Secure Sockets Layer (SSL)**. The principle at the basis of HTTPS is to have authentication of the visited website privacy protection integrity of data exchanged between the communicating parties.

In telecommunications and information technology, it is the result of an asymmetric encryption protocol to HTTP. It is used to ensure confidential transfers of data over the web so as to prevent interception of content.

HTTPS's security is guaranteed by the TLS protocol next, which in practice uses long-term private and public keys to generate short-term session keys. These keys are then used to encrypt the data stream between the client and server. The certificates defined by the X.509 standard are used to authenticate the server (sometimes the client). As a result, the approval authorities and the public key certificates are required in order to verify the relationship that exists between the certificate and its owner, in addition to generating the signature and managing the validity of the certificates.

While this may be more beneficial than verifying identities through a trusted system, mass disclosures on the surveillance network in 2013 drew the attention of the approval authorities as a potential weakness for man-in-the-middle attacks.

An important property in this context is forward secrecy, which ensures that encrypted communications recorded in the past can not be retrieved and deciphered and encryption keys to long-term or passwords are not compromised in the future. Not all web servers provide forward secrecy.

A website must be totally hosted on HTTPS protocol without having any of its content over HTTP--for example, to have an online upload script insecure (unencrypted)--or else you will be vulnerable to certain attacks and subjected to surveillance. Even having just a particular web page of a website that contains sensitive information (such as a login) page under HTTPS protocol and having the rest of the website uploaded to the HTTP protocol will expose you to possible attacks. On a website that has sensitive information somewhere on it, every time the site is accessed in HTTP instead of HTTPS, the user and the session will be exposed on the network. Similarly, cookies on an active web site via HTTPS must have the security attribute enabled.

Undertow has a default X.509 certificate to guarantee HTTPS connection. This certificate is generated automatically by a default keystore. In the main XML file configuration `standalone.xml` in the folder `/standalone/configuration`, you can find the HTTPS configuration provided by the security realm.

Security realm

A security realm comprises mechanisms for protecting resources in an application server. Each security realm consists of a set of configured security providers, users, groups, security roles, and security policies. A user must be defined in a security realm in order to access any resources belonging to that realm. When a user attempts to access a particular resource, the application server tries to authenticate and authorize the user by checking the security role assigned to the user in the relevant security realm and the security policy of the particular resource. In the `standalone.xml` file, we can see the default security realm configuration working with HTTPS:

```
<security-realm name="ApplicationRealm">
  <server-identities>
    <ssl>
      <keystore path="application.keystore" relative-
to="jboss.server.config.dir" keystore-password="password" alias="server"
key-password="password" generate-self-signed-certificate-host="localhost"/>
    </ssl>
  </server-identities>
  <authentication>
    <local default-user="$local" allowed-users="*" skip-group-
loading="true"/>
    <properties path="application-users.properties" relative-
to="jboss.server.config.dir"/>
  </authentication>
  <authorization>
    <properties path="application-roles.properties" relative-
to="jboss.server.config.dir"/>
  </authorization>
</security-realm>
```

The SSL connection is ensured by the default keystore, the `application.keystore` that manages the crypting keys used to encrypt the connection. In this example, the authentication is managed through keys inside the file `application-users.properties`. In this file, you can add a row containing user and password to authenticate in your web apps. Here is a sample:

```
admin=2a0923285184943425d1f53ddd58ec7a
```

The password is an Md5 encrypted string. It's a good practice use this system to preserve the passwords in the filesystem.

The authorization is done by the `application-roles.properties` file:

```
admin=PowerUser,BillingAdmin
```

In this case, the admin user will have the roles `PowerUser` and `BillingAdmin`. Those two files can be updated through the command-line script sited in the bin directory of WildFly `add-user.sh`. When you start this command, you must respond to the following questions:

```
bash-3.2$ ./add-user.sh
What type of user do you wish to add?
 a) Management User (mgmt-users.properties)
 b) Application User (application-users.properties)
(a): b
Enter the details of the new user to add.
Using realm 'ApplicationRealm' as discovered from the existing property
files.
Username : my-user
Password recommendations are listed below. To modify these restrictions
edit the add-user.properties configuration file.
 - The password should be different from the username
 - The password should not be one of the following restricted values {root,
admin, administrator}
 - The password should contain at least 8 characters, 1 alphabetic
character(s), 1 digit(s), 1 non-alphanumeric symbol(s)
Password :
WFLYDM0101: Password should have at least 1 digit.
Are you sure you want to use the password entered yes/no? yes
Re-enter Password :
What groups do you want this user to belong to? (Please enter a comma
separated list, or leave blank for none)[ ]: admin
About to add user 'my-user' for realm 'ApplicationRealm'
Is this correct yes/no? yes
Added user 'my-user' to file '.../application-users.properties'
Added user 'my-user' with groups admin to file '.../application-
roles.properties'
Is this new user going to be used for one AS process to connect to another
AS process?
e.g. for a slave host controller connecting to the master or for a Remoting
connection for server to server EJB calls.
yes/no? yes
To represent the user add the following to the server-identities definition
<secret value="bXktcGFzc3dvcmQ=" />
```

Reopening the `application-user.properties` file, we will find the new user:

```
my-user=5222410df4f506c6ab5637f07624364b
```

And `application-roles.properties` set to `admin`:

```
my-user=admin
```

As we can see in the aforementioned code list, we have two types of users--management users and application users. Management users work only in administrative applications as the web console or JMX systems, while application users work in developed custom applications as webapps or EJB applications.

The web server is configured here in the `standalone.xml` file:

```
<server name="default-server">
  <http-listener name="default" socket-binding="http" redirect-
socket="https" enable-http2="true"/>
  <https-listener name="https" socket-binding="https" security-
realm="ApplicationRealm" enable-http2="true"/>
  <host name="default-host" alias="localhost">
     <location name="/" handler="welcome-content"/>
     <filter-ref name="server-header"/>
     <filter-ref name="x-powered-by-header"/>
  </host>
</server>
```

To the web server is associated a HTTPS listener that will be active for each HTTPS call by the browser or another web client. This listener is configured to use the application realm seen before.

Of course, the default certificate cannot be used in a real situation. An X.509 certificate must not be known by all, so it's always important set your own certificate. After that, it needs to be verified by an authority provider to acquire security. The most famous are VeriSign, GeoTrust and Comodo.

Custom HTTPS configuration

Here is a guide to set HTTPS/TLS in our WebSocket endpoint starting from zero.

As the first thing, we need a new keystore. To create it, we can use via command line the standard Java `keytool` command:

```
keytool -genkey -alias websocket -keyalg RSA -keystore websocket.keystore -
validity 10950
```

```
Enter keystore password: websocket
Re-enter new password: websocket
What is your first and last name?
  [Unknown]:  Luca Stancapiano
What is the name of your organizational unit?
  [Unknown]:  JBoss Middleware
What is the name of your organization?
  [Unknown]:  Vige
What is the name of your City or Locality?
  [Unknown]:  Rome
What is the name of your State or Province?
  [Unknown]:  IT
What is the two-letter country code for this unit?
  [Unknown]:  IT
Is CN=Luca Stancapiano, OU=JBoss Middleware, O=Vige, L=Rome, ST=IT,
C=IT correct?
  [no]:  yes

Enter key password for <websocket>
    (RETURN if same as keystore password):
Re-enter new password:
```

It creates a keystore file. Put the `websocket.keystore` in your WildFly in the `/standalone/configuration` directory and start WildFly.

Once WildFly is started, we can use the command line console of WildFly to create a security realm for WildFly:

```
./bin/jboss-cli.sh -c
[standalone@localhost:9990 /] /core-service=management/security-
realm=WebSocketRealm:add()
{"outcome" => "success"}
```

Once created, we have to configure it:

```
[standalone@localhost:9990 /] /core-service=management/security-
realm=WebSocketRealm/server-identity=ssl:add(keystore-
path=websocket.keystore, keystore-relative-to=jboss.server.config.dir,
keystore-password=websocket)
{
    "outcome" => "success",
    "response-headers" => {
        "operation-requires-reload" => true,
        "process-state" => "reload-required"
    }
}
```

This script adds a new `scriptlet` in the `standalone.xml` file. If we open the configuration file, we will see the newly created security-realm:

```
<security-realm name="WebSocketRealm">
  <server-identities>
    <ssl>
      <keystore path="websocket.keystore" relative-
to="jboss.server.config.dir" keystore-password="websocket"/>
    </ssl>
  </server-identities>
 </security-realm>
```

In the end, we can modify the default server and append the newly created realm. The https listener will become:

```
<https-listener name="https" socket-binding="https" security-
realm="WebSocketRealm" enable-http2="true"/>
```

WebSocket HTTPS connection

See now how start a WebSocket secure connection with a java client. First, create a WebSocket endpoint:

```
@ServerEndpoint(value = "/session")
public class SessionSocketServer {
    ...
    @OnOpen
    public void onOpen(Session session) throws NamingException {
        ...
    }
    @OnMessage
    public String onMessage(String message, Session session) {
     return "Server received [" + message + "]";
    }
    @OnClose
    public void onClose(Session session) {
        ...
    }
    @OnError
    public void onError(Throwable exception, Session session) {
        ...
    }
}
```

And a basic WebSocket client:

```
public class SecureSocketClient extends Endpoint {
    ...
    private static final BlockingDeque<String> queue = new
LinkedBlockingDeque<>();

    @Override
    public void onClose(final Session session, CloseReason closeReason) {
    }
    public static void awake() throws InterruptedException {
        queue.poll(5, SECONDS);
    }
    @Override
    public void onOpen(Session session, EndpointConfig config) {
    ...
        session.getAsyncRemote().sendText("hi");
    }
}
```

This client is different from the previous client we have seen in the paragraph of WebSocket container, because in the first example we have used the annotations. The Java WebSocket specifications provide interfaces too as an alternative. In this case, the interface `javax.websocket.Endpoint` is used instead of the `javax.websocket.ClientEndpoint` annotation.

Undertow, by default, lets us navigate in the enterprise components in both modes, HTTP and HTTPS. If we want to force the server WebSocket endpoint to work only in HTTPS, we must configure the `web.xml` file of the application. This file is the standard descriptor for web applications. Here is a sample to force the transport as confidential to all HTTP URL contexts starting with the work session. Confidential transport is used to guarantee an encrypted channel. Here is the code of the `web.xml` descriptor file:

```
<web-app xmlns="http://xmlns.jcp.org/xml/ns/javaee"
        xmlns:xsi="http://www.w3.org/2001/XMLSchema-instance"
        xsi:schemaLocation="http://xmlns.jcp.org/xml/ns/javaee
http://xmlns.jcp.org/xml/ns/javaee/web-app_3_1.xsd"
        version="3.1">
    <security-constraint>
        <web-resource-collection>
            <web-resource-name>Secure WebSocket</web-resource-name>
            <url-pattern>/session</url-pattern>
        </web-resource-collection>
        <user-data-constraint>
            <transport-guarantee>CONFIDENTIAL</transport-guarantee>
        </user-data-constraint>
    </security-constraint>
```

```
    . . .
</web-app>
```

This configuration allows automatic redirect to a HTTPS connection, even if we run an HTTP call.

To start the HTTPS connection, as the first thing, we need to import an SSL context:

```
private SSLContext createSSLContext() throws Exception {
    SSLContext sslContext = getInstance("TLS");
    TrustManager tm = new X509TrustManager() {
        public void checkClientTrusted(X509Certificate[] chain, String
authType) throws CertificateException {
        }
        public void checkServerTrusted(X509Certificate[] chain, String
authType) throws CertificateException {
        }
        public X509Certificate[] getAcceptedIssuers() {
          return null;
        }
    };
    sslContext.init(null, new TrustManager[] { tm }, null);
    return sslContext;
}
. . .
SSLContext context = createSSLContext();
. . .
```

The SSL context is available from Java standard since the 1.4 version through the `javax.net.ssl.SSLContext` class. Because our X.509 certificate is not verified, we must force the trust manager to accept the connection. To do it, we can simply write a new `X509TrustManager` with empty methods and configure it in the init method of our SSL context.

The same thing is done when we connect to an uncertified site and the browser asks us to connect in anyway though we know its low reliability the possible security problems. In this image, we can see what happens when we connect with to the WildFly default page in HTTPS:

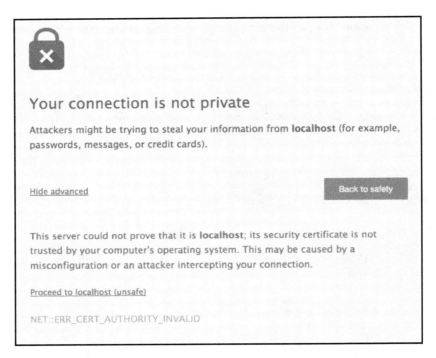

Once we have the SSL context, we can start the connection to the endpoint through our Java WebSocket client:

```
SecureSocketClient endpoint = new SecureSocketClient();
ClientEndpointConfig clientEndpointConfig = create().build();
clientEndpointConfig.getUserProperties().put(SSL_CONTEXT, context);
final WebSocketContainer serverContainer = getWebSocketContainer();
URI uri = new URI("wss://127.0.0.1:8443/secure-test/session");
serverContainer.connectToServer(endpoint, clientEndpointConfig, uri);
```

Another WebSocket component joint to the code is `javax.websocket.ClientEndpointConfig`. It provides a custom configuration for the client. To establish the SSL connection, we must add the SSL context to the user properties of the client. Note the used protocol for the WebSocket. WSS, WebSocket secure, is the secure protocol to use for the HTTPS connections.

8443 is the default SSL port configured in WildFly for the web application. We can customize it in the standalone.xml file:

```
<socket-binding name="https" port="${jboss.https.port:8443}"/>
```

Or simply add a Java property when we start WildFly. Here is a sample:

```
./standalone.sh -Djboss.https.port=8444
```

We can verify the HTTPS connection inside the SessionSocketServer instance:

```
private Logger logger = getLogger(SessionSocketServer.class.getName());
...
@OnOpen
  public void onOpen(Session session) throws NamingException {
      logger.info("session secure: "+session.isSecure());
  }
```

The result of the connection will be true.

Using JavaScript, the connection happens in a simpler manner because the SSL context is managed by the browser. So our JavaScript code will be something similar:

```
var ws = new WebSocket("wss://127.0.0.1:8443/secure-test/session");
ws.onopen = function() {
    alert("Web Socket is connected!!");
};
...
```

Negotiated subprotocols

There are no assumptions about the format of messages in the WebSocket protocol; the message contents are opaque. The only control is over the text or binary type messages, so they can be efficiently decoded by the client and server to improve performance.

Unlike HTTP or XHR requests, which add HTTP headers to the request and the response, the WebSocket message is raw. To resolve this problem, it is mandatory to implement a communication subprotocol between the client and the server. This subprotocol must be able to communicate this data:

- A consistent message header containing instructions to decode the remainder of the payload according the agree between the client and the server.

- The server and client can agree on a custom message format, for example, a communication system via JSON, using encoded messages or a custom binary format. So the metadata will be inside the encoded structure.
- A set of binary and text messages can be used to send and receive the payload and metadata information; for example, a text message can send a binary message with the application payload followed by a set of HTTP headers.

This list is only a simple example of possible strategies. All these strategies can be built in the code of the application, so we have a large set of chooses. Now we have analyzed the issues with serialization and metadata management. The next question we have to resolve is--how do both the client and server understand each other and how do we keep them synchronized?

WebSockets fortunately provide a good set of subprotocol negotiation APIs to address this issue. The client will report to the server, as part of its initial connection handshake, which protocols it supports. Here is an example of a JavaScript client using the negotiation subprotocols:

```
var ws = new WebSocket('ws://localhost:8080/negotiation-test/chat',
                       ['configured-proto']);

ws.onopen = function () {
  if (ws.protocol == 'configured-proto') {
    ...
  } else {
    ...
  }
}
```

As the previous example shows, the WebSocket constructor accepts an optional array of subprotocol names, which reports the list of protocols supported by the client or which it would support. The custom list is sent to the server, and the server can choose one of the protocols reported by the client.

If the subprotocol negotiation is okay, then the onopen callback is activated on the client, and the application can read the protocol attribute on the WebSocket object to use the chosen protocol. Otherwise, if the server supports none of the sent protocols, the WebSocket handshake cannot work. The onError callback is invoked, and the connection is ended with an error message.

The names of the subprotocols are defined in the application the server receives them through the initial handshake as shown before. The chosen subprotocol works only in the application layer so the core implementation of the WebSockets is free from issues.

Here is a sample of server endpoint that accepts three custom protocols:

```
@ServerEndpoint(value = "/chat", subprotocols = { "foo", "bar",
"configured-proto" })
public class MessageEndpoint {
    ...
    @OnMessage
    public String handleMessage(Session session, final String message) {
        String proto = session.getNegotiatedSubprotocol();
        return message + " " + (proto.isEmpty() ? "" : " (protocol=" + proto
+ ")");
    }
    ...
}
```

In the `@ServerEndpoint` annotations, you have to set the available subprotocols. If the subprotocol is not chosen by the client, the server will choose the first of the list.

The `getNegotiatedSubprotol()` method of the WebSocket session shows the chosen subprotocol for the connection.

The chosen negotiated subprotocol is sent through the HTTP header with the key `Sec-WebSocket-Protocol`.

Configurators for requests and responses

An alternative Java client can be found here:

```
@ClientEndpoint(subprotocols = {"foo", "bar", "configured-proto"},
configurator = ClientConfigurator.class)
public class AnnotatedClientEndpointWithConfigurator {
    ...
    public static String message() throws InterruptedException {
        ...
    }
    @OnOpen
    public void onOpen(final Session session) {
        ...
    }
    ...
}
```

The `Configurator` added in the `@ClientEndpoint` annotation is a part of `javax.websocket.ClientEndpointConfig`. It is used to manipulate the request and the response for a connection. Here is a simple implementation:

```
public class ClientConfigurator extends Configurator {
    ...
    @Override
    public void beforeRequest(Map<String, List<String>> headers) {
        ...
        headers.get(SEC_WEB_SOCKET_PROTOCOL_STRING).get(0);
            headers.put(SEC_WEB_SOCKET_PROTOCOL_STRING,
Collections.singletonList("configured-proto"));
        ...
    }
    @Override
    public void afterResponse(HandshakeResponse hr) {
        Map<String, List<String>> headers = hr.getHeaders();
        ...
    }
```

The `beforeRequest(...)` method is used in this case to send the `Sec-WebSocket-Protocol` header to the server endpoint. The server endpoint will read the header and it will establish the preferred subprotocol for the connection.

The Java code to start the connection will be something like this:

```
final WebSocketContainer serverContainer = getWebSocketContainer();
URI uri = new URI("ws://localhost:8080/negotiation-test/chat");
serverContainer.connectToServer(AnnotatedClientEndpointWithConfigurator.class, uri);
```

Request informations and parameters

The session preserves the informations of the request and its parameters:

- Path parameters
- Request parameters
- Query string
- Request URI
- Protocol version
- Is open

Path parameters

Path parameter lets you make a parametric connection path of the WebSockets. As for REST seen in `Chapter 6`, *Creating REST Services* we can use the URL path to make different choices in the flow. Here is a sample of a WebSocket endpoint with a parametric URL:

```
@ServerEndpoint(value = "/chat/{user}",...)
public class MessageEndpoint {
    ...
    @OnMessage
    public String handleMessage(Session session, final String message,
@PathParam("user") String user) {
        String proto = session.getNegotiatedSubprotocol();
        return message + " " + user + (proto.isEmpty() ? "" : "
(protocol=" + proto + ")");
    }
    ...
}
```

EL script seen in `Chapter 6`, *Creating REST Services* can be used to read parameters. The EL parameter `user` cited in the value of the `@ServerEndpoint` annotation, can be sent by the client through a simple connection code:

```
final WebSocketContainer serverContainer = getWebSocketContainer();
URI uri = new URI("ws://localhost:8080/negotiation-test/chat/Bob");
serverContainer.connectToServer(AnnotatedClientEndpointWithConfigurator.cla
ss, uri);
```

Through the URI, the WebSocket container associates with the server end point, passing the parameter valued as `Bob`.

The `javax.websocket.PathParam` annotation is very similar to the `javax.ws.rs.PathParam` annotation seen in `Chapter 6`, *Creating REST Services*. It can be added to any WebSocket endpoint override method, so we can manage the path parameter.

The same session provides a method to manage the path parameters:

```
Map<String, String> pathParameters = session.getPathParameters();
```

It will return:

```
{user=Bob}
```

Request parameters

In our URI connection, we can send HTTP request parameters as with a typical web application. If our client sends a parameter as follows:

```
final WebSocketContainer serverContainer = getWebSocketContainer();
URI uri = new URI("ws://localhost:8080/negotiation-
test/chat?my_request_id=35");
serverContainer.connectToServer(AnnotatedClientEndpointWithConfigurator.cla
ss, uri);
```

It will be received by the session. We can manage the parameter thanks to the getRequestParametersMap method:

```
Map<String, List<String>> requestParameters =
sessionServer.getRequestParameterMap()
```

With the result:

```
{my_request_id=35},
```

Through the query string method:

```
String queryString = sessionServer.getQueryString()
```

With the result:

```
my_request_id=35
```

Or through the request URI:

```
URI uri = sessionServer.getRequestURI()
```

This is the result:

```
/negotiation-test/chat?my_request_id=35
```

Other features

By default, the WebSocket protocol used by Java EE 7 has version 13. Through this method, we can verify the used version protocol:

```
String version = session.getProtocolVersion();
```

This method searches for the parameter `Sec-WebSocket-Version` inside the HTTP headers.

To verify that the session is open, a simple API can be used:

```
boolean open = session.isOpen();
```

Container configuration

The session preserves the information of the WebSocket container:

- **Default async send timeout**: This sets the number of milliseconds the implementation will time out attempting to send a WebSocket message for all `RemoteEndpoints` associated with this container. A non-positive number indicates that the implementation will not time out when attempting to send a WebSocket message asynchronously. Note that this default may be overridden in each `Remote Endpoint`.

- **Default max binary message buffer size**: This sets the default maximum size of incoming binary message that this container will buffer.

- **Default max session idle timeout**: Sets the default time in milliseconds after which any WebSocket sessions in this container will be closed if it has been inactive. A value of 0 or negative indicates the sessions will never time out due to inactivity. The value may be overridden on a per session basis.

- **Default max text message buffer size**: Sets the maximum size of incoming text message that this container will buffer.

- **Installed extensions**: Return the set of extensions installed in the container. An extension is a little part of configuration represented by a name and a map of parameters.

Here is how to set these configurations starting by the session:

```
WebSocketContainer container = session.getContainer();
container.setAsyncSendTimeout(4);
container.setDefaultMaxBinaryMessageBufferSize(5);
container.setDefaultMaxSessionIdleTimeout(6);
container.setDefaultMaxTextMessageBufferSize(7);
```

Here is how to show the extensions used in the WebSocket container:

```
Set<Extension> installedExtensions = container.getInstalledExtensions();
Iterator<Extension> extensions = installedExtensions.iterator();
while (extensions.hasNext()) {
    Extension extension = extensions.next();
    logger.info("extension name: " + extension.getName());
    List<Parameter> parameters = extension.getParameters();
    for (Parameter parameter : parameters) {
        logger.info("extension parameter name: " + parameter.getName());
        logger.info("extension parameter value: " + parameter.getValue());
    }
}
```

Runtime configuration

The session preserves the runtime configuration:

- Max binary message buffer size
- Max idle timeout
- Max text message buffer size

Client WebSockets

From the session, we can get two client types to send messages:

- **Basic**: A simple client where we can send the following messages:
  - Texts
  - Objects
  - Binary contents
  - Ping pong messages as binary contents
- **Async**: It can send the same message types and we can configure how to send them:
  - Send timeout
  - Message handler
  - Batch outgoing messages

Basic client

From the session, we can get the `basic` client. This client has all the functions to send messages. It can be taken like this:

```
Basic basic = sessionClient.getBasicRemote();
```

Here are some examples of sending messages:

```
ByteBuffer byteBuffer = allocate(23);
basic.sendBinary(byteBuffer);
basic.sendBinary(byteBuffer, true);
basic.sendObject(555);
basic.sendText("my text");
basic.sendText("my text 2", false);
```

The `java.nio.ByteBuffer` abstract class is the byte buffer chosen by the WebSocket specification to send binary messages. We can send **Partial** or **Whole** messages according to the used method. Through:

```
basic.sendBinary(byteBuffer);
```

We send Whole messages through the internet. If the byte buffer is too large, we can split it into Partial messages and send them one at a time, like so:

```
basic.sendBinary(byteBuffer1, false);
basic.sendBinary(byteBuffer2, false);
basic.sendBinary(byteBuffer3, false);
basic.sendBinary(byteBuffer, true);
```

The boolean value established when the Partial message is the last sent value so that the server can compose the Whole message.

Text messages can be sent as Partial or Whole too in the same manner.

If we want to only test the net through simpler messages, a ping/pong functionality can be used. The parent class of `Basic`, `javax.websocket.RemoteEndpoint`, manages this type of messages:

```
ByteBuffer byteBuffer = allocate(13);
RemoteEndpoint remoteEndpoint = (RemoteEndpoint)basic;
remoteEndpoint.sendPing(byteBuffer);
remoteEndpoint.sendPong(byteBuffer);
```

More complex objects can be sent through the `sendObject()` method. Remember that only serializable objects can be sent through the internet.

Some systems could be more comfortable to work with the java.io classes. The basic client lets you work with the `java.io.Writer` and `java.io.OutputStream`. They can be invoked in a very simple manner:

```
OutputStream outputStream = basic.getSendStream();
Writer writer = basic.getSendWriter();
```

Async client

The asynchronous client manages the same messages of the basic client but it:

- Doesn't suspend the current thread until the sending of the message
- Can establish a send timeout. After this time, the message expires
- Can batch the messages

Here you can see how to take the asynchronous client:

```
Async async = sessionClient.getAsyncRemote();
```

See some examples of text, binary, and object messages:

```
ByteBuffer byteBuffer = allocate(11);
Future<Void> future = async.sendBinary(byteBuffer);
async.setSendTimeout(45);
future.get();
```

To send asynchronous messages, the `java.util.concurrent.` Future class introduced in Java 7 is used. In this sample, the message will be sent after the execution of the `get()` method of the `Future` class.

Facultatively, we can set the timeout, so after that the message expires and it cannot be sent. If the timeout is set to `-1`, then it is disabled.

 In the previous section, *Container configuration,* we exposed the default timeouts. This last configuration of the timeout is used to override the default.

The alternative to the `Future` class is the `SendHandler`:

```
ByteBuffer byteBuffer = allocate(39);
SendHandler sendHandler = new SendHandler() {
    @Override
    public void onResult(SendResult result) {
        boolean ok = result.isOK();
        Throwable throwable = result.getException();
    }
};
async.sendBinary(byteBuffer, sendHandler);
```

The `javax.websocket.SendHandler` provides a callback method where you can see the status of the result. You can see if the send result is okay. If not, you can monitor it through the thrown exception. The same thing can be done with the text and object messages:

```
future = async.sendObject(666);
future.get();
...
async.setSendTimeout(45);
async.sendObject("my test 2", sendHandler);
future = async.sendText("my text");
future.get();
...
async.sendText("my text 2", sendHandler);
```

Another important feature is the batch. With the batch we can declare all the objects, texts or binaries to send them all together as they are in a transaction. Here is a sample of a send batch:

```
async.setBatchingAllowed(true);
async.sendObject("my test 2", sendHandler);
async.sendText("my text 2", sendHandler);
future = async.sendText("my text");
future.get();
async.flushBatch();
```

If we set the `setBatchingAllowed` method to `true`, then all those messages will be sent only when the `flushBatch()` method is executed. If there is an error, all messages will be terminated.

Message handlers

Message handlers are used to manage messages according to the type.

Developers must implement message handlers so that they can receive incoming messages through a WebSocket conversation. Each WebSocket session works on one thread at a time to call its own message handlers. So, because each message handler instance must be used to handle messages for only one WebSocket session, at most one thread at a time can be calling its methods. Programmers who wish to work with messages from multiple clients inside the same message handlers can add the same instance as a handler on each WebSocket session of the clients. In that case, they must write code while paying attention that their message handler will be called concurrently by multiple threads, each one coming from a different session client side.

WebSocket specifications let you create a custom message handler. Here is a sample:

```
public class SessionMessageHandler implements Whole<PongMessage> {
  private Logger logger = getLogger(SessionMessageHandler.class.getName());
    @Override
    public void onMessage(PongMessage message) {
       logger.info("message: " + message);
    }
}
```

This handler is used, for example, to decorate pong messages logging the message. A message handler can be of two types, Whole and Partial. These types extend the `javax.websocket.MessageHandler` interface, which provides the `onMessage` method. See the details in the next paragraphs.

Whole

This handler is notified by the container when a complete message is received. If the message is received in more parts, the container makes a buffer of it until it is has been completely received before this method is called.

The Whole handler is a generic type. The type is used to establish what messages it can receive. For handling incoming text messages, the allowed types for the type T are:

- `java.io.Reader`
- `java.lang.String`
- Any object for which there are corresponding `javax.websocket.Decoder.Text` or `javax.websocket.Decoder.TextStream` configured objects

To handle binary messages, the allowed types for the type T must be:

- `java.io.ByteBuffer`
- `byte[]`
- `java.io.InputStream`
- Any object for which there are corresponding `javax.websocket.Decoder.Binary` or `javax.websocket.Decoder.BinaryStream` configured objects

To work with the pong messages, the type T must be a class of type `javax.websocket.PongMessage`.

 It is preferable that developers work with simple message types such as `bytes []`, string or other objects other than readers or input streams. The container just works with the readers, so the object messages are automatically read by the readers. The strength of the WebSocket API is its simplicity, so it's better to take advantage of it.

Partial

This handler is notified by the developed implementation because it becomes ready to deliver parts of a Whole message.

For handling parts of text messages, the type T must be declared as a `java.lang.String` class.

The allowable types for binary messages are:

- `byte[]`
- `java.io.ByteBuffer`

 After the completion of the `onMessage` method, it is not recommended to use the byte buffer because it could be taken by the WebSocket implementation and opened or closed. As explained in the previous paragraph, use simple types.

Custom message handler registration

The WebSocket session lets you register the message handler. Here's how to register a message handler:

```
MessageHandler messageHandler = new SessionMessageHandler();
sessionClient.addMessageHandler(messageHandler);
```

Here we can see the registered message handlers in the session:

```
Set<MessageHandler> messageHandlers = sessionClient.getMessageHandlers();
```

As a default, Undertow provides in the message handlers list an annotated endpoint represented by the class `io.undertow.websockets.jsr.annotated.AnnotatedEndpoint`.

It is used to configure all events with the related message types. Each message type uses its own message handlers by default thanks to this class.

To use the message handler, we can simply send a pong message from our client. Here is a sample:

```
final WebSocketContainer serverContainer = getWebSocketContainer();
serverContainer.connectToServer(SessionSocketClient.class,
url.toURI().resolve("session"));
...
session.getBasicRemote().sendPong(allocate(33));
```

Here's how remove it from the session configuration:

```
sessionClient.removeMessageHandler(messageHandler);
```

Ajax versus WebSockets

WebSockets aren't intended to replace AJAX and even a replacement for Comet/long-poll is not strictly on the cards although there are many cases where this makes sense.

The goal of WebSockets is to provide a bi-directional, low-latency, long-running, and full-duplex connection between a server and browser. WebSockets open new application domains to browser applications where previously it was not possible unless AJAX was used. Examples of new applications can be dynamic media streams, interactive games, or bridging to existing network protocols.

However, there are similar goals between WebSockets and AJAX/Comet. For example, when the browser wants to receive events by the server, surely Comet techniques and WebSockets both should be considered. If your application needs low-latency push events, then this would be a factor in favor of WebSockets. Otherwise, if your application needs to work together with existing frameworks and deployed technologies (RESTful APIs, OAuth, load balancers, or proxies), Comet could be a more indicated technique, at least for now.

If we don't need these specific benefits that WebSockets provides, then it's probably better to stick to the existing techniques like Comet and AJAX because they allow you to reuse and integrate with a large set of existing tools, security mechanisms, technologies, and knowledge bases. AJAX is actually more known than WebSockets, and consequently it's easy to find consolidated frameworks that still work with AJAX technologies.

Otherwise, if you are creating a new application that warns of issues in latency and connection constraints of HTTP/Comet/Ajax, then it's better to work with WebSockets.

Summary

With this chapter, you know how to write WebSockets and asynchronous web message systems with a very little code. Java enterprise continues its journey of simplifying the implementation of components and applications. We now know when use Ajax instead of WebSockets and vice versa. Java EE provides many frameworks, often similar, so we must always be skilled at identifying what technology is better for our requests.
We worked on a message system based on HTTP. In the next chapter, we will see the classic message system of Java EE based on JMS. Enjoy!

8
Working with Messaging

WildFly 10 introduces the new JMS 2.0 implementation from Java EE 7. There are new good features in these specifications ranging from easier client writing and streamlined APIs to new messaging features.

JMS was always the object to review in the history of JBoss application server. Since the 2.x version, JBoss used open source products developed internally by the community, starting from JBoss MQ, JBoss Messaging, and HornetQ arriving until ActiveMQ.

Differently by the last engines, ActiveMQ called Artemis as an opensource product provided by the Apache community as well. It fully implements the JMS 2.0 specs. A custom ActiveMQ extended version, the `1.1.0.wildfly-017`, is imported in WildFly and managed through the wrapper project `wildfly-messaging-activemq`.

Following are the features of ActiveMQ:

- It has a full feature set of tools for messaging systems
- It is under open source license. The Apache software license v2.0 is used in Apache ActiveMQ Artemis to minimize barriers of adoption
- It is a pure Java product and runs on any platform with a Java 8+ runtime
- It provides a good performing engine. It manages persistent and not persistent messages
- It is highly usable
- It is elegant and has a clean design with very few third-party dependencies. ActiveMQ Artemis can start standalone, run integrated in any JEE application server, or run embedded inside other products.

- It is clustered. It works on clusters of servers that can load balance messages. It links geographically distributed clusters over unreliable connections to form a global network. The routing of the messages is configured in a highly flexible way.
- It has seamless high availability. It manages the failover so that all data is saved in the other nodes of the cluster. If a node falls down, it automatically finds a substitute node.

JMS 2.0 offers new API to work with minus code and make more robust code; anyway, it maintains compatibility with the old specifications. We will go ahead in this chapter by prioritizing the new mode. These are the key points we will show:

- Installation and configuration of queues and topics
- Implementation of JMS clients
- Notes on ActiveMQ
- Injection of JMS components
- Main JMS annotations
- Message listeners

Queues and topics

JMS works inside channels of messages that manage the messages asynchronously. These channels contain messages that they will collect or remove according the configuration and the type of channel.

These channels are of two types, queues and topics. These channels are highly configurable by the WildFly console. Like all components in WildFly they can be installed through the console command line or directly with maven plugins of the project.

In the next two paragraphs, we will show what they mean and all the possible configurations.

Queues

Queues collect the sent messages that are waiting to be read. The messages are delivered in the order they are sent and when beds are removed from the queue.

Creating the queue from the web console

Let's see the steps to create a new queue through the web console:

1. Connect to `http://localhost:9990/`.
2. Go to **Configuration** | **Subsystems** | **Messaging - ActiveMQ/default**:

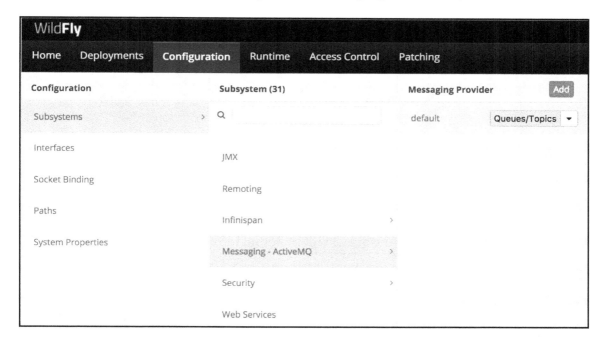

3. Click on **Queues/Topics** and select the **Queues** menu and click on the **Add** button; you will see this screen:

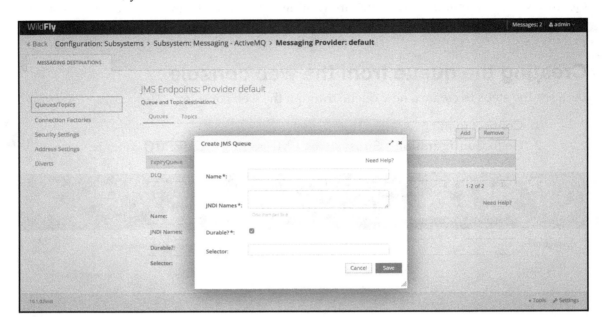

4. The parameters to insert are as follows:

Name	The name of the queue
JNDI names	The JNDI names the queue will be bound to
Durable?	Whether the queue is durable or not
Selector	The queue selector

Like all enterprise components, JMS components are callable through **JNDI (Java Naming Directory Interface)**.

Durable queues keep messages around persistently for any suitable consumer to consume them. Durable queues do not need to concern themselves with which consumer will consume the messages at some point in the future. There is just one copy of a message that any consumer in the future can consume.

Message selector allows us to *filter the messages that a message consumer will receive*. The filter is a relatively complex language similar to the syntax of an SQL WHERE clause. The selector can use all the message headers and properties for filtering operations, but it cannot use the message content.

Selectors are mostly useful for channels that broadcast a very large number of messages to its subscribers. On queues, only messages that match the selector will be returned; the others stay in the queue (and thus can be read by a MessageConsumer with a different selector).

The following SQL elements are allowed in our filters, and we can put them in the Selector field of the form:

Element	Description of the element	Example of Selectors
AND, OR, NOT	Logical operators	`(releaseYear < 1986) AND NOT (title = 'Bad')`
String literals	String literals in single quotes, duplicate to escape	`title = 'Tom''s'`
Number literals	Numbers in Java syntax; they can be double or integer	`releaseYear = 1982`
Properties	Message properties that follow Java identifier naming	`releaseYear = 1983`
Boolean literals	TRUE and FALSE	`isAvailable = FALSE`
( )	Round brackets	`(releaseYear < 1981) OR (releaseYear > 1990)`
BETWEEN	Checks whether the number is in range (both the numbers are inclusive)	`releaseYear BETWEEN 1980 AND 1989`
Header fields	Any headers except JMSDestination, JMSExpiration, and JMSReplyTo	`JMSPriority = 10`
=, <>, <, <=, >, >=	Comparison operators	`(releaseYear < 1986) AND (title <> 'Bad')`
LIKE	String comparison with wildcards '_' and '%'	`title LIKE 'Mirror%'`

IN	Finds value in a set of strings	title IN ('Piece of mind', 'Somewhere in time', 'Powerslave')
IS NULL, IS NOT NULL	Checks whether the value is null or not null	releaseYear IS NULL
*, +, -, /	Arithmetic operators	releaseYear * 2 > 2000 - 18

The next step is to fill the form:

In this chapter, we will implement a messaging service to send the coordinates of the bus means. The queue is created and showed in the queues list:

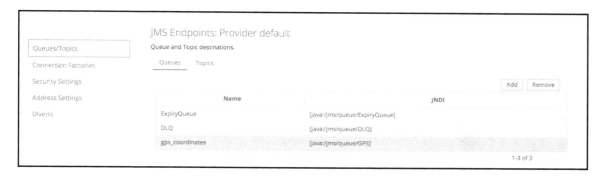

Creating the queue using CLI and Maven WildFly plugin

The same thing can be done with the command-line console. So, start a WildFly instance, go
to the `bin` directory of WildFly, and execute the following script:

```
bash-3.2$ ./jboss-cli.sh
You are disconnected at the moment. Type 'connect' to connect to the server
or 'help' for the list of supported commands.
[disconnected /] connect
[standalone@localhost:9990 /] /subsystem=messaging-
activemq/server=default/jms-
queue=gps_coordinates:add(entries=["java:/jms/queue/GPS"])
{"outcome" => "success"}
```

The same thing can be done through Maven. Simply add this snippet to your `pom.xml`:

```
<plugin>
    <groupId>org.wildfly.plugins</groupId>
    <artifactId>wildfly-maven-plugin</artifactId>
    <version>1.0.2.Final</version>
    <executions>
        <execution>
            <id>add-resources</id>
            <phase>install</phase>
            <goals>
                <goal>add-resource</goal>
            </goals>
            <configuration>
                <resources>
                    <resource>
                        <address>subsystem=messaging-activemq,server=default,jms-
queue=gps_coordinates</address>
                        <properties>
                            <durable>true</durable>
                            <entries>!!["gps_coordinates",
```

```
    "java:/jms/queue/GPS"]</entries>
                    </properties>
                </resource>
            </resources>
        </configuration>
    </execution>
    <execution>
        <id>del-resources</id>
        <phase>clean</phase>
        <goals>
            <goal>undeploy</goal>
        </goals>
        <configuration>
            <afterDeployment>
                <commands>
                    <command>/subsystem=messaging-
activemq/server=default/jms-queue=gps_coordinates:remove
                    </command>
                </commands>
            </afterDeployment>
        </configuration>
    </execution>
</executions>
</plugin>
```

The maven WildFly plugin lets you perform admin operations in WildFly using the same custom protocol used by command line. Two executions are configured:

- `add-resources`: It hooks the installed maven scope and adds the queue passing the name, JNDI, and durable parameters seen in the preceding paragraph
- `del-resources`: It hooks the clean Maven scope and removes the chosen queue by name

Creating the queue through an Arquillian test case

We can also add and remove the queue through an Arquillian test case:

```
@RunWith(Arquillian.class)
@ServerSetup(MessagingResourcesSetupTask.class)
public class MessageTestCase {
    ...
    private static final String QUEUE_NAME = "gps_coordinates";
    private static final String QUEUE_LOOKUP = "java:/jms/queue/GPS";
    static class MessagingResourcesSetupTask implements ServerSetupTask {
        @Override
        public void setup(ManagementClient managementClient, String
```

```
containerId) throws Exception {
getInstance(managementClient.getControllerClient()).createJmsQueue(QUEUE_NA
ME, QUEUE_LOOKUP);
        }
        @Override
        public void tearDown(ManagementClient managementClient, String
containerId) throws Exception {
getInstance(managementClient.getControllerClient()).removeJmsQueue(QUEUE_NA
ME);
    }
      }
      . . .
}
```

The `org.jboss.as.arquillian.api.ServerSetup` Arquillian annotation lets us use an external setup manager used to install or remove new components inside WildFly. In this case, we are installing the queue declared with two variables--QUEUE_NAME and QUEUE_LOOKUP.

When the test ends, the `tearDown` method will be started automatically, and it will remove the installed queue.

To use Arquillian, it's important to add the WildFly test suite dependency in your `pom.xml` project:

```
...
<dependencies>
    <dependency>
        <groupId>org.wildfly</groupId>
        <artifactId>wildfly-testsuite-shared</artifactId>
        <version>10.1.0.Final</version>
        <scope>test</scope>
    </dependency>
</dependencies>
...
```

We will find the created queue in the `standalone-full.xml`, as follows:

```
<subsystem xmlns="urn:jboss:domain:messaging-activemq:1.0">
    <server name="default">
            ...
            <jms-queue name="gps_coordinates" entries="java:/jms/queue/GPS"/>
            ...
    </server>
</subsystem>
```

JMS is available in the standalone-full configuration. By default, WildFly supports four standalone configurations. They can be found in the standalone/configuration directory:

- `standalone.xml`: It supports all components except the messaging and CORBA/IIOP
- `standalone-full.xml`: It supports all components
- `standalone-ha.xml`: It supports all components except the messaging and CORBA/IIOP with the enabled cluster
- `standalone-full-ha.xml`: It supports all components with the enabled cluster

To start WildFly with the chosen configuration, simply add a `-c` with the configuration in the `standalone.sh` script. Here's a sample to start the standalone full configuration:

```
./standalone.sh -c standalone-full.xml
```

Create the Java client for the queue

Now let's see how to create a client to send a message to the queue. JMS 2.0 simplifies the creation of clients; this is a sample of a client inside a stateless EJB:

```
@Stateless
public class MessageQueueSender {
    @Inject
    private JMSContext context;
    @Resource(mappedName = "java:/jms/queue/GPS")
    private Queue queue;

    public void sendMessage(String message) {
        context.createProducer().send(queue, message);
    }
}
```

The `javax.jms.JMSContext` is injectable from any EE component. We will shortly look at the JMS context in detail.

The queue is represented in JMS by the `javax.jms.Queue` class. It can be injected as JNDI resource through the `@Resource` annotation seen in `Chapter 2`, *Working with Dependency Injection*.

The JMS context, through the `createProducer` method, creates a producer represented by the `javax.jms.JMSProducer` class used to send the messages. We can now create a client injecting the stateless and sending a string message, `"hello!"`:

```
...
@EJB
private MessageQueueSender messageQueueSender;
...
messageQueueSender.sendMessage("hello!");
```

Topics

Topics are a distribution mechanism for publishing messages sent to multiple clients. Here are some features of the topics:

- Publish/subscribe model
- Multiple clients subscribe to the message
- There is no guarantee that messages are delivered in the order they are sent
- There is no guarantee that each message is processed only once as this can be sensed from the model
- Topics have multiple subscribers, and there is a chance that the topic does not know all the subscribers; the destination is unknown
- The subscriber / JMS client needs to be active when the messages are produced by the producer, unless the subscription was a durable subscription
- No, every message successfully processed is not acknowledged by the consumer/subscriber

Creating the topic from the web console

In the same mode, we can add the topic through the console:

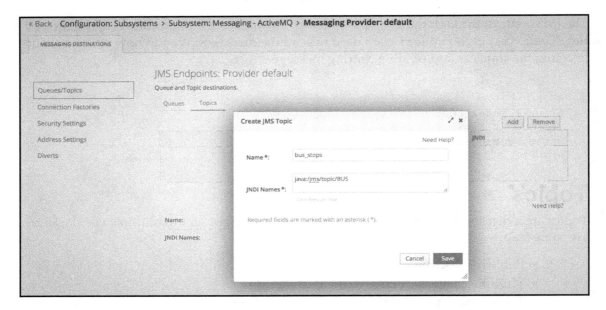

The topic will be found in the **Topics** list:

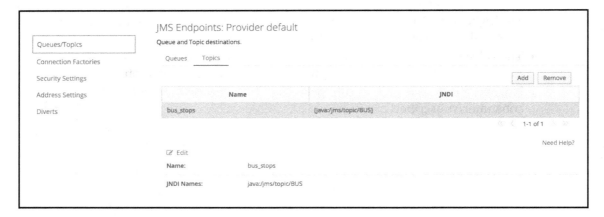

Unlike the queue, the topic is always durable, and it doesn't need selectors because the topic is limited to the subscriptions. Instead, the queue is more adaptable to manage a big set of data for many users.

Creating the topic with the Maven WildFly plugin

With the Maven WildFly plugin, we can do the same thing seen with the queue. Simply, we can move the queue resource with the topic resource to deploy this:

```
<resource>
    <address>subsystem=messaging-activemq,server=default,jms-
topic=bus_stops</address>
    <properties>
        <entries>!!["bus_stops","java:/jms/topic/BUS"]</entries>
    </properties>
</resource>
```

The resource to undeploy:

```
<command>/subsystem=messaging-activemq/server=default/jms-
topic=bus_stops:remove
</command>
```

Creating the topic through an Arquillian test case

Here, you can see the Arquillian method used to create the topic:

```
private static final String TOPIC_NAME = "bus_stops";
public static final String TOPIC_LOOKUP = "java:/jms/topic/BUS";
...
JMSOperations jmsOperations =
getInstance(managementClient.getControllerClient());
jmsOperations.createJmsTopic(TOPIC_NAME, TOPIC_LOOKUP);
...
```

Also, it is used to remove the topic:

```
...
JMSOperations jmsOperations =
getInstance(managementClient.getControllerClient());
jmsOperations.removeJmsTopic(TOPIC_NAME);
...
```

Creating the Java client for the topic

As for the queue, we can create a client for the topic. This is a sample from inside a stateless EJB:

```
@Stateless
public class MessageTopicSender {
    @Inject
    private JMSContext context;
    @Resource(mappedName = TOPIC_LOOKUP)
    private Topic topic;
    public void sendMessage(String message) {
        context.createProducer().send(topic, message);
    }
}
```

The topic is represented in JMS by the `javax.jms.Topic` class. It can be injected as JNDI resource through the `@Resource` annotation seen in Chapter 2, *Working with Dependency Injection*. The following is the client that will send a string `"hello"` message:

```
@EJB
private MessageTopicSender messageTopicSender;
...
messageTopicSender.sendMessage("hello!");
```

Remote clients

Topics and queues can be used remotely. A remote client must use JNDI to get the default JMS connection factory. Here's the code to obtain the connection factory:

```
String CONNECTION_FACTORY = "jms/RemoteConnectionFactory";
...
final Properties env = new Properties();
env.put(INITIAL_CONTEXT_FACTORY,
"org.jboss.naming.remote.client.InitialContextFactory");
env.put(PROVIDER_URL, "http-remoting://127.0.0.1:8080");
Context namingContext = new InitialContext(env);
ConnectionFactory connectionFactory = (ConnectionFactory)
namingContext.lookup(CONNECTION_FACTORY);
```

The remote connection factory is declared in the `standalone-full.xml` property file in the `standalone/configuration` folder of WildFly:

```
<connection-factory name="RemoteConnectionFactory"
entries="java:jboss/exported/jms/RemoteConnectionFactory" connectors="http-connector"/>
```

The connectors field lets the connection factory be called with JNDI through the `http-remoting` protocol. This protocol was created since the JBoss 5 application server, and it lets you execute remote callings directly through the HTTP protocol.

 To declare any remote component callable by JNDI, it's important to configure it through the `java:jboss/exported` naming. Using this naming for any component as connection factory or EJB ensures that the component is remote.

Once we have the connection factory, we can take the destination that can be a queue or a topic. This is how you take a remote queue through JNDI:

```
String REMOTE_QUEUE_LOOKUP = "java:/jms/queue/Questionary";
...
Destination destination = (Destination)
namingContext.lookup(REMOTE_QUEUE_LOOKUP);
```

 As for the connection factory, it's important for the queue to be registered as a `java:jboss/exported/jms/queue/Questionary` JNDI name too. We remind to previous section *Queues and Topics* how to register the destinations.

Once we have the destination, we can send a remote message. Here's a sample:

```
String USER_NAME = "my-user";
String USER_PASSWORD = "my-pass";
...
String question = "how many components in your family?";
String response = "they are four";
// Create the JMS context
JMSContext context = connectionFactory.createContext(USER_NAME,
USER_PASSWORD);
Questionary questionary = new Questionary();
questionary.setQuestion(question);
questionary.setResponse(response);
JMSProducer producer = context.createProducer();
producer.send(destination, questionary);
```

In this example, we started the JMSContext through the connection factory, passing a user and a password. WildFly provides a default authentication for the remote client through the application-users.properties and application-roles.properties, seen in the earlier chapters, so ensure that you create an application user and a role beforehand.

The default realm used is the ApplicationRealm, which can be showed in our standalone-full.xml file:

```
<security-realm name="ApplicationRealm">
    <server-identities>
        <ssl>
            <keystore path="application.keystore" relative-
to="jboss.server.config.dir" keystore-password="password" alias="server"
key-password="password" generate-self-signed-certificate-host="localhost"/>
        </ssl>
    </server-identities>
    <authentication>
        <local default-user="$local" allowed-users="*" skip-group-
loading="true"/>
            <properties path="application-users.properties" relative-
to="jboss.server.config.dir"/>
    </authentication>
    <authorization>
        <properties path="application-roles.properties" relative-
to="jboss.server.config.dir"/>
    </authorization>
</security-realm>
```

The ApplicationRealm sets the default property files where we find the users and the roles sited in the jboss.server.config.dir, a variable representing the configuration/standalone folder of WildFly.

The application.keystore is used to encrypt the password inside the file. Here's a sample of application users.properties with the MD5 encrypted password my-pass:

```
my-user=e0aa5b3d064f986c004d4db12e84334c
```

By default, JMS accepts the guest role. This is how the application roles.properties file should be to authorize the my-user user: my-user=guest.

This client has sent an object message represented, in this case, by the Questionary class. To use object messages, you can simply write a serializable class and send it through the JMSProducer component. Let's examine a sample of Questionary:

```
public class Questionary implements Serializable {
    private static final long serialVersionUID = 7097408487111792846L;
    private String question;
    private String response;
    private boolean approved;
    ...
}
```

To execute the client as a standalone application, simply add this code to your pom.xml maven descriptor file:

```
<dependency>
    <groupId>org.wildfly</groupId>
    <artifactId>wildfly-client-all</artifactId>
    <version>10.1.0.Final</version>
</dependency>
```

This is the default library that WildFly provides for the local and remote clients, and it contains all the client utilities to interact with the enterprise components.

Message listeners

Let's continue with the previous sample client to write a message consumer through the message listener. The message listener is an alternative to the receive method of the JMSConsumer class we saw in the *Queues* and *Topics* sections.

The message listener is represented by the javax.jms interface. MessageListener lets the client listen to the incoming messages and execute an action after the reception of the message. This is a sample of the message listener listening to the questionary messages:

```
public class MessageQueueListener implements MessageListener {
    ...
    private Questionary questionary;

    @Override
    public void onMessage(Message message) {
        ObjectMessage objectMessage = (ObjectMessage) message;
        try {
            Questionary questionary =
objectMessage.getBody(Questionary.class);
            questionary.setApproved(true);
```

```
            this.questionary = questionary;
        } catch (JMSException e) {
            ...
        }
    }
    ...
}
```

The `onMessage` method is started automatically when a message is received by the client.

In this sample, the object message represented by the `javax.jms.ObjectMessage` interface is casted to `Questionary`, and it is updated after that. Now, we'll see how to implement the receiver client and set the message listener:

```
JMSConsumer consumer = context.createConsumer(destination);
MessageQueueListener messageQueueListener = new MessageQueueListener();
consumer.setMessageListener(messageQueueListener);
...
questionary = messageQueueListener.getQuestionary();
```

The `JMSConsumer` class, through the `setMessageListener` method, configures the message listener. Just after the configuration, the `JMSProducer` is ready to receive the questionary messages.

The JMS context

A JMS context is the main interface in the simplified JMS API introduced for JMS 2.0. This adds the functionality of two different objects from the JMS 1.1 API--a connection and a session in a single object.

When an application needs to send messages, we need to use the `createProducer` method to create a `JMSProducer`, which provides methods to configure and send messages. Messages may be sent either synchronously or asynchronously.

When an application needs to receive messages, we need to use one of the several `createConsumer` or `createDurableConsumer` methods to create a JMS consumer . A JMS consumer provides methods to receive messages either synchronously or asynchronously.

According to the JMS 1.1 API, a JMS context should be thought of as representing both a connection and a session. Although the simplified API removes the need for applications to use those objects, the concepts of connection and session remain important. A connection represents a physical link to the JMS server, and a session represents a single-threaded context for sending and receiving messages.

A JMS context may be created by calling one of the several `createContext` methods on a `ConnectionFactory`. A JMS context that is created in this way is described as being managed by the application. A managed JMS context by the application must be closed when no longer needed by calling its close method.

Applications working in the Java EE web and EJB containers may alternatively inject a JMS context into their application using the `@Inject` annotation. A JMS context that is created in this way is described as being container managed. A container-managed JMS context will be closed by the container automatically.

Applications working in the EJB containers and Java EE web are not allowed to create more than one active session on a connection, so their combination in a single object gives an advantage of this restriction to get a simpler API.

However, applications working in the Java EE application, in a Java SE environment, or in the client container are allowed to create multiple active sessions on the same connection. This permits the same physical connection to be used in multiple threads at the same time. Such applications that require multiple sessions to be created on the same connection must use one of the `createContext` methods on the `ConnectionFactory` to create the first JMS context and then use the `createContext` method on the JMS context to create additional JMS context instances that work with the same connection. All these JMS context instances are managed by the application and should be closed when no longer needed. Calling the `close` method of the JMS context is enough to close the instances. Many utilities are provided by the JMS context; this is the list:

- **Acknowledge**: Acknowledges all messages consumed by the session of the JMS context
- **Close**: Closes the JMS context
- **Commit**: Commits all messages worked in the transaction and releases all the locks currently present
- **Create browser**: Creates a `QueueBrowser` instance where peek the messages on a chosen queue; it is possible to specify a message selector too
- **Create bytes message**: Creates a `BytesMessage` instance

- **Create consumer**: Creates a JMS consumer choosing a destination, a message selector, and the `noLocal` parameter that establishes the JMS consumer; it must be remote

- **Create context**: Creates a new JMS context with the chosen session mode through the connection of the JMS context. If the session is not specified, a new session can be created

- **Create durable consumer**: Creates an unshared durable subscription on the chosen topic if one does not already exist and creates a consumer on the subscription

- **Create map message**: Creates a `MapMessage` instance

- **Create message**: Creates a `Message` instance

- **Create object message**: Creates an `ObjectMessage` instance and initializes it

- **Create producer**: Creates a new JMS producer instance, which will be be used to configure and send the messages

- **Create queue**: Creates a queue instance that encapsulates a specified provider-specific queue name

- **Create shared consumer**: Creates a shared, non-durable subscription with the chosen name on the topic if one does not already exist and creates a consumer on the subscription

- **Create shared durable consumer**: Creates a shared, durable subscription on the chosen topic if one does not already exist, choosing a message selector, and creates a consumer on that subscription

- **Create stream message**: Creates a `StreamMessage` instance

- **Create temporary queue**: Creates a `TemporaryQueue` instance

- **Create temporary topic**: Creates a `TemporaryTopic` instance

- **Create text message**: Used to create initialized `TextMessage` objects

- **Create topic**: Creates a topic instance that encapsulates a specified topic name

- **Auto start**: Returns whether the used connection used by the JMS context will be started in an automatic mode when a consumer will be created

- **Client ID**: Gets the client identifier for the connection in the JMS context

- **Exception listener**: Gets the `ExceptionListener` object for the connection in the JMS context. It sets the client identifier and the exception listener for the connection

- **Metadata**: Gets the connection metadata for the connection in the JMS context

- **Session mode**: Returns the session mode of the session in the JMS context
- **Transacted**: Establishes whether the session of the JMS context is in transacted mode
- **Recover**: Stops the delivery of messages in the session of the JMS context and restarts the message delivery with the oldest unacknowledged message
- **Rollback**: Executes the rollback on any messages done in this transaction and releases all the locks currently held
- **Start**: Starts or restarts the delivery of the incoming messages by the connection of the JMS context
- **Stop**: It stops the delivery of incoming messages by the connection of the JMS context for a while
- **Unsubscribe**: Unsubscribes a durable subscription created on the client side

Summary

JMS is a good message system for backend environments. It has a 10 year history, and it is a guarantee of stability. By going through this chapter, we are able to send and receive messages inside our enterprise components and remote clients and understand what configuration we need for our applications.

Now, we are ready for the next chapter, where we will show the mail configuration in WildFly and the instruments used to send the email.

9
Implementing a Mail Client

In this chapter, we will see how to send an email using a simple test SMTP server and a Gmail SMTP protocol in Java; we will use JavaMail API v1.5.2. It is a very robust solution available in the market.

The JavaMail API provides a platform-independent and protocol-independent framework to build mail and messaging applications. Generally, implementing a mail session in a compliant Java EE Application server is very simple because Java EE provides all the required classes to create an SMTP client and send messages.

The JavaMail API is also available as an optional package for use with the Java SE platform. The JavaMail 1.5.2 release contains several bug fixes and enhancements. In this chapter, we will cover the following:

- How to configure the mail server in WildFly
- How to send mails in and out of our enterprise components
- How to test the reception of the emails through SubEtha Mail

Mail client API

Java mail has the API to generate a client to send SMTP messages. In this paragraph, we will see how to write the Java client.

Java example

Here's a sample of the Java client creating a default JavaMail session:

```java
    private Properties mailServerProperties;
    private Session getMailSession;
    private MimeMessage generateMailMessage;

    public void completeClientSend() throws AddressException,
MessagingException {
        // Step1
        logger.info("n 1st ===> setup Mail Server Properties..");
        mailServerProperties = System.getProperties();
        mailServerProperties.put("mail.smtp.port", "587");
        mailServerProperties.put("mail.smtp.auth", "true");
        mailServerProperties.put("mail.smtp.starttls.enable", "true");
        logger.info("Mail Server Properties have been setup successfully..");
        // Step2
        logger.info("nn 2nd ===> get Mail Session..");
        getMailSession = Session.getDefaultInstance(mailServerProperties,
null);
        generateMailMessage = new MimeMessage(getMailSession);
        generateMailMessage.addRecipient(Message.RecipientType.TO, new
InternetAddress("test1@vige.it"));
        generateMailMessage.addRecipient(Message.RecipientType.CC, new
InternetAddress("test2@vige.it"));
        generateMailMessage.setSubject("Greetings from Vige..");
        String emailBody = "Test email by Vige.it JavaMail API example. " +
"<br><br> Regards, <br>Vige Admin";
        generateMailMessage.setContent(emailBody, "text/html");
        logger.info("Mail Session has been created successfully..");
        // Step3
        logger.info("nn 3rd ===> Get Session and Send mail");
        Transport transport = getMailSession.getTransport("smtp");
        // Enter your correct gmail UserID and Password
        // if you have 2FA enabled then provide App Specific Password
        transport.connect("smtp.gmail.com", "<----- Your GMAIL ID ----->",
"<----- Your GMAIL PASSWORD ----->");
        transport.sendMessage(generateMailMessage,
generateMailMessage.getAllRecipients());
        transport.close();
    }
}
```

In this code, you need to remove the comments and put the credential access to connect to Gmail as a server:

```
<----- Your GMAIL ID ----->",
"<----- Your GMAIL PASSWORD ----->
```

The resulting output will be as follows:

```
1st ===> setup Mail Server Properties..
Mail Server Properties have been setup successfully..
2nd ===> get Mail Session..
Mail Session has been created successfully..
3rd ===> Get Session and Send mail
===> Your Java Program has just sent an Email successfully. Check your
email..
```

 Google can block the access by an external application. If it happens, the mail account configured as server will receive the message of access attempt. To allow the access, you must simply configure the Gmail account through the Google web console connecting to `https://www.goog le.com/settings/security/lesssecureapps`.

A simpler example is to inject the mail session of WildFly in your own code. The following is a smarter way of sending emails:

```
@Resource(name = "java:jboss/mail/Default")
private Session session;
...
Message message = new MimeMessage(session);
message.setRecipients(TO, InternetAddress.parse(addresses));
message.setSubject(topic);
message.setText(textMessage);
Transport.send(message);
```

WildFly has a default configured session. The session contains all the information of the SMTP server, such as the server URL, port, and credentials. This configuration will be seen in the next paragraph.

Creating a client with Java SE

If you have a maven project and you want to send an SMTP message, simply add these dependencies to the maven pom file:

```
<dependency>
    <groupid>javax.mail</groupid>
    <artifactid>mail</artifactid>
    <version>1.5.2</version>
</dependency>
<dependency>
    <groupid>javax.mail</groupid>
    <artifactid>javax.mail-api</artifactid>
    <version>1.5.5</version>
</dependency>
```

Configuration of the mail server

The configuration is in the `standalone.xml` file. By default, the mail server points to `localhost`. Here are the configurations that will be imported by the clients through the SMTP session seen in the preceding paragraph:

```
<outbound-socket-binding name="mail-smtp">
    <remote-destination host="localhost" port="25"/>
</outbound-socket-binding>
```

To connect it to Gmail, simply change the `remote-destination host` property, as illustrated:

```
<remote-destination host="smtp.gmail.com" port="587"/>
```

1. Go to the WildFly web console to set the authentication properties:

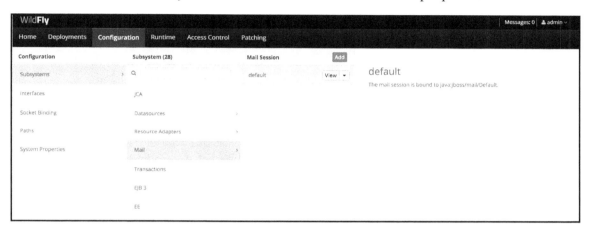

2. Click on the **View** button; you will find this page:

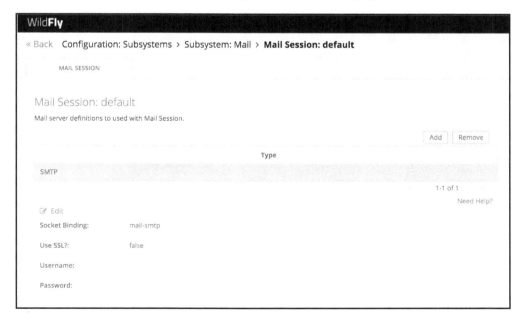

3. You can see the reference to the **mail-smtp** output socket binding configured in the `standalone.xml` file. We can set the three authentication properties by clicking on the **Edit** button:

Use SSL?	Does server require SSL?
Username	Username to authenticate on server
Password	Password to authenticate on server

To use Gmail, simply set SSL to true and put the credentials for a valid Google account.

SMTP local mail server

In the previous paragraph, we used Gmail as SMTP server, but we need a Google account, and we need to set the security options to use it. It can be useful to install a local mail server for internal tests.

SubEtha Mail is a simple SMTP that can be installed directly from the project. To use it, simply add this dependency in the pom file of your maven project:

```
<dependency>
  <groupId>org.subethamail</groupId>
  <artifactId>subethasmtp</artifactId>
  <version>3.1.7</version>
  <scope>test</scope>
</dependency>
```

Thanks to SubEtha Mail, we can start and stop a simple SMTP mail server by code. Here's a sample of test case that starts and stops the mail server through SubEtha Mail:

```
...
private MyMessageHandlerFactory myFactory = new MyMessageHandlerFactory();
private SMTPServer smtpServer = new SMTPServer(myFactory);
...
@Before
public void init() {
 smtpServer.setPort(25000);
 smtpServer.start();
}

@After
```

```
public void end() {
  smtpServer.stop();
}
...
```

We can use the `@Before` and `@After` JUnit annotations to start and stop the server for each test method. To each test method, we set the smtp port--in this case, it is set to `25000`--and then we start the smtp server.

At the start of the test case, we instantiate the mail server through the `org.subethamail.smtp.server.SMTPServer` class.

Before instantiating the mail server, SubEtha Mail asks to implement a message handler factory. Here's an example of message handler factory:

```
public class MyMessageHandlerFactory implements MessageHandlerFactory {
  ...
  public MessageHandler create(MessageContext ctx) {
    return new Handler(ctx);
  }
  class Handler implements MessageHandler {
    MessageContext ctx;
    public Handler(MessageContext ctx) {
      this.ctx = ctx;
    }
    public void from(String from) throws RejectException {
      ...
    }
    public void recipient(String recipient) throws RejectException {
      ...
    }
    public void data(InputStream data) throws IOException {
      ...
    }
    public void done() {
      ...
    }
  }
}
```

This class, implementing the `org.subethamail.smtp.MessageHandlerFactory` interface, allows us to create a message handler that manages the smtp messages of the server.

The message handler is created by implementing the `org.subethamail.smtp.MessageHandler` interface. Each method represents a part of the message. We can implement the from, recipient, and data methods to manipulate the information in the from and recipient mail addresses, the body of the message, and the advice when the message is sent.

As there are policies to open an smtp standard port in your operative system, we choose to open a different smtp port, the `25000`. Remember to set the correct parameters of the mail session to join and point the server address to `localhost` and the server port to `25000`.

Summary

JavaMail is part of the Java enterprise edition since its birth. It's a very simple framework, and it can be used not only inside an application server but in many contexts. Remember that if you work in a Java EE compliant application server as WildFly, you should always use the tools that it provides you with, for example, the mail session. It is considered bad programming to rewrite the existing or available services or components. In the subsequent chapters, we will continue talking about the asynchronous shifting to the REST services. Each architecture described in Java EE 7 has its asynchronous side.

10
Asynchronous REST

The new features of JAX RS 2.0 are the asynchronous calls.

The processing demands on the server work normally in synchronous mode, which means that the client connection of a request is processed by a single thread made available from a container. Once the thread that processed the request comes back to the container, the container can be safely be assumed that the processing of the request is over and that the client connection can be released safely along with all the resources associated with the connection. This model is generally sufficient to process the requests whose execution of resources to process requires a relatively short time.

However, in cases where the execution of an operation on a resource requires much time to calculate the result, a server-side model of asynchronous processing should be used. In this model, there can be no association between a thread processing the request and a client connection. The container that handles the incoming request can no longer assume a client connection to be closed when it returns a request for processing to the thread.

Instead of exposing a plant, it needs to suspend, reactivate, and close client connections explicitly. Note that the use of the server-side asynchronous processing model will not improve the processing of requests received by the customer's time. However, it will increase the throughput of the server, releasing the initial thread of the container processing demand, while demand can be put in a processing queue or stay running on another dedicated thread. The thread released to the container can be used to accept and process new requests from other connections.

In this chapter, we will cover the following:

- Calling asynchronous resources through REST
- Managing timeouts in the REST services
- Working with callbacks
- Asynchronous clients

Asynchronous resources

The following example shows a simple asynchronous resource method using the new JAX-RS async features:

```
@GET
@Path("/simple")
public void asyncGet(@Suspended final AsyncResponse asyncResponse) {
    new Thread(new Runnable() {
        @Override
        public void run() {
          String result = veryExpensiveOperation();
            asyncResponse.resume(result);
        }
      private String veryExpensiveOperation() {
       return new MagicNumber(3) + "";
      }
    }).start();
}
```

We have a JAX-RS `AsyncResponse` class passed as an attribute to a GET method implementation, `asyncGet`. This method injects an instance of `AsyncResponse` using the `javax.ws.rs.container.Suspended` annotation.

This annotation is very similar to the `javax.ws.rs.core.Context` annotation. The `@Context` annotation allows us to inject a REST response. The `@Suspend` annotation does the same with the difference, it declares the resource as part of an asynchronous operation too.

Asynchronous is when a thread is different when starting the thread end operation. In this case, it is not certain that the `AsyncResponse` will return to the same thread. Through the `@Suspend`, we say that the `AsyncResponse` is suspended until a thread can take the response and resume it. The choice and creation of the threads is the work of RESTEasy. The suspend operation of the `AsyncResponse` is transparent to the application. The application must only declare the operation as asynchronous through the `@Suspend` annotation and remember that the response must be resumed before to using it.

Note that the `asyncGet` method returns void in this example. In case of an asynchronous JAX-RS resource methods is lawful, even for a method declared as `@GET`, because the response is never directly returned from the method with a value. Being asynchronous, the response will return when the internal decision of the framework will be confirmed or never done in other cases.

With the `asyncGet` resource method, a new thread is started. Nothing of output streams will be closed at the end of the method until the `resume` method of the `AsyncResponse` is executed.

The one thread candidate to host the resource will go back in the thread pool of the application server once the method executes. In this state, the request processing remains suspended and the started thread can process other new requests.

New threads started in the resource methods may execute expensive operations, which might take a long time to end. When the result is ready, it will be resumed through the `resume()` method of the `AsyncResponse` instance. The resumed response will then be processed in a new thread by RESTEasy in the same way as any other synchronous response. Execution of filters, interceptors, and exception mappers can be included as necessary and then the response is sent back to the client.

We must note that this asynchronous response does not need to be resumed from the starting thread of the resource method. The asynchronous response can be resumed even from other request processing threads. In other examples, the suspended asynchronous response from the GET method can be resumed later on, for example, from a POST method. The suspended asynchronous response can be passed between requests through a static field and then resumed from another method that runs on a different request processing thread.

The asynchronous call response time may be prolonged over time; the factors can be many--complexity in code, different waiting points for resource managers, unconnected connections, or unexpected errors. Timeouts can solve the long wait; REST provides a good system for configuring timeouts on resources and methods. In the next paragraph, we will see the timeout in detail.

REST timeouts

In this example, we will see how to use the timeouts on the JAX-RS asynchronous methods:

```
@GET
@Path("/withTimeout")
public void asyncGetWithTimeout(@Suspended final AsyncResponse
asyncResponse) {
    asyncResponse.setTimeoutHandler(new TimeoutHandler() {
        @Override
        public void handleTimeout(AsyncResponse asyncResponse) {
 asyncResponse.resume(status(SERVICE_UNAVAILABLE).entity("Operation time
out.").build());
        }
    });
  asyncResponse.setTimeout(1, SECONDS);
  new Thread(new Runnable() {
        @Override
    public void run() {
            String result = ...
            asyncResponse.resume(result);
        }
    }).start();
}
```

Timeouts are not defined by default on the suspended resource instance; so, we risk endless expectations in some cases. We can use the setTimeoutHandler method to configure a timeout event handler and the setTimeout(Long, TimeUnit) method directly to the resource. The setTimeoutHandler() method represents a handler that will be invoked when timeout is reached so that we can add additional operations to unlock the endless call. In this sample, the handler resumes the response by sending a **503 Service Unavailable** response code represented by the javax.ws.rs.core.Response.Status.SERVICE_UNAVAILABLE enum.

We can also define a timeout interval without the custom timeout handler, using just the `setTimeout` method. As defined by the JAX-RS specification, a default handler will be used by the RESTEasy runtime after the expiration, throwing a `javax.ws.rs.ServiceUnavailableException` mapped by default with the 503, HTTP error response.

REST server callbacks

As the asynchronous operations in some cases can take a long time and often don't end inside a single method invocation of a resource, the JAX-RS specifications provide utilities to register callbacks to invoke on suspended asynchronous response state changes. We can register two types of callbacks in RESTEasy:

- Completion callbacks executed at the end of the requests or when they fail
- Connection callbacks executed when a client connection is closed or lost

Here a sample of registration of a completion callback:

```
@GET
@Path("/withCallback")
public void asyncGetWithCallback(@Suspended final AsyncResponse
asyncResponse) {
   asyncResponse.register(new CompletionCallback() {
       @Override
       public void onComplete(Throwable throwable) {
        if (throwable == null) {
            numberOfSuccessResponses++;
          } else {
            numberOfFailures++;
            lastException = throwable;
          }
       }
   });
   new Thread(new Runnable() {
       @Override
       public void run() {
        String result = ...
          asyncResponse.resume(result);
       }
   }).start();
}
```

A completion callback is registered through the `register` method on the `AsyncResponse` instance. Only the responses to which the completion callback has been registered will join the registration operation.

In the preceding example, the `javax.ws.rs.container.CompletionCallback` interface is overridden to calculate the number of successful and failed processed responses, and only in the case of exceptions, to store the last exception. This example is a very simple case showing how to use the callbacks. We can use the completion callbacks, for example, to release resources, change the state of internal resources or representations, or manage the failures. The `onComplete` method overridden by our `CompletionCallback` implementation has an argument throwable, which will be set only if an error occurs. Otherwise, the parameter will return as null value, which means that the response operation has ended successfully.

The callback will be executed only if the response is written to the client before, and never just after, the response is resumed.

We have seen a sample of the `register` method of the `AsyncResponse` instance registering single callbacks as objects. Other overloadings offer options to register the callback as a class or even multiple callbacks, thanks to the Java varags.

Connection callbacks

As some asynchronous requests can take a long time for processing, the client can decide to close the connection to the server before the response is resumed or before it is written in time to the client. To prevent these use cases, we can use the `javax.ws.rs.container.ConnectionCallback interface`.

The connection callback will start only if the connection prematurely terminates, or if it is lost while the response returns back to the client. If a response is successfully written, and the client connection is closed as expected, this callback will not even be invoked.

Asynchronous clients

The asynchronous processing works on the client side too; JAX-RS APIs are available for it. The following is a simple example of a client using an asynchronous client API:

```
Client client = newClient();
WebTarget target = client.target(url);
final AsyncInvoker asyncInvoker = target.request().async();
Future<Response> future = asyncInvoker.get();
Response response = future.get();
```

Unlike synchronous invocation, the asynchronous client calls the HTTP get() method through the javax.ws.rs.client.AsyncInvoker instead of the javax.ws.rs.client.SyncInvoker. The AsyncInvoker returns calling the javax.ws.rs.client.Invocation.Builder.async() method as shown earlier.

The AsyncInvoker provides methods similar to the SyncInvoker, with the difference that these methods do not return a synchronous response. The synchronous responses are replaced by the Future class, shown in Chapter 5, *Working with Distributed Transactions* in the *Enterprise Concurrent API* section. The Future class represents the returned response data. You will note that these methods run in a very fast mode because they don't wait till the actual request completes. Unlike the AsyncInvoker, the future.get() method will wait until a response returns.

Asynchronous client callbacks

Like the server side, the client API can add asynchronous callbacks too. We can use these callbacks to receive the responses from the server instead of executing the Future.get() method to receive them. Here's a sample of how to register a client-side asynchronous invocation callback:

```
...
final AsyncInvoker asyncInvoker = target.request().async();
final MyResult myResponse = new MyResult();
asyncInvoker.get(new InvocationCallback<Response>() {
  @Override
  public void completed(Response response) {
    ...
  }
  @Override
  public void failed(Throwable arg0) {
    ...
  }
```

```
});
```

The callback must implement the `javax.ws.rs.client.InvocationCallback` interface and override two methods:

- The `completed(Response)` method is invoked when the operation ends successfully. The resulting response is passed as an attribute of the callback method.
- The `failed(Throwable)` method is invoked when the invocation fails, so an exception showing the failure is passed to the method as an attribute.

In this case, we have a generic type for the `InvocationCallback`, the response. So, the failed method can only be invoked when the invocation has errors because of an internal client-side problem. The failed method cannot be invoked if the server returns an HTTP error code, for example, the 404 error if the requested resource is not found on the server. In such a case, the response can be passed to the complete method of the callback so that it can send the 404 error code. This case happens only using the response directly as generic type. In the next example, an exception is thrown on the invocation callback even if it returns an error not used in HTTP.

Like the synchronous client API, we can directly retrieve the response entity as a Java type without first requesting a response. In an `InvocationCallback`, we need to set a generic type representing the expected response entity type without declaring the response class. Let's take an example:

```
asyncInvoker.get(new InvocationCallback<String>() {
    @Override
    public void completed(String response) {
        . . .
    }
    @Override
    public void failed(Throwable arg0) {
        . . .
    }
});
```

With that, we end the chapter hoping in its usefulness. Java EE 7, along with WildFly, get powerful asynchronous clients and servers.

Summary

With this chapter, we end reading on REST that we started in the Chapter 6, *Creating REST Services*. Now we have a complete vision of these services, and we are able to understand what type of service needs our business logic to be exposed. Never were the REST services so complete as they are now, thanks to the asynchronous services. Performances and wait time improve, and the HTTP services are getting closer and closer to real time. In the next chapter, we will continue with the asynchronous components resuming the speech on EJB started in Chapter 4, *Implementing Business Logic*.

11
Asynchronous EJB

The innovation of Java EE 7 is the increase of the asynchronous part in the enterprise components. We have shown the WebSockets and REST in the earlier chapters. In this chapter, we will complete the discussion on the EJB that was started in Chapter 4, *Implementing Business logic*, making the EJB asynchronous, and we will show the timers and the schedulers introduced in the EJB 3.1 specs according to the following:

- Asynchronous EJB annotations
- Timers and schedulers
- Message driven beans

The asynchronous annotation

The simplest thing to make an EJB asynchronous is through the @Asynchronous annotation. If a client calls an EJB marked with this annotation, it must not wait for the result because all the operations of the EJB will work in asynchronous mode. Here's a sample of an asynchronous singleton EJB:

```
@Singleton
@Asynchronous
public class AsyncBean {
 private static final Logger logger = ...

 public void ignoreResult(int a, int b) {
     logger.info("it's asynchronous");
     // here you can add an heavy payload!
  }

 public Future<Integer> longProcessing(int a, int b) {
     return new AsyncResult<Integer>(a * b);
```

```
      }
   }
```

In this example, we have two methods--one void and one returning a result. The ignoreResult method will be executed in a few milliseconds despite a large amount of data being loaded. All the loading will be executed in an asynchronous mode.

The longProcessing method returns a javax.ejb.AsyncResult class. This class is a simple implementation of typed Future class that we saw in Chapter 5, *Working with Distributed Transactions*. This class wraps the real result.

Let's see how a generic client calls these methods:

```
...
@Inject
private AsyncBean asyncBean;
...
asyncBean.ignoreResult(0, 0);
...
Future<Integer> futureResult = asyncBean.longProcessing(8, 9);
Integer intResult = futureResult.get();
```

When a client thread receives a value, it needs to do a synchronous call until the value is not received. This operation is done when the get() method of the futureResult object is called. So, try not to increase the wait time when you execute the get call.

In the preceding example, we have a whole asynchronous class; all its methods are asynchronous. The @Asynchronous annotation can mark methods as well, in order to have both synchronous and asynchronous methods in our class.

Timers and schedulers

The timer is an object similar to an alarm because it counts the milliseconds since the moment it is started. With a timer, you can, for example, set a time point so that an operation can be performed when it expires.

The timer can act on any method of an EJB. When a method is marked with the `@Timeout` annotation, you are able to work with a timer. The method will automatically start when the configured timeout of the timer expires. Here's a sample of the `timeout` method:

```
@Timeout
public void timeout(Timer timer) {
    ...
    timeoutDone = true;
}
```

The timer object represented by the `javax.ejb.Timer` interface holds the countdown for the start of the method defined in the `getTimeRemaining()` method. The timer is configurable at runtime through the `TimerConfig`, which we will show in the next section.

Here are some other utilities that you can use with the timer object:

- **Next timeout**: If the timer is configured as a scheduler, you can see when the timeout starts. The scheduler will be seen in the next paragraph.
- **Cancel**: You can cancel the timeout at runtime. After this operation on the timer, methods marked with the `@Timeout` annotation can start only manually.
- **Schedule**: You can see the expression used to schedule the operations.
- **Info**: A serializable object that propagates a state to maintain applicative information.
- **Handle**: It returns the `javax.ejb.TimerHandler`. This handle provides a `getTimer()` method, which can be used later to re-obtain the timer reference.
- **Calendar time**: The timer can be a calendar or numeric according to whether it is declared as a scheduler or as a numeric timer.
- **Persistent**: The timer can be persistent. Timers can live days, months, or years! So, a persistent context is very important.

Timer service

EJB provides the timer service ready since the EJB 2.1 specification. This service provides the runtime configuration of a timer.

Here's how to take the `timerService` from an EJB as a resource:

```
@Singleton
public class TimerBean {
  @Resource
  private TimerService timerService;
  ...
}
```

Here's how to take the `timer` object:

```
public void programmaticTimeout() {
  ...
  long duration = 60;
  Timer timer = timerService.createSingleActionTimer(duration, new
TimerConfig());
  ...
}
```

The timer object is one for each thread; each thread can get only one instance of timer. For example, each method marked with the `@Timeout` annotation inside a class will receive the same instance of timer.

The `createSingleActionTimer` method takes the current timer of the thread, so it can be configured. In the preceding example, we are configuring the duration of the timer to 60 milliseconds, so the method marked with the `@Timeout` annotation will start 60 milliseconds after the `programmaticTimeout()` method is called.

We are using a default timer config represented by an instance of the `javax.ejb.TimerConfig` interface. We will shortly see how to use the timer configuration in detail.

File configuration

The timer service is configurable in the file configuration XML of WildFly, `standalone.xml`. Here, we can see the default configuration:

```
<timer-service thread-pool-name="default" default-data-store="default-file-
store">
    <data-stores>
        <file-data-store name="default-file-store" path="timer-service-
data" relative-to="jboss.server.data.dir"/>
    </data-stores>
</timer-service>
```

This configuration, through the data stores, establishes how to make the timers persistent. By default, WildFly uses the filesystem to register the timers; in this case, the `jboss.server.data.dir` is responding to the `data` directory of WildFly under the `/timer-service-data` directory. We can simply move this directory configuration using, for example, a database. Here's a timer service configuration sample using the default HSQL database:

```
<timer-service thread-pool-name="default" default-data-store="hsql-store">
    <data-stores>
        <database-data-store name="hsql-store" datasource-jndi-
name="java:jboss/datasources/ExampleDS" />
    </data-stores>
</timer-service>
```

In this sample, we have used a new timer service component, the `database-data-store`, which works directly with the datasources, and we have set the default datasource just configured in WildFly.

Timer configuration

With the timer config represented by the `javax.ejb.TimerConfig` interface, we are able to configure the timers at runtime. Let's see how to configure a timer through the timer config:

```
public void timerConfig() {
    DateFormat formatter = new SimpleDateFormat("MM/dd/yyyy 'at' HH:mm");
    Date date = null;
    ...
    date = formatter.parse("05/01/2010 at 12:05");
    TimerConfig timerConfig = new TimerConfig();
    timerConfig.setInfo("my configuration");
    timerConfig.setPersistent(false);
    Timer timer = timerService.createSingleActionTimer(date, timerConfig);
}
```

In this sample, we set the timer as a calendar timer because we have created the date when the @Timeout methods will start.

We have created a serializable object as string "my configuration" that will be shared in the timer environment, and we have configured the timer as not persistent.

By default, the timer config sets the timer as persistent. A not-persistent timer must be used when the timeout is very short. It's a good practice to use it under 60 minutes, but it also depends on the use. For example, the application can start a manual timeout on the click of a button. In this case, you don't risk losing the timer because the operation will be done in the moment. Instead, if you work with batches, you have a high risk of losing the timer if the batches are long, so it should be set as persistent. The batches will be shown in the next chapter.

Access timeout

If we don't configure the timer programmatically, there is a very smart annotation to configure the time in the annotation directly. Adding the @AccessTimeout annotation instead of @Timeout to our methods is enough to use this feature. Here's a sample:

```
@AccessTimeout(value = 5, unit = SECONDS)
public void doItSoon() {
    ...
}
```

This method will automatically start after 5 seconds.

Old specs compliant

To use the old EJB style with the timers, a simple interface is provided since EJB 2.1--the javax.ejb.TimedObject. Here's a sample of a stateless implementing the timed object:

```
@Stateless
@Local(value = OldSpecsLocal.class)
public class OldSpecsBean implements OldSpecsLocal, SessionBean,
TimedObject {
    private SessionContext theEJBContext;
    public void setSessionContext(SessionContext theContext) {
        theEJBContext = theContext;
    }
  public void ejbTimeout(Timer theTimer) {
    String whyWasICalled = (String) theTimer.getInfo();
        ...
  }
    ...
    public void fireInThirtySeconds() throws EJBException {
    TimerService theTimerService = theEJBContext.getTimerService();
        String aLabel = "30SecondTimeout";
        Timer theTimer = theTimerService.createTimer(300, aLabel);
```

```
        . . .
    }
}
```

The `TimedObject` provides the `ejbTimeout` method just seen on the `@Timeout` annotation, as the timeout method can read the timer and start when the timer expires.

If we want to configure the timer, we need the timer service. To import the timer service, the EJB must implement the `javax.ejb.SessionBean` interface; it provides the `setSessionContext` method where you can import the `javax.ejb.SessionContext`.

In the `fireInThirtySeconds` method, we can use the `SessionContext` to get the `TimerService` class and configure the timer as in this example, setting the timeout to 300 milliseconds.

Stateful timeout

A particular timeout is provided for the stateful EJB. The `@StatefulTimeout` annotation establishes the duration time of a stateful EJB before returning to the pool when it doesn't receive calls by the clients. This is a sample of stateful timeout:

```
@Stateful
@StatefulTimeout(value = 15, unit = MILLISECONDS)
public class User {
    private boolean registered = false;
    public void register() {
        registered = true;
    }
  public boolean isRegistered() {
        return registered;
    }
    @Remove
  public void remove() {
        registered = false;
    }
}
```

After 15 milliseconds, the container will execute the deletion of the stateful bean. To understand this operation, we can implement a method marked with the `@Remove` annotation seen in Chapter 4, *Implementing Business Logic*, and wait for 15 milliseconds. After this, the `remove` method will be executed. The `remove` can be tested through a client injecting the stateful:

```
...
@EJB
private User user;
...
user.register();
assertTrue("The stateful session is registered", user.isRegistered());
sleep(160);
try {
    user.isRegistered();
    fail();
} catch (NoSuchEJBException e) {
    logger.info("The ejb is expired");
}
```

On the first time, the user represented by the stateful bean is registered because the `register()` method is started. Waiting for a little time, thanks to the `sleep` method of the thread class, we again tried to use the stateless but it was expired, so the `NoSuchEJBException` was thrown.

Schedulers

The scheduler, also called calendar timer, is a particular timer starting after a defined date. Unlike the simple timer, the method needs a special annotation, the `@Schedule`, to be marked with the timeout. Let's take a sample of the scheduled method:

```
@Singleton
public class SchedulerBean {
    @Schedule(minute = "*/3", hour = "*")
    public void automaticTimeout() {
...
    }
    @Schedule(dayOfWeek = "Sun", hour = "0")
    public void cleanupWeekData() {
        ...
    }
...
}
```

In this sample, the singleton has two scheduled methods.

The first is set to start every three minutes. The used expression to set the time is the syntax of the Unix Cron utilities, by now a standard for all types of timers.

The second will start on each Sunday at midnight. You can find all the configuration params for the schedule annotation in this table:

Attribute	Description	Default Value	Allowable values and examples
second	Number of seconds within a minute	0	From 0 to 59. For example, second="30".
minute	Number of minutes within an hour	0	From 0 to 59. For example, minute="15".
hour	Number of hours within a day	0	From 0 to 23. For example, hour="13".
dayOfWeek	Number of days within a week	*	From 0 to 7 (both 0 and 7 refer to Sunday). For example, dayOfWeek="3". Sun, Mon, Tue, Wed, Thu, Fri, and Sat. For example, dayOfWeek="Mon".
dayOfMonth	Number of days within a month	*	From 1 to 31. For example, dayOfMonth="15". From –7 to –1 (a negative number means the nth day or days before the end of the month). For example, dayOfMonth="-3". Last. For example, dayOfMonth="Last". [1st, 2nd, 3rd, 4th, 5th, Last] [Sun, Mon, Tue, Wed, Thu, Fri, Sat]. For example, dayOfMonth="2nd Fri".
month	Number of months within a year	*	From 1 to 12. For example, month="7". Jan, Feb, Mar, Apr, May, Jun, Jul, Aug, Sep, Oct, Nov, and Dec. For example, month="July".
year	The calendar year	*	A four digit calendar year, for example, year="2011".

To see whether the timer is set as scheduler, you can use this method for the timer:

```
Timer timer.....
timer.isCalendarTime();
```

If it returns true, it is a scheduler; otherwise, it is a timer working with the numeric countdown.

The scheduler can be configured programmatically in the timer in this mode:

```
ScheduleExpression scheduleExpression = new ScheduleExpression();
scheduleExpression.hour("10");
scheduleExpression.start(new Date());
Timer timer = timerService.createCalendarTimer(scheduleExpression, new
TimerConfig());
...
```

In this sample, we are configuring a scheduler, starting now, at 10 AM.

If the timer is not a scheduler, a `java.lang.IllegalStateException` will be thrown.

A scheduled method can be configured with multiple expressions using the `@Scheduled` annotation that holds more schedules. Here's a sample of the multiple scheduled annotated method:

```
@Schedules({ @Schedule(dayOfMonth = "Last"), @Schedule(dayOfWeek = "Fri",
hour = "23") })
public void doPeriodicCleanup() {
    ...
}
```

In this case, we are configuring the timer expiring on the last day of each month and each Friday at 11 PM.

A calendar schedule is cumulative; for example, we can add a new schedule expression starting the `createCalendarTimer` method of the `TimeService` class again:

```
...
scheduleExpression = new ScheduleExpression();
scheduleExpression.dayOfWeek("Wed");
timer = timerService.createCalendarTimer(scheduleExpression, new
TimerConfig());
```

 Remember that the timer is always the same for the current thread, so we will get the same timer expiring each Friday at 23 and each Wednesday at the default hour, midnight.

Transactions and timers

Timers are usually used along with the enterprise beans inside a transaction. If the current transaction is rolled back, the timer will also be rolled back. At the same mode, if an EJB removes a timer inside a transaction that must be rolled back because some error occurs, the timer deletion will also be rolled back. In this case, the timer's duration is reset, as if the deletion was never done.

In the beans working with the container managed transactions, the method annotated with the @Timeout annotation is usually set with the REQUIRED or REQUIRES_NEW transaction attributes to preserve the integrity. Through these attributes, the EJB container starts a new transaction to call the @Timeout annotated method. If the transaction ends with a rollback, the EJB container will call the @Timeout method at least one more time.

Message driven beans

A message driven bean is a particular EJB that allows enterprise applications to process asynchronous messages. This type of bean usually works as a JMS message listener, which is an event listener with the difference that it receives JMS messages instead of events.

 More details on the message listener are in Chapter 8, *Working with Messaging*, in the *Message listeners* section.

The messages are usually sent by any Java EE components as a web component, an application client, another enterprise bean, and a JMS application, but also by systems that do not work with Java EE technology. Message driven beans can process JMS messages or other types of messages. Here's a sample of message driven bean:

```
@MessageDriven(mappedName = "jms/queue", activationConfig = {
    @ActivationConfigProperty(propertyName = "destination", propertyValue =
"java:jms/queue/ExpiryQueue"),
    @ActivationConfigProperty(propertyName = "acknowledgeMode",
propertyValue = "Auto-acknowledge"),
    @ActivationConfigProperty(propertyName = "destinationType",
propertyValue = "javax.jms.Queue") })
public class WorkingBean implements MessageListener {
    @Resource
    private MessageDrivenContext mdc;

    @Override
```

```
    public void onMessage(Message message) {
      ...
    } catch (JMSException e) {
      mdc.setRollbackOnly();
    } catch (Throwable te) {
      ...
    }
  }
}
```

The annotations simplify much of the configuration of the message driven bean. The `@MessageDriven` annotation introduced in EJB 3.0 declares the message driven bean. Through this annotation, the bean class is installed in the runtime environment and it listens to the messages.

The bean is configured thanks to the `@ActivationConfigProperty` annotations that add properties to the EJB container. In this case, we set the following:

- `destination`: The JMS destination that the message driven bean listens to. When a message is sent to the declared destination, the bean will be activated, and it will execute its work. In this sample, we use the default queue installed in WildFly, the `ExpiryQueue`.
- `acknowledgeMode`: The acknowledge mode of the message. See the next section, *Acknowledge mode*, for details
- `destinationType`: with it you can specify the accepted message by the bean to be a code or queue declaring the JMS interfaces `javax.jms.Queue` or `javax.jms.Topic`

The message driven bean class must implement the `javax.jms.MessageListener` interface and implement the relative `onMessage` method, where we put the business logic.

Message driven bean context

Message driven beans can inject the message driven bean context represented by `javax.ejb.MessageDrivenBeanContext`. This context inherits all the basic properties of the EJB.

It's very similar to the session context shown in `Chapter 4`, *Implementing Business Logic*, in the *The session context* paragraph. Here's a list of operations that you can do with the message driven bean context:

- **Lookup**: Through this, you can look up EE components and resources using JNDI.
- **Caller principal**: If you are in a secure context, you will get the login information by the `java.security.Principal` interface.
- **User transaction**: If you are in a transactional context, you can get the `javax.transaction.UserTransaction` interface seen in `Chapter 5`, *Working with Distributed Transactions* and operate inside a transaction.
- **Timer service**: This object is used to manage the timer. It will be covered in detail further on in this chapter.
- **Context data**: A map of properties shared in the runtime execution of the bean.
- **Caller in role**: A function to verify if the current logged user is authorized for a defined role.
- **Set rollback only**: In the example, it is used through the `setRollBackOnly(true)` method. It executes the rollback inside a transaction.

Another mode to obtain the message driven bean context is through an interface. For example, our bean can implement the `javax.ejb.MessageDrivenBean` interface:

```
...
public class WorkingBean implements MessageListener, MessageDrivenBean {
   private MessageDrivenContext ctx;
   ...
   @Override
 public void setMessageDrivenContext(MessageDrivenContext ctx) throws
EJBException {
  this.ctx = ctx;
 }
   @Override
 public void ejbRemove() throws EJBException {
     ...
   }
   ...
}
```

The EJB container will automatically set the context through the `setMessageDrivenContext` method.

The `ejbRemove` method is also inherited by the `MessageDrivenBean` interface. Once the message driven bean is not used by the client, the `ejbRemove` method will be executed. It can be used to clean resources that are not used anymore.

Acknowledge mode

A JMS message must be acknowledged, otherwise it is not considered to be correctly consumed. The successful consumption of the messages takes place in three steps:

1. The clients receive the messages.
2. The clients process the messages.
3. The messages are acknowledged. Acknowledgment can be started either by the JMS provider or by the client, according to the session acknowledgment mode configuration.

In sessions using **JMS API Local Transactions**, acknowledgment acts automatically when a transaction is committed. If a transaction is rolled back, all the consumed messages will be redelivered.

In sessions without transactions, the value specified as the second argument of the `createSession` method decides when and how the messages will be acknowledged. Here, we list the three argument values we can put in the `createSession` method:

- `Session.AUTO_ACKNOWLEDGE`: It's an automatic operation where the session acknowledges the correct reception of the message, either when the client has successfully returned from a reception or when the message listener called to process the message has no errors. A synchronous reception in a session marked as `AUTO_ACKNOWLEDGE` is the one exception to the three steps described earlier. In this case, the reception and the acknowledgment will take place in one step, and the processing of the message will be executed at the end.

- `Session.CLIENT_ACKNOWLEDGE`: The acknowledgement operation is done by the client. The client sends a message calling the method of the message's acknowledgement. So, the acknowledgment will take place on the session level. If the client acknowledges a consumed message, then all the other messages will be automatically acknowledged. For example, if a message consumer client consumes sixty messages and then acknowledges the seventh message delivered, then all sixty messages are acknowledged.

- In the Java EE specifications, a CLIENT_ACKNOWLEDGE session can be used only in the application clients and never in web components or enterprise beans.

- Session.DUPS_OK_ACKNOWLEDGE: This type drives the session to acknowledge the delivery of the message in a lazy mode. It's a little dangerous because if the JMS provider fails, a delivery of some duplicate messages will occur, so this configuration should be used only for consumers tolerating duplicate messages. If the JMS provider redelivers a message, it can set the value of the JMSRedelivered message header to true so that the session overhead will be reduced and the session will prevent the duplicate messages.

If a queue receives a message but doesn't acknowledge it when a session ends, the JMS provider redelivers them when a new consumer accesses the queue. The provider also retains unacknowledged messages for a finished session configured with the durable TopicSubscriber. Unacknowledged messages for a non-durable TopicSubscriber will be dropped after the closing of the session.

If we use a queue or durable subscription, we can use the session.recover method to stop a session without transactions and restart it using its first unacknowledged message. The session's set of delivered messages is reset to the point after its last acknowledged message. The messages it now delivers may be different from those that were originally delivered if the messages expire or if higher priority messages are received. In a non-durable TopicSubscriber, the provider can drop the unacknowledged messages if its session is recovered.

Summary

We have now completed the EJB. Now we have a complete vision of the beans working in the background and the business components in Java EE.

EJBs are a recent technology but are the best components to solve issues related to transaction development, competition, and security. We've seen that with a few lines of code, we are able to provide components that are ready to be immediately put into production environments. With EJBs or developers, you just have to focus on the business logic once you choose the component that best suits your situation.

In this chapter, we anticipated the schedulers and timeouts, thanks to the EJB. More complex schedulers will be seen in the next chapter in a deeper mode. Java EE grows increasingly, adapting to the necessary requirements of customers.

12
Batches and Workflows

One good feature that started in Java EE7 is batch management. WildFly supports the implementation of this specification, the JSR 352 batch applications for the Java platform started in the 2011 and now finally integrated into the Java EE specifications.

A batch is a group of records processed as a single unit, usually without input from a user. Batches are important things for the applications because customers need the option to execute scheduled asynchronous operations for example massive data to update automatically for a date in the night.

Batches can be compared to the scheduled singletons seen in `Chapter 11`, *Asynchronous EJB* but they are organized with one scope in mind, guaranteeing the process of a large quantity of data. So the batches work in a domain different to the EJB because they don't need to be called upon by an external component. They don't need a strong security management because the batches can be used only inside the administration domain. Using the batches you have:

- No deployment descriptors
- Portability
- Reusable interfaces
- Used by multiple users
- Runtime API
- Powerful expression language
- Parallel processing

An extension of the batch is the workflow. A workflow is a set of batches that work according to a flow. The programmer is able to design a flow, deciding all the batches that the workflow must execute either on a timer decision than a process decision.

A workflow is composed by steps and jobs:

- A job represents a single process of a workflow. It is represented by a **Job Specification Language** (**JSL**) usually by an XML file. A job (with JSR 352) is a container for steps.
- A step is a domain object represented by a sequential phase of the job. A step contains all the logic and data to perform the processing. The batch specifications deliberately leave the definition of a step vague because the content depends on the application and can be defined as the developer wishes.

JBeret 1.2.1.Final is an opensource product developed by the JBoss community implementing the JSR 352. It is integrated into WildFly 10.1.0.Final.

In this chapter we will analyze, with samples, all features available in WildFly to start batches and workflows according to the following points:

- Differences between workflows and **Business Process Model** (**BPM**)
- Batch types and models
- Jobs, steps and all workflow components provided by WildFly
- Metrics of the jobs and the steps
- Batch listeners and exceptions
- Monitoring of the batches
- Deployment of the batches

Workflows and BPM

Workflows have existed for many years. Different protocols have been defined during these years. The BPM eventually became **Business Process Model and Notation** (**BPMN**).

BPMN usually provides a web console where the analyst designs the flow. The flow can then be exported and directly deployed in a application server, so it's ready to be executed. Different good open source implementations exist, such as **Bonita**, **Activiti**, and **JBPM**. Let's look at a sample of Activiti designed flow:

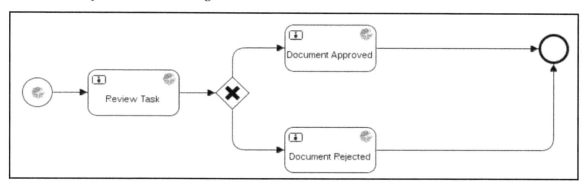

This simple flow is composed of three steps: **Review Task**, **Document Approved**, and **Document Rejected**. Each step executes an operation. The X (cross mark) is a decision. The process will calculate based on the direction the road will take (in this case, left or right).

The same thing can be done in WildFly now. So, what is the difference introduced in these new specifications? The BPM specification limits itself to the design of the flow. When we write the steps, we need the instruments that the BPM doesn't specify. Indeed, each workflow product provides its own classes to set the operations. Moreover, a BPM is not specified to work in Java. Usually, a migration between two different workflow products, for example, takes a considerable time. JSR 352 lets you resolve these problems.

JSR 352 provides a complete set of interfaces, such as Java API, to write a workflow. This thing allows a standard work. You can write, for example, a workflow with Glassfish, the application server of Oracle, and move it in a simple mode in WildFly.

Another important thing is the compatibility with the enterprise components. Usually, the one who writes a BPM workflow product doesn't need to worry about integrating it in a Java EE context. So, you can often see that these products don't work with EJB, CDI or other components, or the Java resource adaptor. With the new JSR, we can write a simple EJB and use it as a batch inside our flow.

Finally, Java has its workflow specification. It will resolve the problems listed.

Batch models

The Java Batch API (JSR 352) allows executing batch activities based on a **Job Specification Language** (**JSL**) using two main programming models: *Chunk steps* and *Batchlets*. The JSL is the XML descriptor file used to configure the processes and all its components as the steps and the Batchlets.

In this section, we will see samples of JSL and two samples of chunks and Batchlets.

Chunks

A chunk is a small part of the process working in a number of processes. It is the right actor to handle batches with large data queues. A set of chunk forms a process. It's very useful in massive boots when you need to organize your work into small steps.

For example, during a data migration, we will need to commit the operation any certain time. The chunk mode is done in three steps:

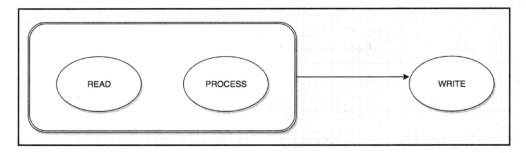

In the first step, an item is read and then processed. According to the chosen number of chunks, the item will be written and the cycle restarted until the payload doesn't end. Here's a sample of JSL code:

```
<job id="PayrollJob" xmlns="http://xmlns.jcp.org/xml/ns/javaee"
version="1.0">
  <step id="process">
    <chunk item-count="2">
      <reader ref="payrollItemReader" />
      <processor ref="payrollItemProcessor" />
      <writer ref="payrollItemWriter" />
    </chunk>
  </step>
</job>
```

Through this XML descriptor, we will write a process with a step that reads the records of a file as the first operation done by the reader, transforms these records into Java objects as the second operation done by the processor, and serializes the objects as the third operation by the writer. For each of the two received items, the serialization operation will proceed until the items end.

Chunk and ETL

Extract, transform, load (**ETL**) is an english expression referring to the process of extraction, transformation, and loading of data into a synthesis system (data warehouses, data marts, and so on). Chunk mode is a form of ETL. In this section, we will explore the key points of an ETL system.

Data can be extracted from source systems, such as a transactional database, also called OLTP, common text files, or from other computer systems, for example, ERP or CRM systems.

They then undergo a process of transformation, which consists of the following:

- Select only those that are of interest to the system
- Normalize the data (for example, eliminating duplicates)
- Translate encoded data
- Derive new data calculated
- Perform pair (join) between data retrieved from different tables
- Group data

Such a transformation has the aim of consolidating data (that is, make homogeneous data from different sources). To do so, it is more adherent to the business logic of the system of analysis for which it is developed.

Finally, they are stored in the synthesis system tables (load).

Pay special attention to the granularity of the information to be stored in the structure downstream. In fact, these must not only be aggregated so they do not contain excessive details (which can lead to deterioration of the performance of queries performed on the system), but must also maintain a granularity that allows us to perform the necessary analysis on the data.

How the implementation of extractors requires a detailed analysis of power systems should be emphasized. The goal is that this process is the same for all synthesis systems. The stratification in more extractors time by the same system for supplying different synthesis systems should be absolutely avoided. Such extractors having small variations in extraction criteria, encoding, or cleanup of data, tend to have, in practice, similar criteria, but not identical, extraction. The result of these layers is to obtain synthesis systems that present high direction results which, representing the same phenomena, instead show different values. This helps generate distrust of the results of the general synthesis systems.

To understand what can happen better, it is enough to think of having to determine the number of customers of a company on a certain date. You need to decide, in the face of a registry office, the name of the customers, after how much downtime do not consider it as such. It may be that the meaning of "customer number" is different for different departments of the same company. For the management control, a customer can be such only if they purchased during the year, but for marketing, it has to send a Christmas card; the basing will certainly be different and superior.

It needs to be delegated to a specific subsystem dedicated to a data integration function between the **Online Transaction Processing** (**OLTP**) systems and the synthesis of **Online Analytical Processing** (**OLAP**) systems, stating the fact that multiple processes are developed to extract the same data.

The exploitation of metadata (for example, data dictionary) will help generate the integration, not only technical, but also cultural in-house.

Having this approach means making independent but integrated, the different business subsystems (vendors, inventory, customers, general accounting, and management) control by creating and maintaining the uniqueness of the data and making the centralized control easier or replacement of one of the systems integration object.

It should be noted how often ETL refers to the instrument with which it is possible to develop this particular power architecture, which in itself can also be developed with standard tools. The ETL, however, being instruments dedicated, provides tangible results in terms of documentation and speed of development. On the other hand, they need a specialized working group in this language and then, in case of turnover or dismissal, the need advances to manage the presence in the company of suitable back-up to the related costs.

Chunk Reader

The operators are defined as Java classes. Here's a sample of the reader:

```
@Named
public class PayrollItemReader extends AbstractItemReader {
    ...
    public final static string INPUT_DATA_FILE_NAME = "payrollDataFileName";
    @Inject
    private JobContext jobContext;
    private int recordNumber;
    private BufferedReader br;
    private string currentLine;
    private Object[] stringLines;
    ...
```

The batch components work in a CDI context, so we use the @Named annotation so that we don't need to instantiate these components. The job context can be injected with a simple annotation. This context implements the javax.batch.runtime.context.JobContext interface, and it has all the information of the current process. There are many more utilities that we will see in the next section *Job context and step context*.

 For more information about CDI, refer to Chapter 2, *Working with Dependency Injection*.

A reader must implement the javax.batch.api.chunk.AbstractItemReader Java abstract class that provides the following methods:

- **Open**: It starts at the beginning of the process. It must execute the init operations, preparing the environment.
- **Close**: It is done at the end of the process to close and dismiss all items that are not used anymore.
- **Read**: It reads an item at a time.
- **Checkpoint**: It can be considered a transaction. A set of chunks can be divided into checkpoints where each checkpoint starts a new transaction.

Let's see how it is implemented in the `open` method:

```
...
@Override
public void open(Serializable prevCheckpointInfo) throws Exception {
    JobOperator jobOperator = getJobOperator();
    Properties jobParameters =
jobOperator.getParameters(jobContext.getExecutionId());
    string resourceName = (string) jobParameters.get(INPUT_DATA_FILE_NAME);
    InputStream inputStream = new FileInputStream(resourceName);
    br = new BufferedReader(new InputStreamReader(inputStream));
  Stream<string> lines = br.lines();
    if (prevCheckpointInfo != null)
        recordNumber = (Integer) prevCheckpointInfo;
    else
        recordNumber = 0;
    stringLines = lines.toArray();
    ...
}
```

The `open` method can get a checkpoint object as input, so if the process is reopened, we can maintain the state and the information about the last operation done, as it is very useful for massive loading.

The job operator defined by the `javax.batch.operations.JobOperator` interface is the main class that lets you perform operations on the current workflow. In this case, it can be taken in a static mode through the following command:

```
JobOperator jobOperator =
javax.batch.runtime.BatchRuntime.getJobOperator();
```

Through the job operator, we find the current properties of the process configured by a client.

When a process is started, it has its own execution ID that represents the process. Thanks to the job context, we take the execution ID of the process and pass it to the job operator to get the properties. Once we have the desired property, we start reading a file and extract the lines that will be registered in the `stringLines` variable.

The file can have content such as the following:

```
1  4
2  33
3  21
```

The open method then initializes the `recordNumber` variable, which we will use to register the current item to process.

Let's now see the `close()` method, which deletes the unused variables and closes the input stream:

```
@Override
public void close() throws Exception {
 br.close();
   recordNumber = 0;
   currentLine = null;
}
```

Here's the `readItem` method:

```
@Override
public Object readItem() throws Exception {
 Object record = null;
   if (stringLines.length > recordNumber) {
  currentLine = stringLines[recordNumber] + "";
     string[] fields = currentLine.split("[, trn]+");
     PayrollInputRecord payrollInputRecord = new PayrollInputRecord();
     payrollInputRecord.setId(parseInt(fields[0]));
     payrollInputRecord.setBaseSalary(parseInt(fields[1]));
     record = payrollInputRecord;
     recordNumber++;
   }
   return record;
}
```

Thanks to the `recordNumber` variable, the reader chooses a record from the input file to process and puts it in a custom Java class, the `PayrollInpuRecord`.

This is the `checkpointInfo` method:

```
@Override
public Serializable checkpointInfo() throws Exception {
   return recordNumber;
}
```

It will maintain the number of the records of the input file to be read. According to the XML JSL descriptor, each read will be followed by the processor. Now, let's see how to write the processor.

Chunk processor

The processor will first receive the read item and then process it:

```
@Named
public class PayrollItemProcessor implements ItemProcessor {
    @Inject
private JobContext jobContext;

public Object processItem(Object obj) throws Exception {
    PayrollInputRecord inputRecord = (PayrollInputRecord) obj;
PayrollRecord payrollRecord = new PayrollRecord();
int base = inputRecord.getBaseSalary();
float tax = base * 27 / 100.0f;
float bonus = base * 15 / 100.0f;
    payrollRecord.setEmpID(inputRecord.getId());
    payrollRecord.setBase(base);
    payrollRecord.setTax(tax);
    payrollRecord.setBonus(bonus);
    payrollRecord.setNet(base + bonus - tax);
    return payrollRecord;
}
```

The processor must then implement the `javax.batch.api.chunk.ItemProcessor`
interface. The interface then provides the `processItem` method, which receives the read
item. In this sample, the `PayrollInputRecord` will be transformed in a `PayrollRecord`
class.

When the second record is processed according to the item-count variable seen in the JSL
descriptor file, the writer will be enabled.

Chunk writer

Here's a sample of writer implementing
the `javax.batch.api.chunk.AbstractItemWriter` abstract class:

```
@Named
public class PayrollItemWriter extends AbstractItemWriter {
    public final static string PAYROLL_TEMP_FILE =
"target/payroll_serialized";
    @Override
public void writeItems(List<Object> list) throws Exception {
for (Object obj : list)
        serialize(obj)
}
```

The `writeItems` method receives the list of items to write. In our process, it will receive all the items two at a time. As the items are three, this method will be started twice, the first time importing two items and the second and last time importing one item.

Client

Now, we'll look at a sample of a client starting the process:

```
...
private final static string JOB_NAME = "PayrollJob";
public final static string INPUT_DATA_FILE_NAME = "payrollDataFileName";
private final static string INPUT_PROPERTIES =
"src/main/resources/input.properties";
...
JobOperator jobOperator = getJobOperator();
Properties props = new Properties();
props.setProperty(INPUT_DATA_FILE_NAME, INPUT_PROPERTIES);
long executionId = jobOperator.start(JOB_NAME, props);
...
```

It's very simple. As seen in the *Chunk reader* section, the first thing we receive is the job operator. Then, we put the properties that will be used inside the process, and at the end, we use the `start()` method of the job operator to start the process passing the name of the process. In this case, it is PayrollJob as seen in the JSL descriptor and the properties. The start method returns the execution ID described earlier.

Batchlets

The Batchlet, unlike the chunk, doesn't read sequential items. It can be a global executor of items. Unlike the chunk that requires a default set of reading, processing, and writing operations, the batch is more suitable for less powerful but sophisticated dynamic processes and free of ETL schema. Examples of Batchlets can be sending mail and notifications. A Batchlet is atomic, so it is not divided into different operations as per the chunk. We will introduce Batchlets through a more complex process. Here's the JSL descriptor:

```
<job id="Sendmail" xmlns="http://xmlns.jcp.org/xml/ns/javaee"
version="1.0">
    <flow id="mainprocess" next="sendemail">
        <step id="copyfiles" next="decider1">
            <Batchlet ref="copyFilesBatchlet" />
        </step>
        <decision id="decider1" ref="decisionNode">
            <next on="DSK_SPACE_LOW" to="sendemail" />
```

```
            <end on="DSK_SPACE_OK" />
        </decision>
    </flow>
    <step id="sendemail">
        <properties>
            <property name="mail.from" value="SENDER-EMAIL" />
            <property name="mail.to" value="DESTINATION-EMAIL" />
        </properties>
        <Batchlet ref="mailBatchlet" />
    </step>
</job>
```

In this process, we see how the flow is designed in detail. As we saw in the *Workflows and BPM* section, the flow is a set of steps that work through decisions. The decision is the component that decides the next step to take. This is a graphical representation of the flow:

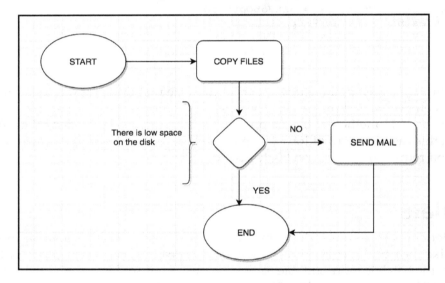

COPY FILES and **SEND MAIL** are Batchlets that will first execute a copy through files and then send a mail. The square figure represents the decision. If the space is low, the process will get out, else Batchlet will be executed before sending the mail and then the process will get out.

Let's take a look at the code of the first Batchlet:

```
@Named
public class CopyFilesBatchlet extends AbstractBatchlet {
    ...
    @Inject
    private JobContext jobContext;
    @Override
    public string process() {
        Properties parameters = getParameters();
        string source = parameters.getProperty("source");
        string destination = parameters.getProperty("destination");
        try {
            copy(new File(source).toPath(), new File(destination).toPath(),
REPLACE_EXISTING);
            return COMPLETED.name();
        } catch (IOException e) {... }
        return FAILED.name();
    }
    private Properties getParameters() {
        JobOperator operator = getJobOperator();
        return operator.getParameters(jobContext.getExecutionId());
    }
}
```

Batchlets must extend the `javax.batch.api.AbstractBatchlet` abstract class. This abstract class provides two methods:

- **Process**: Contains the operations of the batch
- **Stop**: Invoked for each Batchlet when the job operator executes the stopping of the process

The process method returns the state of the process as a string. The states are described in the `javax.batch.runtime.BatchStatus` enum. They can be STARTING, STARTED, STOPPING, STOPPED, FAILED, COMPLETED, or ABANDONED. In our example, we set a COMPLETE status if there are no errors and a FAILED status when there are errors in the execution of the operations.

So, this Batchlet will simply copy a file passed as input and described in a property of the job operator in a destination directory.

Decision

This is how the decision is implemented:

```
@Named
public class DecisionNode implements Decider {
    @Inject
  private JobContext jobContext;
    @Override
  public string decide(StepExecution[] ses) throws Exception {
  Properties parameters = getParameters();
  string fs = parameters.getProperty("filesystem");
  File file = new File(fs);
  long totalSpace = file.getTotalSpace();
  if (totalSpace > 100000) {
          return "DSK_SPACE_OK";
        } else {
          return "DSK_SPACE_LOW";
      }
    }
   private Properties getParameters() {
  JobOperator operator = getJobOperator();
  return operator.getParameters(jobContext.getExecutionId());
   }
 }
```

The decision must implement the `javax.batch.api.Decider` interface. This interface provides the `decide()` method, returning the exit status.

The exit status is a string that represents a value generated by a decision. In our decision, we set the value DSK_SPACE_OK if there is space in the filesystem, while DSK_SPACE_LOW is set if there is not enough space. These values are read by the process through the JSL file. You can refer to it earlier in the chapter, where the decision is configured. If it returns a DSK_SPACE_OK, the flow will end, while the flow will execute the next Batchlet, the sendmail Batchlet, if it returns the DSK_SPACE_LOW.

Mail example

Another good feature of the JSR-352 is that the mail management is implemented by Java mail. Whoever implements these specifications doesn't need to use an external mail session because it is present in the application server. The work of writing a service that send mail results is very simple. Here's a sample of a Batchlet that sends an email if the decision returns a positive control:

```
@Named
public class MailBatchlet extends AbstractBatchlet {
    ...
    @Resource(mappedName = "Java:jboss/mail/Default")
    private Session mailSession;
    @Inject
    private StepContext stepContext;
    @Inject
    private JobContext jobContext;
    @Override
    public string process() {
        string fromAddress =
stepContext.getProperties().getProperty("mail.from");
        string toAddress =
stepContext.getProperties().getProperty("mail.to");
        try {
            MimeMessage m = new MimeMessage(mailSession);
            Address from = new InternetAddress(fromAddress);
            Address[] to = new InternetAddress[] { new
InternetAddress(toAddress) };
            m.setFrom(from);
            m.setRecipients(TO, to);
            m.setSubject("Batch on wildfly executed");
            m.setSentDate(new Java.util.Date());
            m.setContent("Job Execution id " + jobContext.getExecutionId() + "
warned disk space getting low!","text/plain");
            send(m);
        } catch (javax.mail.MessagingException e) { ... }
    return COMPLETED.name();
}
```

As you can see, the `Java.mail.Session` can be taken through the `@Resource` annotation, returning the session configured in the application server with the JNDI name `Java:jboss/mail/Default`. The step context is very similar to the job context. It will be seen along with the job context in the *Job context and step context* section.

When the mail is sent, a `COMPLETE` status will return.

Client

This is a simple client starting the send mail process:

```
...
private final static string INPUT_PROPERTIES =
"src/main/resources/input.properties";
...
JobOperator jobOperator = getJobOperator();
Properties p = new Properties();
p.setProperty("source", INPUT_PROPERTIES);
p.setProperty("destination", "target/output.properties");
p.setProperty("filesystem", "target");
executionId = jobOperator.start(JOB_NAME, p);
...
```

Job context and step context

Batches provide two contexts: job context, which provides information about the current job (called also process) execution, and step context, containing informations for the single step of the job. The common properties for both the job context and the step context are as follows:

- **Transient user data**: A transient data object belonging to the current Job XML execution element.
- **Properties**: The properties propagated by the client. They will be always in the job and in the steps.
- **Name**: Name of the job or step described in the JSL.
- **Execution id**: Identifier for the current job or step. Identifiers are different for more jobs or more steps.
- **Batch status**: The status of the execution. Refer to the *Batchlets* section for more details.
- **Exit status**: A variable used to decide the direction of the flow; it is custom.

The other property of the job context is the following:

- **Instance id**: Batch specifications have two different concepts of job instance and job execution. The job instance is created when the job is deployed. We cannot get two equal job instances in the application server. The job instance is identified through the `javax.batch.runtime.JobInstance` interface through the instance id. At the same time, we can get more job executions for the same job instance.

The other properties of the step context are these:

- **Persistent user data**: A persistent data object belonging to the current step. The user data type must implement `Java.util.Serializable`. This data is saved as part of a step's checkpoint. For a step that does not do checkpoints, it is saved after the step ends. It is available upon restart.
- **Exception**: In case of an exception during a step, a step maintains the last exception error as the `Java.lang.Exception` class, so it can be managed by the application and the error is notified to the users or to other enterprise components. It is very useful to manage the errors in the steps.
- **Metrics**: A set of measures to monitor the operations done in the step. Refer to the *Metrics and step execution* section for more details.

Both the job context and the step context can be injected in any batch component. Here's a sample of injections inside a Batchlet:

```
@Inject
private JobContext jobContext;
@Inject
private StepContext stepContext;
```

`JobContext` is declared by the interface `javax.batch.runtime.context.JobContext` batch while the step context is declared by `javax.batch.runtime.context.StepContext`.

Metrics and step execution

Through the metrics, you can monitor the following properties described in
the `javax.batch.runtime.Metric` enum:

- `READ_COUNT`: How many times the item is read inside a step. In the case of the Payroll job seen in the *Chunks* section, we will have three read items for the job at the end.
- `WRITE_COUNT`: How many times the item is written inside a step. In the case of the payroll job seen in the *Chunks* section, we will have three written items for the job at the end.
- `COMMIT_COUNT`: How many commits are done to write the items. In the case of the payroll job seen in the *Chunks* section, we have two commits 2+1 at the end.
- `ROLLBACK_COUNT`: The number of rollbacked items. If we get errors in the write of the items, it will increment.
- `READ_SKIP_COUNT`: An item can be skipped according to the batch status returned by the read of item.
- `PROCESS_SKIP_COUNT`: An item can be skipped according to the batch status returned by the process of item.
- `WRITE_SKIP_COUNT`: An item can be skipped according to the batch status returned by the write of item.
- `FILTER_COUNT`: Returns the current number of items filtered out of this execution.

To get the metrics, it is enough to receive the step executions by the job operator. A step execution represents the step and contains all its runtime information as the metrics. Here's the code to get the metrics for a step:

```
...
List<StepExecution> stepExecutions =
jobOperator.getStepExecutions(executionId);
for (StepExecution stepExecution : stepExecutions) {
   Metric[] metrics = stepExecution.getMetrics();
   for (Metric metric : metrics)
 switch (metric.getType()) {
        case COMMIT_COUNT:
            logger.log("Metric commit count value", metric.getValue());
 break;
        case READ_SKIP_COUNT:
            logger.log("Metric read skip count value", metric.getValue());
 break;
        case WRITE_SKIP_COUNT:
```

```
                logger.log("Metric write skip count value", metric.getValue());
    break;
            case WRITE_COUNT:
                logger.log("Metric write count value", metric.getValue());
    break;
            case ROLLBACK_COUNT:
                logger.log("Metric rollback count value", metric.getValue());
    break;
            case READ_COUNT:
                logger.log("Metric read count value", metric.getValue());
    break;
            case FILTER_COUNT:
                logger.log("Metric filter count value", metric.getValue());
    break;
            case PROCESS_SKIP_COUNT:
                logger.log("Metric process skip count value",
metric.getValue());
  break;
        }
    }
}
```

We simply need to pass the execution id of the started process and get all the step executions. Each step execution has its metrics.

The following is the other information you can get by the step execution:

- **Start time**: The start time of the step.
- **End time**: The end time of the step if it is ended; returns null if it is not started or it is currently on execution.

 Other information is the same as seen in the step context in the *job context and step context* section.

Listeners

Listeners are very useful in the batch specifications because through them, you can externalize the operations decoupled by the processes or other batch elements in other parts of your code. For example, you can write a listener that embraces more processes, and it starts after one particular operation of each process.

The following are the types of listeners we can write in WildFly. WildFly 10, through JBeret, supports three types of listeners, which we list in the following sections.

Job listener

This listener starts at job level. Here's a sample of `JobListener`:

```
@Named
public class JobCheckpointListener implements JobListener {
    public final static string STARTED_BEFORE_JOB = "started before job";
    ...
    @Inject
 private JobContext jobContext;

    @Override
public void beforeJob() throws Exception {
  CheckpointUserData checkpointUserData = new CheckpointUserData();
  checkpointUserData.setStartedBeforeJob(STARTED_BEFORE_JOB);
  jobContext.setTransientUserData(checkpointUserData);
        ...
}
    @Override
public void afterJob() throws Exception {
  Properties jobProperties = jobContext.getProperties();
        ...
}
}
```

The `javax.batch.api.listener.JobListener` interface provides two important methods: `beforeJob()`, which starts at the start of the job, for example, when we launch the job through the start command of the job operator, and a `afterJob()` method that starts when the job has ended.

 In a listener, we can inject all enterprise components as for the processes seen in the earlier sections.

The `afterJob` method will start every time for any status returning from the steps, either `COMPLETE` or `FAILED`.

In this sample, the `beforeJob()` method creates a transient user data seen in the *Job context and step context* section, and it will be accessible to all the components of the job. When the job ends, the transient user data will expire because it is not persistent. Here, we have a sample of the `CheckpointUserData` class:

```
public class CheckpointUserData {
    private string startedBeforeJob;
    private string startedAfterStep;
    private int counter;

    public string getStartedBeforeJob() {
        return startedBeforeJob;
    }
  public void setStartedBeforeJob(string startedBeforeJob) {
        this.startedBeforeJob = startedBeforeJob;
    }
  public string getStartedAfterStep() {
        return startedAfterStep;
    }
  public void setStartedAfterStep(string startedAfterStep) {
        this.startedAfterStep = startedAfterStep;
    }
  public int getCounter() {
        return counter;
    }
  public void setCounter(int counter) {
   this.counter = counter;
  }
}
```

Now, let's look at how job listeners are declared in the JSL descriptor file:

```
<job version="1.0" id="CheckpointJob" restartable="true"
xmlns="http://xmlns.jcp.org/xml/ns/javaee">
    <properties partition="0">
        <property name="name1" value="value1" />
        <property name="name2" value="value2" />
    </properties>
    <listeners>
        <listener ref="jobCheckpointListener">
            <properties partition="0">
                <property name="name1" value="value1-jobcheckpointlistener" />
                <property name="name2" value="value2-jobcheckpointlistener" />
            </properties>
        </listener>
    </listeners>
    ...
```

It's important for the job listener to be written inside the job element. The position will indicate the type of working listener. Any listener can receive configuration properties to use inside the listener through the job context. The `afterJob()` method is seen over read the properties declared in the JSL descriptor file in the properties tag.

Step listener

The step listener acts on a single step. Like the job listener, for each step, we have two methods: a start and an end:

```
@Named
public class StepCheckpointListener implements StepListener {
...
    public final static string STARTED_AFTER_STEP = "started after step";
    public final static string BEFORE_STEP_PROPERTY = "beforeStepProperty";
    @Inject
 private JobContext jobContext;
    @Inject
 private StepContext stepContext;
    @Override
 public void beforeStep() throws Exception {
  Properties jobProperties = jobContext.getProperties();
  Properties stepProperties = stepContext.getProperties();
      stepProperties.put(BEFORE_STEP_PROPERTY, "Before step property");
      ...
    }
    @Override
 public void afterStep() throws Exception {
  CheckpointUserData checkpointUserData = (CheckpointUserData)
jobContext.getTransientUserData();
   checkpointUserData.setStartedAfterStep(STARTED_AFTER_STEP);
      ...
      PersistentCheckpointUserData persistentCheckpointUserData = new
PersistentCheckpointUserData();
      persistentCheckpointUserData.setStartedAfterStep
(STARTED_AFTER_STEP);
      stepContext.setPersistentUserData
(persistentCheckpointUserData);
      ...
    }
}
```

The listener implements the `javax.batch.api.listener`. The `StepListener` interface provides the `beforeStep()` and `afterStep()` methods. As for the job listener, it will be executed for each returning state, either with or without errors. In this sample, the `beforeStep()` method adds a property in the step context, so it can be read and elaborated only inside the step. After the end of the current step, a persistent user data is created. This object is alive only inside the step context. When it closes and another step is created, this object will be hibernated and reused in the next start of the job because it is persistent. Here's the `PersistentCheckpointUserData` object:

```
public class PersistentCheckpointUserData extends CheckpointUserData
implements Serializable {
    . . .
}
```

It simply extends the `CheckpointUserData` class seen in the *Job listener* section. The important thing is that this class implements the `Java.io.Serializable` interface to guarantee the persistence and serialization of the object.
This is the declaration of the step context in the JSL descriptor file:

```
<job version="1.0" id="CheckpointJob" restartable="true"
    xmlns="http://xmlns.jcp.org/xml/ns/javaee">
    . . .
    <step id="step1">
        <listeners>
            <listener ref="stepCheckpointListener">
                <properties partition="0">
                    <property name="name1" value="value1-
stepcheckpointlistener" />
                    <property name="name2" value="value2-
stepcheckpointlistener" />
                </properties>
            </listener>
    . . .
```

As for the job listener, the position of the declaration inside the step tag is important. The name of the listener reference is the name of the class declared as `@Named`, in lowercase. Automatically, the beans are referenced in this mode if the name of the reference is not declared. Refer to `Chapter 2`, *Working with Dependency Injection*, for more details.

Chunk listener

The chunk listener, as the name says, is made for listening to the chunks. It has two methods tied to the start and end of the chunk, and it helps in managing errors:

```java
@Named
public class PayrollListener implements ChunkListener {
    ...
    public final static string CHUNK_EXIT_STATUS = "chunkExitStatus";
    @Inject
    @BatchProperty(name = "name1")
    private string listenerProp;
    @Inject
    private JobContext jobContext;
    @Inject
    private StepContext stepContext;
    private CountDownLatch latch = new CountDownLatch(1);
    @Override
    public void beforeChunk() throws Exception {
        ...
    }
    @Override
    public void onError(Exception ex) throws Exception {
        ...
    }
    @Override
    public void afterChunk() throws Exception {
        Properties jobProperties = jobContext.getProperties();
        Properties stepProperties = stepContext.getProperties();
        ...
    }
}
```

This listener implements the `javax.batch.api.chunk.listener.ChunkListener` interface.

It starts with the `beforeChunk()` method on the first checkpoint of the chunk and ends with the `afterChunk()` method when all the items of the chunk are released.

The `onError()` method starts automatically when an exception is generated inside the chunk. We can, hence, implement this method and elaborate the error.

Now, let's see how the chunk listener is declared in the JSL file descriptor:

```xml
<job version="1.0" id="CheckpointJob" restartable="true"
    xmlns="http://xmlns.jcp.org/xml/ns/javaee">
    ...
```

```
<step id="step1">
    <listeners>
        ...
        <listener ref="payrollListener">
            <properties partition="0">
                <property name="name1" value="value1-payrolllistener" />
                <property name="name2" value="value2-payrolllistener" />
            </properties>
        </listener>
    </listeners>
    ...
```

The declared position must be the same as, or for the step listeners under the step tag. The batch specifications provide another three particular chunk listener types, one for each component of the chunk. Here's the list:

- `javax.batch.api.chunk.listener.AbstractItemProcessListener`: Used in the chunk processes
- `javax.batch.api.chunk.listener.AbstractItemReadListener`: Used in the chunk readers
- `javax.batch.api.chunk.listener.AbstractItemWriteListener`: Used in the chunk writers

JBeret 1.2.1.Final in WildFly 10.1.0 doesn't support them.

Batch property

A nice feature in the batches is the `javax.batch.api.BatchProperty` annotation. Through this annotation, we can inject the values of the properties declared in the JSL descriptor file.

In the case of the chunk listener, we inject the batch property, as shown:

```
@Inject
@BatchProperty(name = "name1")
private string listenerProp;
```

We are specifying the name of the property we want to inject; in this case, `name1`. As a result, we will get the `listenerProp` variable valued as `value1-payrolllistener`, now declared in the JSL descriptor file.

Checkpoint Algorithm

To show the other features of the chunks, we show this new element for the chunks called **Checkpoint Algorithm**.

In the *Chunk reader* section, we exposed the checkpoints and the `checkpointInfo()` method, which manages the checkpoint objects that are changing according to the item-count parameter declared in the chunk in the JSL descriptor file. It's a default strategy. Through the Checkpoint Algorithm, we can create new strategies to manage the checkpoints.

The Checkpoint Algorithm is represented by the `javax.batch.api.chunk.AbstractCheckpointAlgorithm` abstract class.

 This component, if used, rewrites the item-count property and the `checkpointInfo()` method, so these last also if declared will be ignored.

Here's a simple Checkpoint Algorithm:

```
@Named
public final class PayrollCheckpoint extends AbstractCheckpointAlgorithm {
    public final static string REAL_EXIT_STATUS = "myRealExitStatus";
    @Inject
  private JobContext jobContext;
    @Override
  public int checkpointTimeout() throws Exception {
  CheckpointUserData checkpointUserData = (CheckpointUserData)
jobContext.getTransientUserData();
    if (checkpointUserData.getCounter() == 6)
    return 1;
       else
      return 0;
  }
    @Override
  public void beginCheckpoint() throws Exception {
  super.beginCheckpoint();
  }
    @Override
  public void endCheckpoint() throws Exception {
  super.endCheckpoint();
  }
    @Override
  public boolean isReadyToCheckpoint() throws Exception {
  CheckpointUserData checkpointUserData = (CheckpointUserData)
```

```
jobContext.getTransientUserData();
   if (checkpointUserData.getCounter() % 3 == 0) {
         jobContext.setExitStatus(REAL_EXIT_STATUS);
         return true;
      } else
         return false;
   }
}
```

Now, let's analyze the methods:

- **Begin checkpoint**: It starts each time the checkpoint is declared ready to be restarted.
- **End checkpoint**: It ends each time the checkpoint is declared ready to be restarted.
- **Is ready to checkpoint**: In this method, we write the logic where we decide when to start or end the checkpoint. In our case, we read the transient user data and according to the counter option, if is a multiple of 3, we decide whether to start or not to start the checkpoint.
- **Checkpoint timeout**: Here, we declare the transaction timeout of the checkpoint. Remember that each checkpoint cycle is a transaction. If the timeout expires, a rollback exception will be thrown and the batch status of the job will be marked as FAILED. See the *Chunk reader* section for more details on the checkpoint. In this sample, we set a timeout of a second if the counter is equal to 6, while the timeout is not set (timeout = 0) for other cases.

Let's now continue our sample by adding the Checkpoint Algorithm and a new chunk to manage in our JSL descriptor file:

```
<step id="step1">
   <listeners>
      ...
   </listeners>
   <chunk checkpoint-policy="custom" item-count="5" time-limit="5" skip-
limit="5" retry-limit="5">
      <reader ref="checkpointItemReader">
         <properties partition="0">
            <property name="name1" value="value1" />
            <property name="name2" value="value2" />
         </properties>
      </reader>
      <processor ref="checkpointItemProcessor">
         <properties partition="0">
            <property name="name1" value="value1" />
            <property name="name2" value="value2" />
```

```
            </properties>
        </processor>
        <writer ref="checkpointItemWriter">
            <properties partition="0">
                <property name="name1" value="value1" />
                <property name="name2" value="value2" />
            </properties>
        </writer>
        <checkpoint-algorithm ref="payrollCheckpoint">
            <properties partition="0">
                <property name="name1" value="value1" />
                <property name="name2" value="value2" />
            </properties>
        </checkpoint-algorithm>
        ...
    </chunk>
```

Here, we have declared the reader, writer and processor classes of the chunk more the Checkpoint Algorithm showed before. To enable the Checkpoint Algorithm is important declare in the chunk the checkpoint policy that can be:

- **Default**: No need for a checkpoint algorithm. The algorithm will be executed by the item properties of the chunk and by the `checkpointInfo()` method.
- **Custom**: The custom checkpoint algorithm is enabled.

We have already seen that the policy of the checkpoint is ruled by the counter object of the transient user data. We have set an increment to this counter in the read method of the chunk reader. Here's the reader:

```
@Named
public class CheckpointItemReader extends AbstractItemReader {
    @Inject
 private JobContext jobContext;
    private int counter;
    @Override
 public Object readItem() throws Exception {
        counter++;
        CheckpointUserData checkpointUserData = (CheckpointUserData)
jobContext.getTransientUserData();
        checkpointUserData.setCounter(counter);
        if (counter < 20)
            return "ok read";
        else
            return null;
    }
    public int getCounter() {
        return counter;
```

```
        }
   }
```

The `readItem()` method increments the counter and establishes the end of the chunk when the counter reaches the number 20.

In the following diagram, we found a resume that shows the flow of the listeners working along the Checkpoint Algorithm:

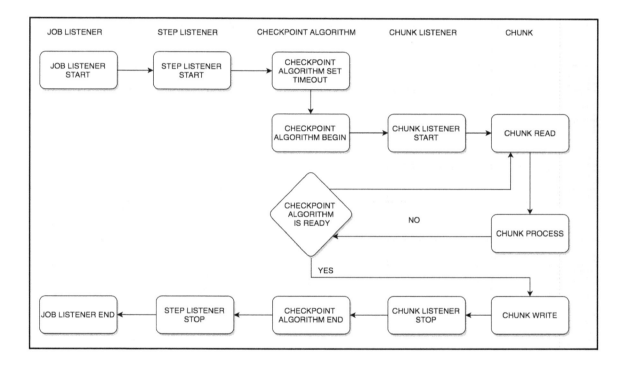

So, as always, start the **JOB LISTENER**, followed by the **STEP LISTENER**.

After the set of the transaction timeout done by the **CHECKPOINT ALGORITHM SET TIMEOUT**, start the transaction and all the chunks inside the transaction. The transaction will end when the **CHECKPOINT ALGORITHM IS READY** is ready and will help in deciding to write the chunks.

After the close of the transaction, the chunk reader will decide to stop the step through the step listener, stopping or opening a new transaction.

Checkpoint timeout

Now, let's test the timeout method. The Checkpoint Algorithm establishes the counter six to make the transaction available for 1 second. To be sure, we force a wait time over 1 second in the chunk. We can put it in the `beforeChunk` of the chunk listener, which we saw in the *Chunk listener* section:

```
    @Override
 public void beforeChunk() throws Exception {
        ...
        CheckpointUserData checkpointUserData = (CheckpointUserData)
jobContext.getTransientUserData();
   if (checkpointUserData.getCounter() == 6)
   latch.await(2, SECONDS);
        ...
    }
```

So when the counter reaches the number 6, the timeout will be set to 1 second and the `beforeChunk()` will wait for 2 seconds.

Let's see how, and what happens when the `beforeChunk` is executed:

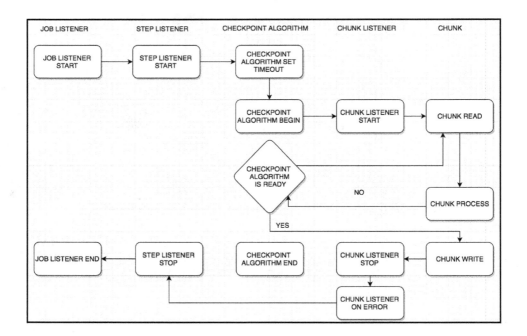

This is what happens:

- On the sixth chunk, the timeout is set to one by the **CHECKPOINT ALGORITHM SET TIMEOUT** and the transaction starts
- The **CHUNK LISTENER START** waits for more than a second
- The transaction ends after the first write
- The **CHUNK LISTENER STOP** is executed
- The **CHUNK LISTENER ON ERROR** starts to manage a `javax.transaction.RollbackException`
- The step and the job are closed

The Checkpoint Algorithm end doesn't work because the transaction is rolled back.

Exceptions

There are many exceptions that can be managed by the batches. The JSL descriptor file introduces three types of exception:

- **Skippable exceptions**: In this tag, we can put the exceptions that will not be reported by the listener. The skipped exceptions will allow the transaction continue.
- **Retryable exceptions**: If an exception is added here, the transaction will be restarted, and the process will again attempt to execute the work.
- **No rollback exceptions**: The exceptions of this tag will be reported by the listener, but the transaction will continue to work until the end, allowing the partial write of the process.

Here's a sample of JSL configuration inside the chunk:

```
<chunk>
...
    <skippable-exception-classes>
        <include class=
"it.vige.realtime.batchesworkflow.checkpoint.exception.SkippedException" />
        <exclude class=
"it.vige.realtime.batchesworkflow.checkpoint.exception.NoSkippedException"
/>
    </skippable-exception-classes>
    <retryable-exception-classes>
        <include class=
"it.vige.realtime.batchesworkflow.checkpoint.exception.RetriedException" />
        <include class="javax.transaction.RollbackException" />
```

```
        <exclude class=
"it.vige.realtime.batchesworkflow.checkpoint.exception.NoRetriedException"
/>
    </retryable-exception-classes>
    <no-rollback-exception-classes>
        <include class=
"it.vige.realtime.batchesworkflow.checkpoint.exception.NoRollbackException"
/>
        <exclude class=
"it.vige.realtime.batchesworkflow.checkpoint.exception.RollbackException"
/>
    </no-rollback-exception-classes>
</chunk>
```

In this JSL, we can find the three categories of exceptions. Each category has two tags:

- `include`: Here, we can put the exceptions that will be included in the category
- `exclude`: Here, we can put the exceptions that will be excluded from the category

Let's now try a new scenario, starting with the listener samples seen in the *Listeners* section, adding this JSL file descriptor to the flow and adding a item processor, as follows:

```
@Named
public class CheckpointItemProcessor implements ItemProcessor {
    @Inject
 private JobContext jobContext;
    @Override
 public Object processItem(Object item) throws Exception {
  CheckpointUserData checkpointUserData = (CheckpointUserData)
jobContext.getTransientUserData();
  if (checkpointUserData.getCounter() == 10)
    throw new SkippedException();
  if (checkpointUserData.getCounter() == 12)
    throw new NoRollbackException();
     return "process ok";
 }
```

In this processor, we are forced to throw exceptions managed by our JSL descriptor file. So, if we start the process again, we will get this situation:

- On the sixth chunk, the timeout is set to 1 by the **CHECKPOINT ALGORITHM SET TIMEOUT** and the transaction starts.
- The **CHUNK LISTENER START** waits for more than a second.
- The transaction ends after the first write.

- The **CHUNK LISTENER STOP** is executed.
- The **CHUNK LISTENER ON ERROR** is not executed because the `javax.transaction.RollbackException` is skipped by the JSL configuration, and the transaction is started again, without errors, because the chunk reader continues reading the seventh chunk.
- The transactions go on until the tenth chunk that throws a `SkippedException`. All go on because the `SkippedException` is ignored by the chunk listener.
- We arrive at the twelfth chunk and a `NoRollbackException` is thrown. In this case, the **CHUNK LISTENER ON ERROR** is executed but no rollback is executed, so the previous loaded data will be saved in the persistent system by the chunk writer.
- The step and the job are closed.

Monitoring of the batches

WildFly provides a simple default console to monitor the batches. In this console, you can monitor through the following metrics:

Active count	**The complete number of threads that are currently executing tasks.**
Completed task count	The total number of tasks that have completed the execution.
Current thread count	The current number of threads inside the pool.
Largest thread count	The largest number of threads that have ever been in the pool at the same time.
Queue size	The size of the queue size.
Rejected count	The number of rejected tasks.
Task count	The total number of the scheduled tasks ready for execution.

To enter the console, simply connect to the WildFly web console on `localhost:9990` and click on **Runtime** | **Standalone Server** | **Subsystems** | **Batch**:

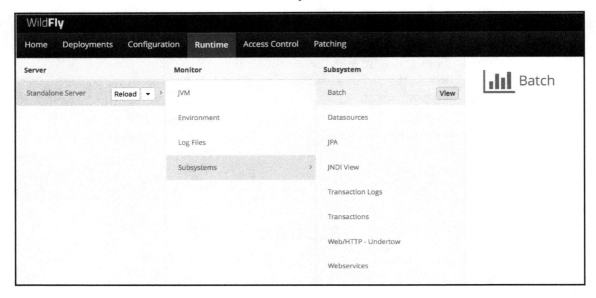

Click on **View**. You will see the runtime parameters monitoring the executed or executing batches:

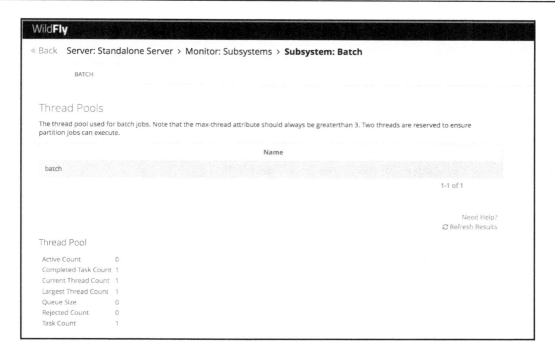

Deploying the workflows

A flow can be deployed as Web Archive or JAR. The important thing about packages is the presence of the JSL descriptor as an XML file. Here, you can see the structure of a Web Archive containing batches:

- **WAR**:
    - Batch classes
    - WEB-INF
        - Classes
            - META-INF
                - Batch-jobs
                    - `descript orProces s.xml`

- **JAR**:
  - Batch classes
  - META-INF
    - Batch-jobs
      - `descriptorProcess.xml`

Be careful of the location of the XML file. The XML will not be imported by WildFly if it is put in a different directory. Pay attention must also be paid to the batch-jobs folder name. A different name will cause the workflow to be cancelled.

Summary

We have completed the discussion about the batches and workflows. We are now able to understand when and how to write a workflow and how to configure it in WildFly 10. Thanks to the different standard specifications made during recent years, the use of workflows is increasing. Now Java also has its specifications. This will make writing workflow more simple, while ensuring greater stability in the process. It is precisely the specifications that make more widespread language of others, and to allow the diffusion of useful products for trade. Java is still the most common.

13
Working with Servlets and JSP

The web is a fundamental part of a Java application server. The main component representing the web in Java is the servlet. Servlet is the oldest component present since the first version of enterprise Java.

A servlet is a web component managed by a container, which generates dynamic web content.
The servlet can be considered as a communication point between a Java server and a web page that can be retrieved from an HTTP browser.
With the subsequent versions of Java EE, in view of the needs and the development of the web and web components and following the growth of the Java language, the mentioned arguments have increased and improved:

- An improved way to develop components thanks to more and more use of annotations, allowing you to write applications with less and less code.
- From Java EE 6 onward, the asynchronous part of the web was introduced, while it was improved in Java EE 7 by exploiting the novelty of the HTTP 1.1 protocol.

In this chapter, we will look at the following points thoroughly:

- Servlets (JSR-340: Java Servlet 3.1) and other web components
- Component annotations
- Security
- **JavaServer Pages** (**JSP**) pages (JSR-245: JavaServer Pages 2.3), what they are, and when they are used
- Web asynchronous

Enjoy reading!

Undertow

WildFly was born with the ambitious aim of replacing Tomcat, the historical web server of Java, with a newer and more intelligent web server, now known as Undertow. Undertow is a project born with WildFly and developed at the same time. The need was born with the advent of HTTP 1.1, which includes the asynchronous web.

Undertow is born by taking into account that every web component always carries with it an asynchronous way of working. For example, the WebSockets that we saw in Chapter 7, *Implementing WebSockets*, are no longer in accordance with Undertow's philosophy as asynchronous servlet.

The old Tomcat structure for the previous version of JBoss 7 does not allow the web asynchronous, except through additional libraries. Undertow is a young project that does not start from old specifications and is, therefore, faster and easier to configure.

The Undertow version that we are using in the book and is included in WildFly 10.1.0 is the version 1.4.0.

Servlets and web components

In this section, we begin the study of web components present in Java EE 7 and supported by WildFly 10, starting from the servlets. Let's start with a simple example of a servlet:

```
@WebServlet("/SimpleServlet")
public class SimpleServlet extends HttpServlet {
    @Override
    protected void doGet(HttpServletRequest request, HttpServletResponse
response) throws ServletException, IOException
    {
        response.getWriter().print("my GET");
    }
```

```
    @Override
    protected void doPost(HttpServletRequest request, HttpServletResponse
response) throws ServletException, IOException
    {
 response.getWriter().print("my POST");
    }
}
```

This servlet represents two HTTP methods, GET and POST, represented by the doGet and doPost methods inherited by the javax.servlet.http.HttpServlet abstract class.

 More information on the HTTP methods can be seen in Chapter 6, *Creating REST Services*, in the *REST and HTTP* paragraph.

According to the chosen HTTP method, a web page written by a Writer will return. The Writer is obtained by the HTTP response.

For example, we will get the following result for a GET call through the browser:

The javax.servlet.annotation.WebServlet annotation declares the class as a servlet. In the annotation, you can add the identifier name where you can call the servlet. In the preceding image, you can see how the servlet is called in GET with the localhost:8080/servlets-jsp/SimpleServlet URL.
SimpleServlet is the declared name in the annotation, while servlets-jsp is the context root of the application. Localhost is the server name and 8080 is the default port used to call a web component in WildFly.

Ports and security

The server name depends on the operative system and the network configuration, while the port can be changed simply by the `standalone.xml` WildFly configuration file. To change the port where it is declared, simply replace `8080` with another number:

```
<socket-binding name="http" port="${jboss.http.port:8080}"/><socket-binding
name="https" port="${jboss.https.port:8443}"/>
```

The `8443` is the default SSL port used to connect to the secured applications. Each application we deploy in WildFly is automatically configured to be called in HTTP and HTTPS (HTTP + SSL).

 Remember that the HTTPS is strictly tied to the application realm and keystore configuration showed in `Chapter 7`, *Implementing WebSockets*, in the section *Security*.

Another way to configure the port is through external application variables. For example, when we start WildFly, we can add the chosen ports:

```
standalone.sh –Djboss.http.port=8081 –Djboss.https.port=8444
```

Request and response

Each HTTP method of the servlet is available with a request represented by the `javax.servlet.http.HttpServletRequest` interface and a response represented by the `javax.servlet.http.HttpServletResponse` interface.
The request contains all the input information, for example, the HTTP headers, web parameters, and web attributes:

- **Headers**: Available through the `request.getHeaders(String headerName)` method, headers contain the information inserted directly by the browser. They can be manipulated inside the servlet.
- **Parameters**: Available through the `request.getParameterMap()` method, parameter are passed at URL level, for example, with `localhost:8080/servlets-jsp/SimpleServlet?param1=pvalue1&param2=value2`.
- **Attributes**: Available through the `request.getAttribute(String attributeName)` method, attributes can be passed only through Java by a servlet to another servlet that share the same request.

The response is used to manage the output information sent to the client. With the response, you can manage the following:

- **Headers**: The servlet can add headers to send to client through the `response.addHeader(String name, String value)` method.
- **Cookies**: The servlet can create cookies to send to the client with the `response.addCookie(Cookie cookie)` method.
- **Status**: The servlet can set the HTTP status of the response through the `response.setStatus(int status)` method. The possible statuses are described in the HTTP protocol. Here are some examples:
    - **405** : Method not allowed
    - **406** : Not acceptable
    - **408** : Request timeout
- **Errors**: The servlet sets the status and redirects the page to an error through the `response.sendError(int status)` method.
- **Writer**: The writer allows us to write the result of the page visible to the user in the browser; it is available through the `response.getWriter()` method.

Cookies

In this section, we will show how to work with the cookies in the servlets in depth. As mentioned in the preceding section, we need the `addCookie` method of the response. To make a complete sample of an operation with the cookies, we must first introduce the JSP pages.

JSP pages

JSP is a technology that is present since the first J2EE 1.2, and it has been created to simplify the development of web pages.

What the servlet writes through the writer of the response in a JSP page is just rendered automatically. To understand this better, let's take the servlet seen in the servlets and Web components paragraph as an example. To render the page in a servlet, we need the following code in our Java code:

```
response.getWriter().print("my GET");
```

We can write the same result using a JSP page represented as a file with the `.jsp` extension by putting the following code:

```
my GET
```

The result is the same and simpler. So the question is, when do we use JSP and servlets. JSPs are born exclusively to show something to the browser. So, they are oriented to write markup code. Unlike the servlet, they can write markup code to the browser, but it is done mainly to manipulate the information of requests and responses.
Here's a sample of a JSP calling a servlet:

```
<%@page contentType="text/html" pageEncoding="UTF-8"%>
<!DOCTYPE HTML PUBLIC "-//W3C//DTD HTML 4.01 Transitional//EN"
    "http://www.w3.org/TR/html4/loose.dtd">
<html>
    <head>
        <meta http-equiv="Content-Type" content="text/html; charset=UTF-8">
        <title>Servlet : Cookies</title>
    </head>
    <body>
        <h1>Servlet : Cookies</h1>
            Call <a
href="${pageContext.request.contextPath}/CookiesServlet">Servlet</a> to see
the pre-defined cookie, and set two cookies - one normal, another HttpOnly.
    </body>
</html>
```

As you can see, it is a simple markup HTML language. In a JSP, we can write Java code using the `<% %>` operators. Inside the `%`, we can write Java code and it will be executed at the loading of the page.

EL Expressions

Another interesting thing we can use in a JSP page is the **Expression Language** (**EL**) Expression. EL is a simple way to call the Java attributes present in the memory. The example in the preceding code in the `${}` annotations adds the context path of the application and appends the `/CookiesServlet` string dynamically. As a result, we obtain a markup code similar to `<a href="servlets-jsp/CookiesServlet">...</a>`.

Through EL, we can take the `pageContext` represented by the `javax.servlet.jsp.PageContext` abstract class. With this class, we can access the HTTP request and take the context path of the application.

The `.request` calls the `getRequest()` method of the page context, while the `.contextPath` calls the `getContextPath()` method of the `HttpServletRequest` interface. This is because the EL automatically translates the calls in the `get` methods.

Cookies operations

Now, let's analyze a new servlet that we will use to work with the cookies:

```
@WebServlet(urlPatterns = { "/CookiesServlet" })
@MultipartConfig(location = "/tmp")
public class CookiesServlet extends HttpServlet {
  ...
    protected void doGet(HttpServletRequest request, HttpServletResponse
response) throws ServletException, IOException {
      response.setContentType("text/html;charset=UTF-8");
      try (PrintWriter out = response.getWriter()) {
        out.println("<!DOCTYPE html>");
        out.println("<html>");
 out.println("<head>");
        out.println("<title>Servlet Cookies</title>");
        out.println("</head>");
 out.println("<body>");
 out.println("<h1>Servlet TestServlet at " + request.getContextPath() +
"</h1>");
 SessionCookieConfig cookies =
request.getServletContext().getSessionCookieConfig();
 out.println("Found cookie: " + cookies.getName());
        Cookie cookie = new Cookie("myCookieKey", "myCookieValue");
        cookie.setMaxAge(60);
 response.addCookie(cookie);
        out.println("<br><br>Set a new cookie");
        cookie = new Cookie("myHttpOnlyCookieKey", "myHttpOnlyCookieValue");
        cookie.setHttpOnly(true);
 cookie.setMaxAge(60);
 response.addCookie(cookie);
        out.println("<br>Set a new HTTPOnly Cookie<br><br>");
        out.println("Check what cookies are visible by");
        out.println("<a href=\"http://" + request.getServerName() + ":" +
request.getServerPort() + request.getContextPath() + "/view/index-
cookies.jsp\">clicking here</a>");
        out.println("</body>");
 out.println("</html>");
 }
 }
```

This servlet produces the following output:

The `javax.servlet.SessionCookiesConfig` interface represents the default cookie written to represent the web session. It is called *JSESSIONID*; let's see what a web session is in depth.

Web session and other scopes

A web session is a permanent memory that starts when a web URL is called by the browser and usually ends after the closing of the browser. The life of a web session is tied to the user. The web session provides two important operations:

- **Activation**: It is activated when the session starts, by default, when a user connects to the web application for the first time. This operation can be forced, thanks to the *activate* method of the web session.
- **Passivation**: It is triggered when the session ends, by default, when a user closes the browser. This *passivate* can be forced, thanks to the activate method of the web session.

The web session is represented by the `javax.servlet.http.HttpSession` interface. In addition to the web session, three important scopes exist in the web:

- **Request scope**: It ends after the first call to a web URL. After the call, all information parameters will be loose. It provides good performances but less registered information.
- **Page scope**: It collects the information present inside a web page, and is used only in JSP.

- **Application scope**: All information is in memory for the complete duration of the web application. By duration, we mean the time after the deployment of the application until the undeploy. It's more persistent but more expensive at the performance level.

Now, let's continue with the analysis of the servlet. The next step is to create a cookie.

Creation of a cookie

A cookie is an object defined with a key and a value as string. The cookie works in the web response. It is persistent because it can be registered as a file in the PC of the user. To create a cookie, simply instantiate it and register it in a response. Here's a sample:

```
Cookie cookie = new Cookie("myCookieKey", "myCookieValue");
cookie.setMaxAge(60);
response.addCookie(cookie);
```

We have created a cookie called myCookieKey with the value myCookieValue and a maximum duration of 60 seconds. In the preceding code, we create a second cookie, myHttpOnlyCookieKey, setting a more secure level. Thanks to the setHttpOnly(true) method, the cookie will never be registered on the client side.

Cookies and JavaScript

JavaScript can read the cookies. The following is a simple command we can put in our JSP page to read the current used cookies:

```
<body>
    <script type="text/javascript">
        document.write(document.cookie);
    </script>
</body>
```

We have written the content of the cookie represented by the document.cookie JavaScript command in the page.

Tests with Selenium

In Chapter 6, *Creating REST Services*, in the paragraph *Selenium and Drone*, we introduced **Selenium** and **Drone** to test the web application. Now, take a deep look into a sample to navigate inside a web page. The first step is to execute the injection of the current URL of the web application and the Selenium driver used to navigate in the application:

```
@ArquillianResource
private URL url;
@Drone
private WebDriver driver;
```

Now, we enter the cookies.jsp page:

```
driver.get(url + "view/cookies.jsp");
```

Then, we search the href tag of the JSP page using xpath and click on href:

```
driver.findElement(xpath("html/body/a")).click();
```

After clicking, we search the body of the resulting page and get it as a String, as illustrated:

```
String textPage1 = driver.findElement(xpath("html/body")).getText();
```

It's a very practical mode to navigate in the HTML pages and test the results.

Error mappings

Servlet technologies provide a good way to redirect the errors in the web pages. In this section, we will show some cases to do it.

File configuration

An alternative to the annotations is file configuration. Actually, file configuration allows a more complete set of configurations compared to annotations. Firstly, we will see how to configure a servlet through the web.xml file, the default configurator file available in the Java web applications. Take this servlet sample:

```
public class ErrorMappingServlet extends HttpServlet {
    ...
    protected void doGet(HttpServletRequest request, HttpServletResponse
response) throws ServletException, IOException
```

```
    {
        throw new RuntimeException();
    }
    ...
}
```

This servlet doesn't declare the servlet annotation seen in the preceding paragraphs, so it needs to be configured in the web.xml. This is a simple web.xml with the declaration of the servlet:

```
<web-app version="3.1"
    xmlns="http://xmlns.jcp.org/xml/ns/javaee"
    xmlns:xsi="http://www.w3.org/2001/XMLSchema-instance"
    xsi:schemaLocation="http://xmlns.jcp.org/xml/ns/javaee
http://xmlns.jcp.org/xml/ns/javaee/web-app_3_1.xsd">
    <servlet>
        <servlet-name>ErrorMappingServlet</servlet-name>
        <servlet-
class>it.vige.webprogramming.servletjsp.errormapping.ErrorMappingServlet</s
ervlet-class>
    </servlet>
    <servlet-mapping>
        <servlet-name>ErrorMappingServlet</servlet-name>
        <url-pattern>/ErrorMappingServlet</url-pattern>
    </servlet-mapping>
    ...
</web-app>
```

The declaration is done by two tags:

- servlet-name: The name of the servlet that will be used in the URL to connect to the servlet
- servlet-class: The name of the class implementation tied to the servlet name

 We can use both annotations and file descriptor to declare a servlet. Just remember that the file descriptor is the priority. So, if your servlet is annotated with a name different than the file descriptor, the name declared in the file descriptor will be the right mapped name.

A JSP page has the same properties of a servlet, and it can be declared as a servlet too in the web.xml descriptor file. Here's a sample:

```
<servlet>
    <display-name>index</display-name>
    <servlet-name>index</servlet-name>
    <jsp-file>/view/secure-programmatic.jsp</jsp-file>
</servlet>
```

With this code, we are declaring a servlet index and mapping it with a JSP page instead of a servlet class.

Now we add the error mapping to the servlet. The error mapping allows us to redirect an error on a chosen page. As you can see in the servlet implementation, we have forced a RuntimeException in our doGet method to simulate an error. Our example will execute the servlet and will then be a redirect on a error page. To configure the error mapping, we need to add the following code to the web.xml:

```
...
<error-page>
    <error-code>404</error-code>
    <location>/view/error-404.jsp</location>
</error-page>
<error-page>
    <exception-type>java.lang.RuntimeException</exception-type>
    <location>/view/error-exception.jsp</location>
</error-page>
...
```

In this configuration, we are configuring two error pages:

- The first will be executed when a 404 HTTP error will be generated. The 404 error starts when we try to connect to an inexistent URL. In this case, when a 404 error starts, the JSP page error-404.jsp will be loaded.
- The second configuration maps the RuntimeException. When an any web component will generate a RuntimeException, automatically our web application will be redirect to the error-exception.jsp page.

File upload

A more efficient and simple upload method has evolved in Java EE 7. Now, we can upload files through our web forms with little code. In this section, we will see a very practical sample. Now, let's start creating an upload form through a JSP page:

```
<form action="${pageContext.request.contextPath}/FileUploadServlet"
method="post" enctype="multipart/form-data">
    <input type="file" name="file" size="50" /> <br />
    <input type="submit" value="Upload File" />
</form>
```

With this code, we can upload files on a chosen platform. The web form allows us to interact with a server. In this case, we can attach a file through the input file tag. To send the file to the server, we need to configure the form with a particular `enc` type, the `multipart/form-data`. It is the standard mode used to send the files. Here's a list of the available `enc` types of the forms:

Value	Description
application/x-www-form-urlencoded	Default; all characters are encoded before they are sent (spaces are converted to "+" symbols, and special characters are converted to ASCII HEX values)
multipart/form-data	No characters are encoded; this value is required when you are using forms that have a file upload control.
text/plain	Spaces are converted to "+" symbols, but no special characters are encoded

The second input type is the button that will submit the file to the server.
This is how the page will be shown in our web application:

We have created the form that will send the file. Now we need the server that will receive the file. We implement it through a servlet:

```
@WebServlet(urlPatterns = { "/FileUploadServlet" })
@MultipartConfig(location = "/tmp")
public class FileUploadServlet extends HttpServlet {
    protected void processRequest(HttpServletRequest request,
HttpServletResponse response) throws ServletException, IOException {
    response.setContentType("text/html;charset=UTF-8");
    try (PrintWriter out = response.getWriter()) {
        out.println("<!DOCTYPE html>");
        ...
        out.println("Received " + request.getParts().size() + " parts
...<br>");
    String fileName = "";
    for (Part part : request.getParts()) {
    fileName = part.getSubmittedFileName();
        out.println("... writing " + fileName + " part<br>");
        part.write(fileName);
        out.println("... written<br>");
    }
        out.println("... uploaded to: /tmp/" + fileName);
        out.println("</body>");
    out.println("</html>");
    }
}
```

The `javax.servlet.annotation.MutipartConfig` automatically configures the properties of the `multipart/form-data`, which is an `enctype`. In our case, we configure the default location in the filesystem for multipart data. Our uploaded file will automatically be put into the `/tmp` folder.

From the request, we can directly take the file data uploaded by the form through the `javax.servlet.http.Part` interface after we get the filename through the `getSubmittedFileName()` method. At the end, we put the file in the default folder of the server configured through the `MultipartConfig` annotation through the `write(String filename)` method of the part. The file is now uploaded.

Filters

Filters are web components that intercept the web requests of the Servlet according to a path and manipulate the request or response.

The filter must implement the `javax.servlet.Filter` interface and implement at least one of the following three methods:

- `init`: This starts when the web application is deployed, and it is usually used to configure initial properties
- `doFilter`: This is the main method that manipulates the request before the servlet is called by the client
- `destroy`: This starts after the undeploy of the web application to close all unused instances or reset internal properties.

This sample manipulates the web response, adding some rows to the resulting page:

```
@WebFilter(filterName = "MyBarFilter", urlPatterns = { "/filtered/*" })
public class MyBarFilter implements Filter {
...
 private FilterConfig filterConfig;
 private void doBeforeProcessing(ServletRequest request, ServletResponse
response) throws IOException, ServletException {
 try (PrintWriter out = response.getWriter()) {
 out.print("my--");
 out.flush();
 }
  }
  private void doAfterProcessing(ServletRequest request, ServletResponse
response) throws IOException, ServletException {
 try (PrintWriter out = response.getWriter()) {
 out.print("--bar");
 out.flush();
 }
 }
  @Override
 public void doFilter(ServletRequest request, ServletResponse response,
FilterChain chain) throws IOException, ServletException {
 PrintWriter out = response.getWriter();
 ResponseCharacterWrapper wrappedResponse = new
ResponseCharacterWrapper((HttpServletResponse) response);
 doBeforeProcessing(request, wrappedResponse);
     chain.doFilter(request, wrappedResponse);
     doAfterProcessing(request, wrappedResponse);
 out.write(wrappedResponse.toString());
  }
```

```
    @Override
    public void init(FilterConfig filterConfig) {
        this.filterConfig = filterConfig;
    }
```

The `javax.servlet.annotation.WebFilter` annotation configures the filter and establishes when the filter will start. In this case, it will start after the calling of any URL containing the `/filtered/` path in the context path.

When the `doFilter` method is activated, the response will be caught and the filter will add a prefix and a suffix to the print stream of the response.

The filter works inside a filter chain. Many filters can intercept an HTTP call, so they need to be executed in a cascade mode. Each filter has the responsibility to call the next filter, otherwise the filter chain will be interrupted. To continue the filter chain, you must simply launch the `doFilter()` method of the `javax.servlet.FilterChain` interface included in the `doFilter()` method of the filter.

HTTP servlet response wrapper

A wrapper for the response is very useful to implement the new features of the response. In our example, we write an implementation that prints the response as a string. To do it, we can implement the `javax.servlet.http.HttpServletResponse` interface, as follows:

```
public class ResponseCharacterWrapper extends HttpServletResponseWrapper {
  private CharArrayWriter output;
  public String toString() {
  return output.toString();
  }
public ResponseCharacterWrapper(HttpServletResponse response) {
        super(response);
        output = new CharArrayWriter();
  }
  public PrintWriter getWriter() {
  return new PrintWriter(output);
  }
}
```

Now, add a servlet mapped with a `/filtered/` path:

```
@WebServlet(urlPatterns = { "/CharacterServlet",
"/filtered/CharacterServlet" })
public class CharacterServlet extends HttpServlet {
    @Override
    protected void doGet(HttpServletRequest request, HttpServletResponse
response) throws ServletException, IOException
```

```
    {
        response.setContentType("text/html;charset=UTF-8");
        try (PrintWriter out = response.getWriter()) {
            out.print("bar");
        }
    }
}
```

Without filters, if we do a `GET HTTP` call through the
`http://localhost:8080/servlets-jsp/filtered/CharacterServlet` URL, we
should obtain a page with a row bar. As the filter intercepts all the `/filtered/` paths, we
will obtain a page as illustrated:

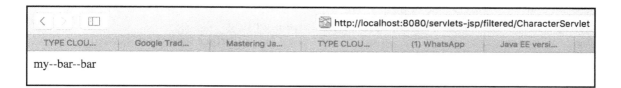

Event listeners

Event listeners are similar to the filters seen in the *Filters* section. The difference is that event
listeners start after a particular event instead of intercepting the path. The servlet
specifications include a wide set of events that we will analyze in this section.

Session listener

The session listener works on the creation of the web session and also destroys it. Here's a
simple example that logs the two events:

```
@WebListener
public class SampleSessionListener implements HttpSessionListener {
    private static final Logger logger =
getLogger(SampleSessionListener.class.getName());
    @Override
    public void sessionCreated(HttpSessionEvent se) {
        logger.info("MySessionListener.sessionCreated: " +
se.getSession().getId());
    }
    @Override
    public void sessionDestroyed(HttpSessionEvent se) {
```

```
        logger.info("MySessionListener.sessionDestroyed: " +
se.getSession().getId());
    }
}
```

Each listener must declare the `javax.servlet.annotation.WebListener` annotation. The session listener must implement the `javax.servlet.http.HttpSessionListener` interface.

Session ID listener

Each session has an identifier that certificates the univocity of the session. When the web session changes, the ID also changes. The `sessionIDlistener` is used to monitor the changes of the session in the web application implementing the `javax.servlet.http.HttpSessionIDListener` interface and the following method:

```
...
@Override
public void sessionIdChanged(HttpSessionEvent event, String oldSessionId) {
  logger.info("MySessionIdListener.sessionIdChanged: new=" +
event.getSession().getId() + ", old=" + oldSessionId);
}
...
```

This example controls the change and prints the new and old session IDs.

Servlet request listener

Like the session listener, servlet request listener intercepts the events of the creation and destroying of a request. Unlike the session listener, it will be executed more number of times depending upon the nature of the request because it is faster and lighter. To use it, simply implement the `javax.servlet.http.ServletRequestListener` interface:

```
@WebListener
public class SampleServletRequestListener implements ServletRequestListener
{
 private static final Logger logger =
getLogger(SampleServletRequestListener.class.getName());
   @Override
 public void requestDestroyed(ServletRequestEvent sre) {
  logger.info("MyServletRequestListener.requestDestroyed: " +
sre.getServletContext().getContextPath());
 }
```

```
    @Override
  public void requestInitialized(ServletRequestEvent sre) {
    logger.info("MyServletRequestListener.requestInitialized: " +
sre.getServletContext().getContextPath());
  }
}
```

Servlet request attribute listener

Servlet request attribute listener interacts with the operations of an attribute of the request. We can add, replace, or delete attributes on a request. The `javax.servlet.http.ServletRequestAttributeListener` interface provides three methods for it. Here's a sample:

```
@WebListener
public class SampleServletRequestAttributeListener implements
ServletRequestAttributeListener {
    private static final Logger logger =
getLogger(SampleServletRequestAttributeListener.class.getName());
    @Override
    public void attributeAdded(ServletRequestAttributeEvent srae) {
        logger.info("MyServletRequestAttributeListener.
        attributeAdded: " + srae.getName());
    }
    @Override
    public void attributeRemoved(ServletRequestAttributeEvent srae)
    {
        logger.info("MyServletRequestAttributeListener.
        attributeRemoved: " + srae.getName());
    }
    @Override
    public void attributeReplaced(ServletRequestAttributeEvent srae)
    {
        logger.info("MyServletRequestAttributeListener.
        attributeReplaced: " + srae.getName());
    }
}
```

Session attribute listener

Like the request, attributes are also in the session. An appropriate listener is ready to work when the attributes change. To use it, simply implement the `javax.servlet.http.HttpSessionAttributeListener` and implements the three methods.

Session binding listener

Another form to check the attributes of a session is through session binding. We can extend any object that will get in the session as an attribute and check it each time it is managed. The `javax.servlet.http.HttpSessionBindingListener` interface provides two methods for the object:

- The `valueBound` method starts when the `MyAttribute` object is taken through the `session.setAttribute(...)` method
- The `valueUnbound` starts when the `session.removeAttribute(...)` method is executed on the `MyAttribute` object

Here a sample of Session binding listener implementation:

```
public class MyAttribute implements HttpSessionBindingListener {
 private static final Logger logger =
getLogger(MyAttribute.class.getName());
    @Override
 public void valueBound(HttpSessionBindingEvent event) {
        logger.info("MyAttribute.valueBound: " + event.getName());
    }
    @Override
 public void valueUnbound(HttpSessionBindingEvent event) {
        logger.info("MyAttribute.valueUnbound: " + event.getName());
    }
}
```

 The class implementing the `HttpSessionBindingListener` cannot have the `WebListener` annotation because it is not really a listener but only an object to intercept.

Session activation listener

The session can be migrated when you work inside a cluster. WildFly will move the current session on a more efficient machine or virtual machine if needed. In this type of migration, a passivation of the Session will be executed in the old VM and an activation will be executed on the new VM. The session activation listener can be used to monitor these two operations. Here's an example:

```
public class SampleHttpSessionActivationListener implements
HttpSessionActivationListener {
 private static final Logger logger =
getLogger(SampleHttpSessionActivationListener.class.getName());
    @Override
 public void sessionWillPassivate(HttpSessionEvent se) {
        logger.info("MyHttpSessionActivationListener.
        sessionWillPassivate: " + se.getSession().getId());
    }
    @Override
 public void sessionDidActivate(HttpSessionEvent se) {
        logger.info("MyHttpSessionActivationListener.
        sessionDidActivate: " + se.getSession().getId());
    }
}
```

Servlet context listener

The servlet context works in the application scope. In the servlet Context represented by the `javax.servlet.ServletContext` interface, we can put all attributes that need to be persistent for all the life of the application when it will be undeployed. As for the request and the session, the servlet context listener, represented by the `javax.servlet.http.SevletContextListener` interface, provides two methods to monitor the creation and the destroying.

Servlet context attribute listener

Attributes can also be added in the servlet context so that a proper listener can be set to monitor the three operations, add, replace, and remove, for an attribute as for the request and the session. To do it, simply implement the `javax.servlet.http.ServletContextAttibuteListener` interface. Let's take the following example:

```
@WebListener
public class SampleContextAttributeListener implements
ServletContextAttributeListener {
 private static final Logger logger =
getLogger(SampleContextAttributeListener.class.getName());
   @Override
 public void attributeAdded(ServletContextAttributeEvent event) {
      logger.info("MyContextAttributeListener.attributeAdded: " +
event.getName());
    }
   @Override
   public void attributeRemoved(ServletContextAttributeEvent event)
   {
      logger.info("MyContextAttributeListener.attributeRemoved: " +
event.getName());
    }
   @Override
   public void attributeReplaced(ServletContextAttributeEvent event)
   {
      logger.info("MyContextAttributeListener.attributeReplaced: " +
event.getName());
      sampleContextAttributeSet.add(3);
    }
}
```

Asynchronous servlet

The servlets we have seen so far work in sync. That is, when a client connects to a servlet, the container assigns a server-side thread to the client and keeps it available until a response is generated and sent to the client.

If the client performs operations that require a long waiting time, the thread will remain busy for a long time, leaving a certain amount of memory space busy. If there are many connected users, the space will increase in proportion.

To solve these problems, there are asynchronous servlets. Asynchronous servlets allow dynamic thread management, allowing the container to fully utilize the available resources and avoid memory leaks.

There are several algorithms that calculate the available resources, allowing thread management that is best suited to cases.

The technology behind the asynchronous servlet is the same as that behind the WebSockets. Also, for this reason, Undertow proves to be faster and lighter compared to the predecessor web servers.

To declare an asynchronous servlet, simply add the `asyncSupported` parameter to the `WebServlet` annotation:

```
@WebServlet(urlPatterns = "/AsynchronousServlet", asyncSupported =
true)
```

Here's an example of the `doGet` method:

```
@Resource
private ManagedExecutorService executor;
...
@Override
protected void doGet(HttpServletRequest request, HttpServletResponse
response) throws ServletException, IOException
{
 AsyncContext ac = request.startAsync();
 ac.addListener(new AsyncListener() {
        @Override
        public void onComplete(AsyncEvent event) throws IOException
        {
 event.getSuppliedResponse().getWriter()
            .println(onComplete);
        }
        @Override
        public void onTimeout(AsyncEvent event) throws IOException
        {
            event.getSuppliedResponse().getWriter()
            .println(onTimeout);
            event.getAsyncContext().complete();
        }
        @Override
        public void onError(AsyncEvent event) throws IOException
        {
            event.getSuppliedResponse().getWriter()
            .println(onError);
        }
        @Override
```

```
        public void onStartAsync(AsyncEvent event) throws IOException
        {
            event.getSuppliedResponse().getWriter()
            .println(onStartAsync);
        }
    });
    executor.submit(new MyAsyncService(ac));
}
...
```

The servlet takes an `AsyncContext` by the request. The `AsyncContext`, represented by the `javax.servlet.AsyncContext` interface, allows us to set the listener in an asynchronous mode that will execute the implemented operations. The listener can be implemented through the `javax.servlet.AsyncListener` interface as an anonymous class implementing the following four methods:

- `onComplete`: This starts when the web response is released.
- `onTimeout`: This starts when the asynchronous operation has timed out. The default configuration is 60 seconds.
- `onError`: If an error status returns from the web response.
- `onStartAsync`: This is called when the asynchronous operation starts.

Here's a simple custom `enum` representing the states:

```
public enum State {
    onComplete, onError, onStartAsync, onTimeout, running
}
```

In our asynchronous servlet, it is lawful to use the managed executor service to manage the concurrency with the thread. Here's an example of a `Runnable` class submitted by an injected `ManagedExecutorService`. This thread will be used to show the running status during the loading of the servlet in the browser:

```
...
class MyAsyncService implements Runnable {
    AsyncContext ac;
    public MyAsyncService(AsyncContext ac) {
        this.ac = ac;
    }
    @Override
    public void run() {
        try {
            ac.getResponse().getWriter().println(running);
        } catch (IOException e) {
            throw new IllegalStateException(e);
```

```
        }
        ac.complete();
      }
  }
```

Further details of the Managed Executor Service are in Chapter 5, *Working with Distributed Transactions*, in the *Managed Executor Service* section. The following is the result of the loaded servlet in the browser:

If the system is slow, or if we load big charges, the operation can time out after 60 seconds. Here's the result of the time-out in the browser:

Non blocking I/O

Real-time web features require a long idle connection time per user. In a classic synchronous web server, it implies to devote one thread to each user, which will be very expensive.

Concurrent connections have a memory and CPU-level cost. To minimize this cost, WildFly uses a single threaded event loop. In this mode, all application code should be asynchronous and non blocking because only one operation can be active at a time.

The terms asynchronous and non-blocking are closely related and it often results in confusion, but they are not exactly the same thing.
Programs that use non blocking I/O have a rule that every function has to return immediately, for example, all the functions in such programs are non-blocking. Thus, control passes very quickly from one operation to the next.

Protocol handler

In `Chapter 7`, *Implementing WebSockets*, in the *Negotiated subprotocols* section, we introduced the multiprotocol function. With this function, we can establish what protocol to use for the client-server communication, and even use of a custom protocol to use in secure system, for example.

Servlets 3.1 introduce the `javax.servlet.http.HttpUpgradeHandler` interface. This interface encapsulates the upgrade protocol processing. The upgrade protocol allows us to switch from the HTTP base protocol to another new protocol.

In the following example, we will call a servlet accepting an header, and it will upgrade the current HTTP base protocol to a custom echo protocol. This is the servlet implementation:

```
@WebServlet(urlPatterns = { "/UpgradeServlet" })
public class UpgradeServlet extends HttpServlet {
 ...
    protected void doGet(HttpServletRequest request, HttpServletResponse
response) throws ServletException, IOException
    {
        response.setContentType("text/html;charset=UTF-8");
        try (PrintWriter out = response.getWriter()) {
 ...
            out.println("<h1>Servlet UpgradeServlet at " +
request.getContextPath() + "</h1>");
            if (request.getHeader("Upgrade").equals("echo")) {
                response.setStatus(SC_SWITCHING_PROTOCOLS);
                response.setHeader("Connection", "Upgrade");
                response.setHeader("Upgrade", "echo");
                request.upgrade(SampleProtocolHandler.class);
                ...
    }
```

```
. . .
            }
}
```

This servlet, when it receives an HTTP header `Upgrade:echo`, thanks to the upgrade method of the web request, it will execute the upgrade to a new custom protocol implemented by the `SampleProtocolHandler` class. Now, let's see the details of the protocol handler implementation:

```java
public class SampleProtocolHandler implements HttpUpgradeHandler
{
    public static final String CRLF = "\r\n";
    @Override
    public void init(WebConnection wc) {
    try (
            ServletInputStream input = wc.getInputStream();
            ServletOutputStream output = wc.getOutputStream();
        ) {
    output.write(("upgrade" + CRLF).getBytes());
            output.write(("received" + CRLF).getBytes());
            output.write("END".getBytes());
        } catch (IOException ex) {}
    }
    @Override
    public void destroy() {
    throw new UnsupportedOperationException("Not supported yet.");
    }
}
```

This simple protocol implements the `init` and `destroy` methods of the `HttpUpgradeHandler` interface and adds a row to the web response--*Upgrade received*. When the browser calls the servlet, a simple self-generated page with the row of the web response will return it to the browser.

To test the example, it's important to set the upgrade echo header. For secure issues, headers cannot be sent directly by the browser unless you use a web agent. A web agent can be written in Java. Here's an example that sends an upgrade header to the `UpgradeServlet`:

```java
public static final String CRLF = "\r\n";
. . .
Socket socket = new Socket("localhost", "8080");
BufferedWriter out = new BufferedWriter(new
OutputStreamWriter(socket.getOutputStream()));
out.write("GET /servlets-jsp/UpgradeServlet HTTP/1.1" + CRLF);
out.write("Host: " + host + ":" + port + CRLF);
out.write("Upgrade: echo" + CRLF);
```

```
out.write("Connection: Upgrade" + CRLF);
out.write(CRLF);
out.flush();
```

Dynamic context registration

In the preceding servlets and web components section, we saw how to declare a servlet and its context path through the @WebServlet annotation or through the web.xml descriptor file. The same thing can be done dynamically at the programming level. As an example, we will write a servlet without context path and a context listener that dynamically registers the servlet. Here's the servlet:

```
public class RegistrationDynamicServlet extends HttpServlet {
    @Override
    protected void doGet(HttpServletRequest req, HttpServletResponse resp)
throws ServletException, IOException {
        resp.getWriter().print("dynamic GET");
    }
}
```

This is the context listener:

```
@WebListener
public class RegistrationContextListener implements ServletContextListener
{
    @Override
    public void contextInitialized(ServletContextEvent sce) {
        ServletRegistration.Dynamic registration =
sce.getServletContext().addServlet("dynamic",RegistrationDynamicServlet.cla
ss);
        registration.addMapping("/dynamic");
    }
    ...
}
```

With this code, we have mapped the RegistrationDynamicServlet named dynamic with a /dynamic path. Now we can call our servlet using the /dynamic context path:

External resources and themes

External resources can be plugged in to our web applications in a theme style typical by the portal systems. We can include additional themes included inside JAR files in the WEB-INF/lib directory of our war, and they can automatically be used by the web application. So, as an example, we can create a JAR file containing the following files:

Now zip it in a JAR file, put in the WEB-INF/lib of our web application, and deploy the web application. Now we are able to read the styles.css inside the context root of the web application:

```
                                          http://localhost:8080/servlets-jsp/styles.css
body {
    background-color: #ff0000;
    font-size: 12px;
    color: #000000;
    margin: 10px;
}

h1 {
    border-bottom: 1px solid #AFAFAF;
    font-size:   16px;
    font-weight: bold;
    margin: 0px;
    padding: 0px;
    color: #FFFFFF;
}

a:link, a:visited {
  color: #045491;
  font-weight : bold;
  text-decoration: none;
}

a:link:hover, a:visited:hover   {
  color: #045491;
  font-weight : bold;
  text-decoration : underline;
}
```

Web fragments

We can even do the same thing for external web components. The included web component inside a web application is called web fragment. To declare a web fragment, we need to put the `web-fragment.xml` descriptor file in an external JAR archive. Here's a sample that declares a filter:

```
<web-fragment version="3.1"
    xmlns="http://xmlns.jcp.org/xml/ns/javaee"
    xmlns:xsi="http://www.w3.org/2001/XMLSchema-instance"
    xsi:schemaLocation="http://xmlns.jcp.org/xml/ns/javaee
http://xmlns.jcp.org/xml/ns/javaee/web-app_3_1.xsd">
    <filter>
        <filter-name>LoggingFilter</filter-name>
        <filter-
class>it.vige.webprogramming.servletjsp.filters.LoggingFilter</filter-
class>
    </filter>
    <filter-mapping>
        <filter-name>LoggingFilter</filter-name>
        <url-pattern>/logging/*</url-pattern>
    </filter-mapping>
</web-fragment>
```

This is the JAR file structure of the web fragment:

Classes must be included in the same JAR file. Here's a sample of `LoggingFilter` declared in the web fragment:

```
@WebFilter(filterName = "LoggingFilter", urlPatterns = { "/logging/*" })
public class LoggingFilter implements Filter {
    ...
    protected void doFilter(ServletRequest request, ServletResponse
response) throws IOException, ServletException {
  if (debug) {
        log("LoggingFilter:DoBeforeProcessing");
    }
  }
    ...
}
```

Once we put the JAR in the `WEB-INF/lib` folder of the web application, we can call a servlet running in the logging context path:

```
@WebServlet(urlPatterns = "/logging/WebFragmentServlet")
public class WebFragmentServlet extends HttpServlet {
 protected void doGet(HttpServletRequest request, HttpServletResponse
response) throws ServletException, IOException
    {
        response.setContentType("text/html;charset=UTF-8");
        PrintWriter out = response.getWriter();
        out.println("<h1>Web Fragment with output from Servlet
Filter</h1>");
        out.println("<br><br>Check server log for output from
LoggingFilter");
    }
 ...
}
```

As a result, we will see the following row generated by the filter of the web fragment in the log file of WildFly:

```
23:42:07,520 INFO [io.undertow.servlet] (default task-20)
LoggingFilter:DoBeforeProcessing
```

Security

In this section, we will see some examples of how to make security to the servlets and configurations provided by the `web.xml` descriptor file.

Any enterprise component needs an application realm to configure the type of security, the location of the credentials, and the protocols to use. The default realm works with the properties files inside the configuration folder of WildFly, but it's simply configurable in the `standalone.xml` file descriptor of WildFly, as seen in `Chapter 7`, *Implementing WebSockets*, in the paragraph *Security Realm*.

File descriptor security

Now, let's see the configuration in the `web.xml`:

```
...
<security-constraint>
  <web-resource-collection>
        <web-resource-name>SecureServlet</web-resource-name>
```

```
            <url-pattern>/SecureServlet</url-pattern>
            <http-method>GET</http-method>
            <http-method>POST</http-method>
    </web-resource-collection>
    <web-resource-collection>
            <web-resource-name>SecureOmissionServlet</web-resource-name>
            <url-pattern>/SecureOmissionServlet</url-pattern>
            <http-method-omission>POST</http-method-omission>
    </web-resource-collection>
    <web-resource-collection>
            <web-resource-name>SecureDenyUncoveredServlet</web-resource-name>
            <url-pattern>/SecureDenyUncoveredServlet</url-pattern>
            <http-method>GET</http-method>
    </web-resource-collection>
    <user-data-constraint>
            <transport-guarantee>NONE</transport-guarantee>
    </user-data-constraint>
    <auth-constraint>
            <role-name>g1</role-name>
    </auth-constraint>
</security-constraint>
<login-config>
    <auth-method>BASIC</auth-method>
    <realm-name>file</realm-name>
</login-config>
<security-role>
    <role-name>g1</role-name>
</security-role>
...
```

All the configuration is picked up by the security-constraint tag. We can put in a series of configurations through the web-resource-collection tags. Each resource collection must have a name through the web-resource-name tag, the servlet URL to set the configuration through the url-pattern tag, and the HTTP methods where security is enabled through the http-method tag.

In the first resource collection called SecureServlet, we restrict the access only for the GET and POST methods; other methods will not get the access.

In the SecureOmissionServlet resource, we disabled all the HTTP methods except the POST declared in the http-method-omission tag.

The `auth-constraint` tag establishes the role that the user must have to get the access. Even if the user puts the correct credentials in the login, he cannot get access because he is registered with a different role. In the `auth-constraint` tag, we can only put the roles declared in the `security-role` tags. It's an old convention that's still current.

The `login-config` tag establishes the type of login enabled when we call a secured servlet. In the `web.xml` file, it is set as `BASIC`, so when we call the Servlet, the login window of the browser will automatically compare.

User data constraints establish a requirement that the constrained requests be received over a protected transport layer connection. This guarantees that the data will be transported between client and server. The strength of the required protection is defined by the value of the transport guarantee. A transport guarantee of `INTEGRAL` is used to establish a requirement for content integrity, and a transport guarantee of `CONFIDENTIAL` is used to establish a requirement for confidentiality. The transport guarantee of `NONE` indicates that the container must accept the constrained requests when received on any connection, including an unprotected one.

Programmatic security

Since the servlet 3.0, the `HttpServletRequest` interface provides a `login` method to use in the programmatic login. Each servlet can directly execute the login. Here's a sample of login in a servlet, passing the credentials as `GET` parameters:

```
@WebServlet(urlPatterns = { "/LoginServlet" })
public class LoginServlet extends HttpServlet {
    protected void doGet(HttpServletRequest request, HttpServletResponse
response) throws ServletException, IOException {
        response.setContentType("text/html;charset=UTF-8");
        PrintWriter out = response.getWriter();
        String user = request.getParameter("user");
        String password = request.getParameter("password");
        if (user != null && password != null) {
            request.login(user, password);
        }
        userDetails(out, request);
    }
    private void userDetails(PrintWriter out, HttpServletRequest request) {
        out.println("isUserInRole?" + request.isUserInRole("g1"));
        out.println("getRemoteUser?" + request.getRemoteUser());
        out.println("getUserPrincipal?" + request.getUserPrincipal());
        out.println("getAuthType?" + request.getAuthType());
    }
```

The login method will execute the login, interrogating the application realm, and in case of error of credentials, it will throw a `javax.servlet.ServletException` with the message `UT010031: Login failed`.

The following is a sample of JSP sending the `GET` parameters to the servlet:

```
<a
href="${pageContext.request.contextPath}/LoginServlet?user=u1&password=p1">
Servlet</a>
```

We now list the other useful secure methods of the `HttpServletRequest`:

- `isUserInRole`: Verifies if the chosen role is permitted in the current secure context.
- `getRemoteUser`: Returns the information of the calling user.
- `getUserPrincipal`: Returns the information of the logged user.
- `getAuthType`: Returns the authentication type. It can be `BASIC`, `DIGEST` if encrypted with MD5, or FORM if managed by an external HTML or JSP page. It will be shown shortly.

Form login

As anticipated in the preceding paragraph, we can declare a form login page directly in the `web.xml` descriptor file. So automatically, when a login must be used, it compares in the browser. The configuration is very simple:

```
...
<servlet>
    <display-name>secure-form</display-name>
    <servlet-name>secure-form</servlet-name>
    <jsp-file>/view/secure-form.jsp</jsp-file>
</servlet>
<security-constraint>
    <web-resource-collection>
        <web-resource-name>SecurityConstraint</web-resource-name>
        <url-pattern>/*</url-pattern>
    </web-resource-collection>
    <auth-constraint>
        <role-name>g1</role-name>
    </auth-constraint>
</security-constraint>
<login-config>
    <auth-method>FORM</auth-method>
```

```
        <realm-name>file</realm-name>
        <form-login-config>
            <form-login-page>/view/loginform.jsp</form-login-page>
            <form-error-page>/view/loginerror.jsp</form-error-page>
        </form-login-config>
    </login-config>
    <security-role>
        <role-name>g1</role-name>
    </security-role>
    ...
```

We only need to declare the form through the `form-login-config` tag. In the form-login-page, we declare the JSP page used to login. In case of a login error, we can define a different JSP to show the error through the `form-error-page` tag. Here's an example of the login form in a JSP page:

```
<%@page contentType="text/html" pageEncoding="UTF-8"%>
<!DOCTYPE HTML PUBLIC "-//W3C//DTD HTML 4.01 Transitional//EN"
    "http://www.w3.org/TR/html4/loose.dtd">
<html>
    <head>
        <meta http-equiv="Content-Type" content="text/html; charset=UTF-8">
        <title>Form-Based Login Page</title>
    </head>
    <body>
        <h1>Form-Based Login Page</h1>
        <form method="POST" action="j_security_check">
            Username: <input type="text" name="j_username"><p />
            Password: <input type="password" name="j_password"
autocomplete="off"><p />
            <input type="submit" value="Submit" name="submitButton">
            <input type="reset" value="Reset">
        </form>
    </body>
</html>
```

The important things of this page are the form declaration through the HTML *form* tag, the action of the form set with the default value `j_security_check`, the input text named `j_username`, and the *password* tag named `j_password`. These three values are managed by Undertow implementing the **Java Authentication Authorization Service (JAAS)** specifications.

JAAS specifies the directives for the login methods in Java. Through JAAS, this form knows what services call when the user executes the login.

The JAAS configuration can be seen in the WildFly default descriptor file, `standalone.xml`. Here's a piece:

```
<security-domain name="other" cache-type="default">
   <authentication>
      <login-module code="Remoting" flag="optional">
         <module-option name="password-stacking" value="useFirstPass"/>
      </login-module>
      <login-module code="RealmDirect" flag="required">
         <module-option name="password-stacking" value="useFirstPass"/>
      </login-module>
   </authentication>
</security-domain>
```

This configuration declares two login modules (`Remoting` and `RealmDirect`) that will be executed in sequence until the login is verified.

Create a custom JAAS module

The following steps will give you an idea of the basic steps involved in creating a custom login module. The following example extends the `UsernamePasswordLoginModule` out-of-the-box module:

1. Create a security domain in `standalone.xml`, as follows:

```
<security-domain name="customSecurity" cache-type="default">
   <authentication>
       <login-module code="com.CustomModule" flag="required"/>
   </authentication>
   <authorization>
       <policy-module code="PermitAll" flag="required"/>
   </authorization>
</security-domain>
```

2. Create a custom login module, as shown:

```
public class CustomModule extends UsernamePasswordLoginModule{
   @Override
   protected Group[] getRoleSets() throws LoginException {
       SimpleGroup group = new SimpleGroup("Roles");
       try {
          group.addMember(new SimplePrincipal("noGroup"));
       } catch (Exception e) {
          throw new LoginException("Failed to create group member for " +
group);
```

```
        }
        return new Group[] { group };
    }
    @Override
    protected boolean validatePassword(String inputPassword, String
expectedPassword) {
        return true;
    }
    @Override
    protected String getUsersPassword() throws LoginException {
        return "sri";
    }
}
```

3. Ways to deploy Custom Login Module:
   - Adding a new module in WildFly
   - If the WAR artifact uses this Login Module, we have to package this as a JAR within the artifact

4. If the WAR artifact uses this Login Module, make it aware of this security domain through jboss-web.xml, and place this xml inside the WEB-INF directory of the application. Consider the following example:

```
<jboss-web>
    <security-domain>java:/jaas/customSecurity</security-domain>
</jboss-web>
```

5. Invoke the custom login module from filter or servlet to perform authentication after clicking on the login button of any custom UI login screen, for example, httpRequest.login("wildfly", "mypassfly");.

6. Once validated by login module using the validatePassword() and getRoleSets() methods, it matches the roles declared in standalone.xml. The principal object would automatically be available to EJBs and interceptors. Consider this example:

```
@Resource
private javax.ejb.SessionContext sessionContext;
...
String caller = sessionContext.getCallerPrincipal().getName();
```

These steps can help override other out-of-the-box JAAS login modules.

Summary

We are now ready to write a web application using the simpler technologies available in WildFly. We can write web pages used for reports and information, or to upload files. However, there exist complex applications that need navigation. For example, a user will navigate in the application, find objects, choose page details or between a list of items, update one of them. MVC is the pattern used to write a more robust web application and manage the navigation. It will be covered by `Chapter 14`, *Writing a JSF Application*.

14
Writing a JSF Application

JSF (**Java Server Faces**) was born to give MVC a Java enterprise solution. MVC 2 is the most common paradigm for writing web applications. Through MVC, you can easily write quite complex web applications.

The JSF implementation engine in WildFly 10 is **Mojarra 2.2.13.SP1**. Mojarra is the historical JSF engine written with the first JSF specifications at the beginning by the Sun Microsystems and then released to the JSF open source community. The developments were started in 2004, and it is now the most used in the world.

In this chapter, we will start from the beginning covering the newness and strengths of JSP 2.2. In this chapter, we will cover the following:

- MVC basic
- JSF components
- JSF annotations
- JSF tag pages
- Descriptor configuration

MVC

The **Model-View-Controller** (**MVC**) in computer science is a very popular architectural pattern in the development of software systems, especially in object-oriented programming. It is suitable to separate the logic of presenting data from business logic. This pattern is positioned in the presentation level in a multi-tier architecture.

Components

The central component of the MVC--the model--captures the behavior of the application in the domain of the problem, regardless of the user interface. The model directly handles the data, logic, and application rules. A view can be in any form of output of information, such as a graph or diagram. Multiple views of the same information, such as a management bar chart and chart view, are possible. The third party, the controller, accepts input and converts it into commands for the model and/or view.

Use

Historically, the MVC pattern has been implemented on the server side. Recently, with the development and partial standardization of JavaScript, the first client implementations were born.

Originally used by the Smalltalk language, the pattern was explicitly or implicitly married to many modern technologies such as PHP, Java (Spring, JSF, and Struts) frameworks, Objective C, or .NET.

Due to the growing spread of MVC-based technologies in framework or middleware platforms for web applications, MVC or MVC framework expression is also being used to specifically indicate this category of systems (including Ruby on Rails, Struts, Spring, Tapestry, and Catalyst).

In the recent years, rich internet applications have been increased by making asynchronous calls to the server (AJAX) without redirecting to display the processing results. With the growing number of JavaScript code executed on the client, the need to create the first framework to implement MVC in pure JavaScript was felt. One of the first ones created was Backbone.js, followed by an endless series of other frameworks, including JavaScriptMVC, Ember, and AngularJS.

Structure

The pattern is based on the separation of tasks between software components that interpret three main roles:

- The model provides the methods for accessing the data useful to the application
- The view displays the data in the model and interacts with users and agents
- The controller receives the commands of the user (usually through the view) and performs them by modifying the status of the other two components

This scheme, among other things, also involves the traditional separation between application logic (often referred to as *business logic* in this context) charged by the controller and the model, and the view-load user interface.

The details of the interactions between these three software objects depend heavily on the technologies used (programming language, any libraries, middleware, and so on) and the type of application (for example, whether it's a web application or a desktop application). Almost always, the relation between view and model is also described as an instance of the observer pattern. Sometimes, when you need to change the standard behavior of the application depending on the circumstances, the controller also implements the strategy pattern.

Configuring and developing your application

A JSF application needs an XML descriptor file inside your WAR in addition to the `web.xml` descriptor file shown in `Chapter 13`, *Working with Servlets and JSP*. The `faces-config.xml` file must be put in the `WEB-INF` folder application as the `web.xml`. It manages the application according the main points of internationalization, navigation, and listener management. We will analyze these points further on in the chapter. Here's a basic sample of `faces-config.xml`:

```
<?xml version="1.0" encoding="UTF-8"?>
<faces-config xmlns="http://xmlns.jcp.org/xml/ns/javaee"
xmlns:xsi="http://www.w3.org/2001/XMLSchema-instance"
xsi:schemaLocation="http://xmlns.jcp.org/xml/ns/javaee
http://xmlns.jcp.org/xml/ns/javaee/web-facesconfig_2_2.xsd" version="2.2">
  ...
</faces-config>
```

In this chapter, we will see the creation of a forum application calling EJB services provided by Rubia Forums. **Rubia Forums** is a complete open source JSF application representing a forum. In addition to the frontend tier, it provides REST and EJB implementations. This product, once called Jobs Forum and managed by the Jobs community, is now managed by Vige, an Italian open source community.

Internationalization

You can configure the languages supported in your application, adding custom files called resource bundles to declare in the descriptor file. Through this configuration, a web application can manage the language of the client and show translated resources. The configuration in the faces --config.xml--is like this:

```
<application>
   <locale-config>
       <default-locale>en</default-locale>
       <supported-locale>it</supported-locale>
   </locale-config>
</application>
```

This configuration configures two supported languages--English and Italian. This configuration enables the Java resource bundles in the web application. In the root of the WEB-INF/classes folder of our application, we can put two resource bundle descriptor files--one containing the English words and one for the Italian words that will be used inside the application.

The resource bundle descriptor file can be named as you want, but it must end with the .properties extension and according to the chosen language, it must represent the initials of the language in the end, optionally followed by an underscore (_) and the initials of the chosen country. These are the two example files--ResourceJSF.properties:

```
Forum=Forum
Category=Category
Topics=Topics
...
Powered_by=Developed by
```

and--`ResourceJSF_it.properties`:

```
Forum=Forum
Category=Categoria
Topics=Topics
...
Powered_by=Sviluppato da
```

The resource bundle files are done in a key/value format. The key will be used in the pages of the web application to show the values. Automatically, the values will be chosen according to the used language.

 The `ResourceJSF.properties` doesn't need the initial of the languages because it is set by the JSF descriptor file by default.

Here's an example of a page by a client connecting from the UK to a JSF application:

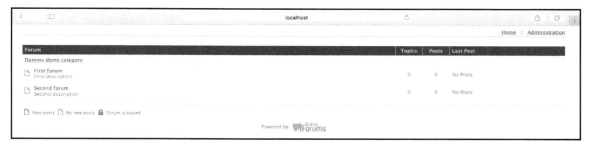

This is a sample of a connection from Italy:

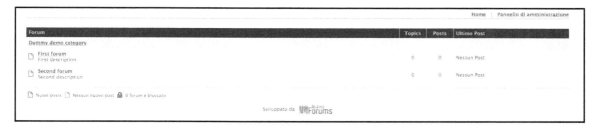

Now, see how the resource bundle is called in the pages. As an example, we can extract the logo image of the page:

```
<div xmlns="http://www.w3.org/1999/xhtml"
...
xmlns:f="http://java.sun.com/jsf/core"
...
```

```
>
    . . .
    <f:loadBundle basename="ResourceJSF" var="resourcebundle" />
    <div class="PoweredBy">
        ${resourcebundle.Powered_by} <a
href="https://github.com/flashboss/rubia-forums">
    <img border="0" src="..." /></a>
    </div>
    . . .
</div>
```

To call the resource bundle, JSF provides the loadBundle tag in its core library. To install it in the page, you need to import the JSF core libraries in your div tag through the XML attribute. It must point to the official JSF XSD page online.

Then, add the tag passing as basename, the name of the descriptor file excluding the suffix, and the language information, and declare a variable through the var attribute to use in the page.

Then, you can use the created variable in all your pages, directly calling the chosen key seen in the descriptor file. The translated value will be returned.

Navigation

In this section, we will configure the navigation of our web application. In this sample, we have two pages--an index page and a category management page. The navigation allows the two pages to communicate, exposing the links to click and move between the pages.

In the preceding figure of the last section, we can see the index page. Now, we would like to see that on the administration link we are redirected to on the categories management page. Here's the configuration that we need in the faces-config.xml descriptor file:

```
    . . .
<navigation-rule>
    <from-view-id>/views/category/viewcategory_body.xhtml</from-view-id>
    <navigation-case>
        <from-outcome>adminPanel</from-outcome>
        <to-view-id>/views/admin/index.xhtml</to-view-id>
    </navigation-case>
</navigation-rule>
    . . .
```

With this navigation rule, we are telling that in the view `category_body.xhtml` JSF page, there must be a link called `adminPanel`; clicking on it will redirect you to the new `index.xhtml` page, in our case it is the categories management page.

Now, let's see how to write the `viewcategory_body.xhtml` index page so that it can use the configured link. Here, we can see the form containing the two links: home and administration:

```
<div
...
xmlns:h="http://java.sun.com/jsf/html"
...
>
...
<h:form>
 <div class="forumsectionhdr">
    <ul>
        <li><h:commandLink value="${resourcebundle.Home}"
 action="viewCategory" /></li>
        ...
        <li>  |    <h:commandLink
 action="adminPanel" value="${resourcebundle.Admin_panel}" />
        </li>
        ...
        </h:panelGroup>
    </ul>
 </div>
</h:form>
...
</div>
```

JSF provides several HTML component tags installed through the **xmlns XSD** online schema. The `commandLink` component reads the `from-outcome` value configured in the `faces-config.xml` descriptor file and uses it in its action tag. This configuration allows the application to redirect to the correct page.

The same thing is done from the category management page to the index page by clicking on the home link. Here's the configuration of this redirection:

```
<navigation-rule>
    <from-view-id>/views/admin/index.xhtml</from-view-id>
    <navigation-case>
        <from-outcome>viewCategory</from-outcome>
        <to-view-id>/views/category/viewcategory_body.xhtml</to-view-id>
    </navigation-case>
    ...
</navigation-rule>
```

Navigation inside the page

Not all links need the navigation configuration; links can point to the same page, so they do not need redirects. As an example, we can take the category management page:

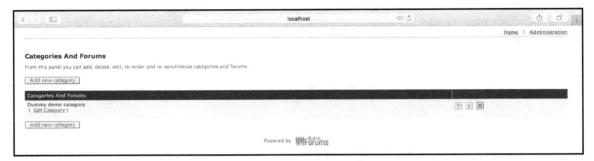

The **Add new category** button opens a window inside the page where we can put the name of the new category and insert it through a **Submit** button:

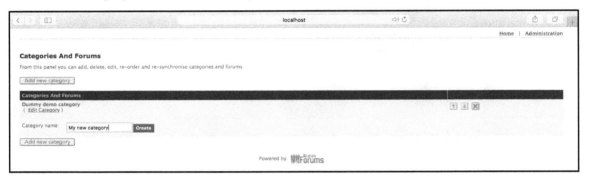

Now, see how the insertion of a category is developed in the page. The form containing the **Add new category** button is like this:

```
<h:form>
  <input type="hidden" name="addCategory" value="true" />
  <div class="actionbuttons">
  <ul>
    <li><h:commandLink>
        <img src="..." alt="${resourcebundle.Create_category}"
name="newCategory" border="0" />
        </h:commandLink></li>
  </ul>
  </div>
</h:form>
```

In this case, the `commandLink` doesn't have a configured action, so if you click on the link, you will again be redirected to the current page by default. The `commandLink` needs a form to work. Automatically after the click, the hidden input--`addCategory`--declared in the second row, will be sent to the page. The action will set the hidden input component to true.

When the page is reloaded, the JSF components and all the EL expressions will be evaluated again, so a new valorised input component can generate new events in the page.

See what happens if we add this code in the same page:

```
<div
  ...
  xmlns:c="http://java.sun.com/jsp/jstl/core"
  xmlns:h="http://java.sun.com/jsf/html"
  xmlns:f="http://java.sun.com/jsf/core"
  ...
>
...
<c:if test="${adminController.addCategoryMode}">
  <h:form id="addCategoryForm">
    <tr class="editRow">
      <td><input type="hidden" name="addCategory" value="true" />
      <label for="categoryname"
class="categorylabel">${resourcebundle.Category_name}:</label>
      <h:inputText id="Category" required="true"
value="#{adminController.categoryName}" />
      <h:message for="Category" styleClass="inlinefailure" />
      <h:commandButton id="editinline" value="${resourcebundle.Create}"
styleClass="buttonMed" action="#{adminController.addCategory}" /> </td>
      <td class="forumlistlast"> </td>
    </tr>
  </h:form>
</c:if>
...
</div>
```

In this code, we introduce **JavaServer Pages Standard Tag Library** (**JSTL**). It is a set of utilities working in JSP pages and other formats as `.xhtml`. The first tag that we see--`<c:if>`--starts a conditional code. If the value inside the test attribute is confirmed, the markup will be included.

In this case, the code searches through an EL expression, a component called adminController. Here's a sample of a component declared through CDI:

```
@Named
@RequestScoped
public class AdminController ... {
  private boolean addCategoryMode;
  ...

  @PostConstruct
  public void startService() {
    ...
      Map<String, String> requestParameterMap =
FacesContext.getCurrentInstance().getExternalContext().getRequestParameterM
ap();
      String addCatStr = requestParameterMap.get("addCategory");
      if (addCatStr != null && addCatStr.trim().length() > 0) {
        addCategoryMode = Boolean.valueOf(addCatStr).booleanValue();
    }
  }

  public boolean isAddCategoryMode() {
    return addCategoryMode;
  }
  ...
}
```

We refer to the details of this component in Chapter 2, *Working with Dependency Injection*, where CDI is explored deeply. We only learn to explain the RequestScope declaration. This scope allows the component to be called for each loading of the page. On each call, the component will be created and the startService method will be executed, thanks to the @PostConstruct annotation. In this method, we call the static javax.faces.context.FacesContext.getCurrentInstance method to get the current faces context. The faces context is the environment instance that we take for the entire duration of the application. Through the faces context, we read the request parameters, and we find the addCategory parameter sent through the JSF page. It will receive the true value, so the addCategoryMode attribute of the component will be valued.

The `.xhtml` page calls the attribute through
the `${adminController.addCategoryMode}` EL expression. It is true, so the
`addCategoryForm` form will be rendered.

Once we put the name of the new category in our form, we can push the **Create** button. This
button is declared in the JSF page through the `commandButton` component. This
component calls the `addCategory` method of our `AdminController` in its action. Here's
the method:

```
...
@EJB
private ForumsModule forumsModule;
...
public String addCategory() {
   boolean success = false;
   try {
      int forumInstanceId = 1;
      ForumInstance forumInstance =
forumsModule.findForumInstanceById(forumInstanceId);
      forumsModule.createCategory(categoryName, forumInstance);
      String start = getBundleMessage("ResourceJSF", "Category_created_0");
  String end = getBundleMessage("ResourceJSF", "Category_created_1");
      setMessage(FEEDBACK, start + " \"" + categoryName + "\" " + end);
      success = true;
   } catch (Exception e) {
handleException(e);
   } finally {
      if (success) {
cleanup();
      }
   }
   return null;
}
```

This method simply calls the `ForumsModule` EJB provided by Rubia Forums and creates the category in the database, returning a message. As a rule, the methods called in the actions of the `commandButton` components must return a string representing the resulting outcome seen in the `faces-config.xml` descriptor file in case of a redirect. If null, it will redirect to the current page. The category is now created:

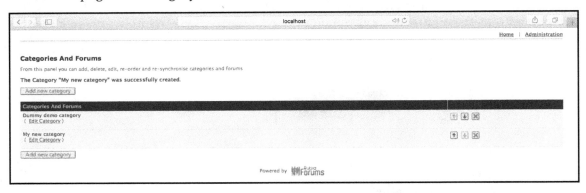

Now, try to delete the new category by clicking on the X (cross) button. The deletion can be configured in the `faces-config.xml`, just as for the others:

```
<navigation-rule>
    <from-view-id>/views/admin/index.xhtml</from-view-id>
...
    <navigation-case>
        <from-outcome>deleteCategory</from-outcome>
        <to-view-id>/views/admin/deletecategory.xhtml</to-view-id>
    </navigation-case>
</navigation-rule>
```

After deleting you will be presented with this page:

The **Confirm** button is very similar to the add category operation, so that won't be explained. More interesting is the **Cancel** button, which we will see shortly.

Phases and listeners

JSF works under different phases. Here, we explain what happens when we receive a JSF page from our browser and we execute some operation. All the JSF phases can be summarized through the following image:

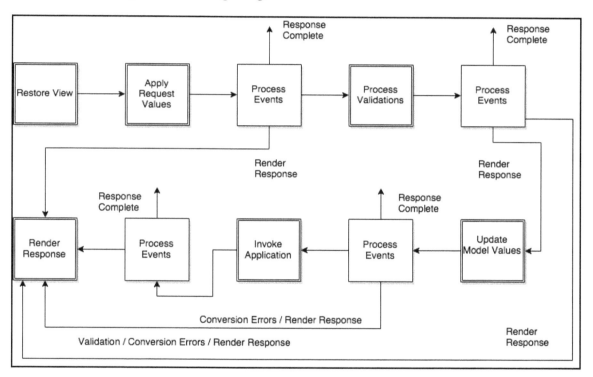

JSF is completely integrated to the servlet specifications, so it works in a request/response system. Usually, requests and responses are wrapped by the JSF implementation engine to allow the faces context to work better.

When we connect to the JSF application to receive the first web page, the **Restore View** starts to find the correct page to send through the response.

If the page has buttons or links, we can use them inside a form and pass to the **Apply Request Values** phase, where the request is created and all the parameters and attributes are collected.

JSF provides validators, a very useful self interface to validate the data of the forms. If no validators are in the application, the application will elaborate a response. This response, according to the configuration, will pass directly to the **Render Response** phase, elaborating a complex JSF page for rendering or send a simple resource not managed by JSF.

If validators are present, the validation of the forms will be done by the **Process Validations** phase. If the form results in an error state, the current page will be rendered; otherwise, the next phase, **Update Model Values**, will be started. This phase has the important role of collecting all the data of the form and executing the configured converters. The converters are particular objects used to convert the values of the forms in Java objects.

For example, a file sent through the HTTP file upload function can be converted into a Java object representing it or a date value form can be converted into a `java.util.Date` object.

At the end, the **Invoke Application** phase will call the actions and relative beans, representing the action declared in the form and elaborating all that the backend needs to execute the action.

JSF provides different listeners to manage the events; a very important one is the Phase Listener. This listener is invoked automatically for any JSF phase. In our example, we can use this listener to make the back function of the **Cancel** button shown in the last part of the previous section *Navigation inside the page*. Here's a sample of Phase Listener used to make the previous state clicking of the **Cancel** button:

```
public class BackButton implements PhaseListener {
    ...
    public static final String BACK_BUTTON = "backButton";
    private PhaseId phaseId = INVOKE_APPLICATION;
    private String oldViewId;

    ...
    @Override
    public void afterPhase(PhaseEvent arg0) {
        FacesContext facesContext = arg0.getFacesContext();
        UIViewRoot uiViewRoot = facesContext.getViewRoot();
        if (getCancelButton(uiViewRoot) != null)
            facesContext.getViewRoot().setViewId(oldViewId);
    }
    @Override
    public void beforePhase(PhaseEvent arg0) {
```

```
            FacesContext facesContext = arg0.getFacesContext();
            UIViewRoot uiViewRoot = facesContext.getViewRoot();
            if (getCancelButton(uiViewRoot) == null)
                oldViewId = uiViewRoot.getViewId();
        }
        @Override
        public PhaseId getPhaseId() {
            return phaseId;
        }
        private UIComponent getCancelButton(UIViewRoot uiViewRoot) {
            List<UIComponent> result = new ArrayList<UIComponent>();
            findComponents("cancel", uiViewRoot.getChildren(), result);
            UIComponent cancelButton = result.isEmpty() ? null :
result.get(0);
            return cancelButton;
        }
        private void findComponents(String id, List<UIComponent> children,
List<UIComponent> result) {
            for (UIComponent child : children) {
                if (child.getId().equals(id))
                    result.add(child);
                else
                    findComponents(id, child.getChildren(), result);
            }
        }
    }
```

This listener must implement the `javax.faces.event.PhaseListener` interface.
Through the `getPhaseId()` method, we establish the phase the listener will be active on.
We have chosen the `javax.faces.event.PhaseId.INVOKE_APPLICATION` phase for the
cancel button; it's the phase executed just before sending the request to the JSF application
action beans. The `beforePhase` and `afterPhase` methods are executed before and after
this phase.

The `beforePhase` operation is used in this case to register the previous page before
reaching the page containing the cancel
button. The `javax.faces.component.UIViewRoot` is the class representing the set of
components in the current page. Here, we search for the cancel button in the current page. If
it is not on the page, it means that we are on the previous page, so we can register it as the
page for redirection. Note how the cancel button is represented by a JSF object through the
`javax.faces.component.UIComponent` abstract class.

Instead, the `afterPhase` redirects the current page to the previously registered page through the `beforePhase` method. The `setViewId` method of the `UIViewRoot` class allows us to redirect to the chosen JSF component, the previous page registered in the `beforePhase` method in this case.

Working with Facelets

Facelets is a historical open source project written to manage web graphic templates and other utilities to write better web applications. It was started by the Apache community and is now integrated in JSF, so all its baggage can be used inside the application servers. The version supported by WildFly 10 and all Java EE 7 compliant application servers is 2.2. It is the candidate to write web templates, custom functions, and custom tags.

Web templates

Web templates allow us to create portions of pages that can be included several times in other pages. The common uses for them are the header and the footer of a website. We looked at the pages of Rubia Forums earlier. Here's the category page:

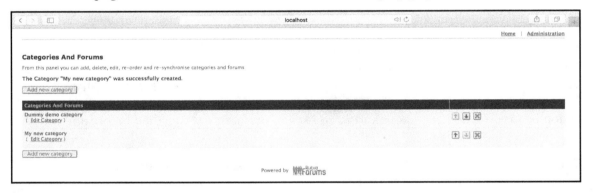

The breadcrumbs at the top are a header that can be shown on several pages. The same thing goes for the **Powered by** image at the bottom. Now, see how to implement the header with the breadcrumbs starting with the category page:

```
<div
...
xmlns:ui="http://java.sun.com/jsf/facelets"
...
>
  <ui:composition template="/views/common/common.xhtml">
```

```
    <ui:define name="mainContent">
        <h:form>
            ...
        </h:form>
    </ui:define>
  </ui:composition>
</div>
```

The `ui` namespace declared through the `xmlns` attribute is used to create the templates. In this page, we started a composition based on a template declared on an external JSF page.

This template defines a piece of the page called `mainContent`. The category page calls the `mainContent`, where it is implemented as a part of markup to render. We don't know where the `mainContent` will be put in the page. This information is on the template page.

Now see how the `common.xhtml` template is declared:

```
...
<ui:composition>
    <h:head>
        ...
    </h:head>
    <h:body class="bodyStyle">
        <h:form>
            <div class="forumsectionhdr">
                <ul>
                    <li><h:commandLink value="${resourcebundle.Home}"
action="viewCategory" /></li>
                    ...
                    <li>   |   <h:commandLink action="adminPanel"
value="${resourcebundle.Admin_panel}" />
                    </li>
                </ul>
            </div>
        </h:form>
        <div class="forumscontainer">
            <ui:insert name="mainContent" />
        </div>
        <div class="PoweredBy">
${resourcebundle.Powered_by} <a
href="https://github.com/flashboss/rubia-forums"><img border="0"
src="${themeHelper.getURL('resourceIconForumsLogoURL')}" /></a>
        </div>
    </h:body>
</ui:composition>
...
```

This page, being included in all the pages, will be the only page declaring a head and a body tag in all the web applications. As you can see on this page, there are three important declarations:

- The breadcrumbs (Home | Administration in the image over) represented by the forumsectionhdr CSS class.
- The **Powered by** at the bottom represented by the PoweredBy CSS class.
- The mainContent section included the previous page. It is declared through the insert UI component. In this part of the code, all pages including the section, can implement our HTML markup.

Templates work hierarchically. We can make the template even more modular, ensuring that the template also includes other templates. In this case, we do not need it because we only represent a page with headers and footers; however, there are many other cases that use more pages. In this way, code reuse becomes high, and we will always get a more readable code for our applications.

Custom functions

Until now, we have configured beans and called them through EL expressions in our JSF pages. It could be useful to use static functions too without the need to create CDI beans. JSF provides the creation of custom functions. We can declare functions tied to Java static methods, so they can be called through EL expressions from our JSF pages.

The main Facelets configuration file must be put in the WEB-INF directory, and it must end with the .taglib.xml suffix. Let's look at a sample of forums.taglig.xml, including a custom function:

```
<?xml version="1.0"?>
<facelet-taglib xmlns="http://xmlns.jcp.org/xml/ns/javaee"
xmlns:xsi="http://www.w3.org/2001/XMLSchema-instance"
xsi:schemaLocation="http://xmlns.jcp.org/xml/ns/javaee
http://xmlns.jcp.org/xml/ns/javaee/web-facelettaglibary_2_2.xsd"
version="2.2">
    <namespace>
        http://www.jboss.com/products/jbossportal/forums
    </namespace>
    <function>
        <function-name>message</function-name>
        <function-class>
            it.vige.webprogramming.javaserverfaces.ui.JSFUtil
        </function-class>
        <function-signature>
```

```
            java.lang.String getMessage(java.lang.String)
      </function-signature>
   </function>
   ...
</facelet-taglib>
```

All you need to work is the declared class through the `function-class` tag and declare the signature in the `function-signature` tag. Here's a sample of the method:

```
public class JSFUtil {
   ...
   public static String getMessage(String id) {
String msg = null;
Iterator<FacesMessage> msgs = getCurrentInstance().getMessages(id);
if (msgs != null) {
if (msgs.hasNext()) {
FacesMessage message = msgs.next();
msg = message.getDetail();
}
}
      return msg;
   }
}
```

This function is used to restore a message sent by a JSF component after an action and show it on the screen. Here's how the page calls the custom function:

```
<div ... xmlns:forums="http://www.jboss.com/products/jbossportal/forums"
...
>
   ...
   <div class="forumtitletext">
      ...
   <p class="successtext">#{forums:message('feedback')}</p>
   </div>
   ...
</div>
```

Simply import the function set with the `xmlns` descriptor tag paying attention to the name declared in the `.taglib.xml` descriptor file with the `namespace` tag seen over it.

Custom tags

Another important feature of Facelets is the custom tag. The custom tag technology, once declared in the Servlets specifications and now in the JSF specifications, allows the developer to write tags similar to HTML page tags in their own JSF pages, implementing particular graphic operations as needed. This is how we can declare a custom tag using Facelets:

```
<?xml version="1.0"?>
<facelet-taglib xmlns="http://xmlns.jcp.org/xml/ns/javaee"
xmlns:xsi="http://www.w3.org/2001/XMLSchema-instance"
xsi:schemaLocation="http://xmlns.jcp.org/xml/ns/javaee
http://xmlns.jcp.org/xml/ns/javaee/web-facelettaglibary_2_2.xsd"
version="2.2">
    <namespace>
        http://www.jboss.com/products/jbossportal/forums
    </namespace>
    ...
    <tag>
        <tag-name>isAllowed</tag-name>
        <handler-class>
     it.vige.webprogramming.javaserverfaces.auth.ACLTagHandler
        </handler-class>
    </tag>
    ...
</facelet-taglib>
```

We have declared a custom tag, called isAllowed. Here's the class implementing the custom tag:

```
public class ACLTagHandler extends TagHandler {
    private TagAttribute fragment;
    private TagAttribute contextData;
    private TagAttribute forumsACLProviderAttr;
    private TagAttribute userModuleAttr;
    public ACLTagHandler(TagConfig config) {
        super(config);
        fragment = getRequiredAttribute("fragment");
        contextData = getAttribute("contextData");
        forumsACLProviderAttr = getAttribute("forumsACLProvider");
        userModuleAttr = getAttribute("userModule");
    }
    @TransactionAttribute
    public void apply(FaceletContext ctx, UIComponent parent) throws
IOException, FacesException, ELException {
        ...
        boolean isAccessAllowed = new
```

```
ACLRenderingController().aclCheck(resource, contextStr,
forumsACLProvider,userModule, ctx);
     if (isAccessAllowed) {
         nextHandler.apply(ctx, parent);
  }
    }
}
```

The class must extend the `javax.faces.view.facelets.TagHandler` abstract class. This class allows us to override the `apply` method where we can add graphical components, or as in this case, filter the access to the resources.

As with any HTML tag, the `TagHandler` class supports the attributes represented by the `javax.faces.view.facelets.TagAttribute` abstract class. In this case, we can configure these four attributes in our JSF page: fragment, `contextData`, `forumsACLProviderAttr`, and `userModuleAttr`.

The `nextHandler` object represented by the `javax.faces.view.facelets.FaceletHandler` interface has the power to prevent the rendering of other tags inside it. If we don't execute the `apply` method of the `nextHandler`, we are blocking a chain of components. If this chain cannot end, nothing will be rendered in the JSF page. To understand better, let's see an example of a page calling this custom tag:

```
<forums:isAllowed fragment="acl://addCategory"
forumsACLProvider="#{forumsACLProvider}" userModule="#{userModule}">
    <h:form>
        ...
    </h:form>
</forums:isAllowed>
```

As you can see, we declare the `isAllowed` custom tag, passing three of the attributes as beans we declare in the class. These beans will take part in the validation of the user, and they will contribute to deciding on the permission access. If the access is not permitted, the form component declared inside the custom tag will be not rendered. We will analyze this solution in detail in a short while to guarantee more exhaustive permissions.

Security

Now, we'll see a solution to make our JSF pages and components secure. In Chapter 13, *Working with Servlets and JSP*, we exposed the security configuration of a web application in the web.xml descriptor file. As the Servlet specifications represent the base structure for the JSF applications, the web.xml remains an important configuration.

So, consider this security configuration in the web.xml descriptor file:

```
<security-constraint>
   <web-resource-collection>
      <web-resource-name>Authenticated</web-resource-name>
      <description></description>
      <url-pattern>/*</url-pattern>
   </web-resource-collection>
   <auth-constraint>
      <role-name>user</role-name>
      <role-name>admin</role-name>
      <role-name>guest</role-name>
   </auth-constraint>
</security-constraint>
<login-config>
   <auth-method>BASIC</auth-method>
   <realm-name>Rubia Forums</realm-name>
</login-config>
<security-role>
   <role-name>user</role-name>
</security-role>
<security-role>
   <role-name>admin</role-name>
</security-role>
<security-role>
   <role-name>guest</role-name>
</security-role>
```

Summing up, the configuration secures all the pages of the web application through a default basic login form and by giving access only for the user, admin, and guest roles.

This configuration guarantees only access to the application. It doesn't cover the single access to a page or a piece of a page that an unauthorized user must not access despite them having generic permission to access the application.

ACL permissions and PicketBox

This type of permission is called **ACL (Access Control List)**. Through ACL, we can configure a set of actions enabled for a particular user of a role. In case of the forum, an administrator can add a post and a category of forum, while a simple user can only add the post. In this section, we will see all the technologies to use to allow these access types.

Earlier, we used a custom tag to manage the ACL permissions in the pages of the applications. Now, we can deepen the topic by showing a full implementation of ACL permissions.

We have seen the preceding custom tag to add a `forumACLProvider` in its attribute. So, we can start with this EJB component candidate to give a response for a permission request. This is a part of the implementation:

```
@Named("forumsACLProvider")
@Stateless
public class JBossACLProvider implements ForumsACLProvider {
    @PersistenceContext(unitName = "forums")
    private EntityManager em;
    private ACLProvider provider = new ACLProviderImpl();
    ...
    public boolean hasAccess(UIContext context) {
    ForumsACLResource resource = null;
        resource = em.find(ForumsACLResource.class, aclContextStr);
        if (resource == null)
            resource = new ForumsACLResource(aclContextStr);
        ...
        return provider.isAccessGranted(resource, identity, READ);
    }
    ...
}
```

This component introduces the default ACL classes in WildFly 10, the `org.jboss.security.acl.ACLProvider` interface and its `org.jboss.security.acl.ACLProviderImpl` relative implementation class. These classes are part of a project of WildFly since the old JBoss 7. It is PicketBox. PicketBox is in WildFly 10 under the 4.9.6. final version, and it provides the security permissions management. It is the right module to use if you need more sophisticated authentication and authorization in your web application.

PicketBox can be defined as a DAO pattern containing its database and all functions to manage several types of permissions, users, and roles. It can be used in standalone applications too.

The `ACLProvider` interface provides an `isAccessGranted` method, where the permissions are calculated querying the database. The following are the attributes it needs:

- `resource`: An object represented by the `org.jboss.security.authorization.Resource` interface. It is the resource to process. The developer needs to write the implementation. It's recommended as an entity bean so that it can be persisted.
- `identity`: The identity representing the logged user and its roles. Represented by the `org.jboss.security.identity.Identity` interface, its simple implementation is in PicketBox, the `org.jboss.security.identity.plugins.SimpleIdentity`.
- `ACLPermission`: It represents the type of permission to evaluate. Possible types are CREATE, READ, UPDATE, and DELETE from the `org.jboss.security.acl.BasicACLPermission` enum. We can, for example, establish whether a user has the permission to delete, create, update, or read a chosen resource.

So, it's important to persist a set of resources in our database so that PicketLink can do the check and verify if the user can access the resource. Considering the resource implementation entity can be something like this:

```
@Entity
@Table(name = "ACL_RESOURCE")
public class ForumsACLResource implements Resource {
  ...
  @Id
  private String id;
  @Column(name = "criteria")
  private String criteria;
  ...
}
```

We can add a set of resources using SQL:

```
insert into ACL_RESOURCE (id, criteria) values ('acl://editPost',
'param[0].poster.userId.equals(identity.id)');
insert into ACL_RESOURCE (id, criteria) values
('it.vige.rubia.ui.action.EditPost:execute',
'param[0].post.poster.userId.equals(identity.id)');
```

Optionally, these resources can have the criteria. With the criteria, we have set an expression where the resource will be accepted only if verified.

The ACL table is managed directly by PicketLink. We need to associate an internal ID to our resource:

```
insert into ACL (aclID, resource) values ('11',
'it.vige.rubia.auth.ForumsACLResource:acl://accessAdminTool');
insert into ACL (aclID, resource) values ('12',
'it.vige.rubia.auth.ForumsACLResource:acl://viewCategory');
insert into ACL (aclID, resource) values ('16',
'it.vige.rubia.auth.ForumsACLResource:acl://addCategory');
```

So, we can associate the user/role to the resource. This is the table that associates the two objects:

```
insert into ACL_ENTRY (entryID, bitMask, identityOrRole, acl_aclID) values
('1', '2', 'users', '11');
insert into ACL_ENTRY (entryID, bitMask, identityOrRole, acl_aclID) values
('2', '2', 'users', '12');
insert into ACL_ENTRY (entryID, bitMask, identityOrRole, acl_aclID) values
('3', '2', 'users', '16');
```

So, consider that our custom tag is something like this:

```
<forums:isAllowed fragment="acl://addCategory"
...>
   ...
</forums:isAllowed>
```

Also, consider that the current user does not have the users role, the condition will be not verified and the code inside the custom tag will be not shown then.

Summary

For years, JSF has been a good framework to use for those who are unfamiliar with the Javascript and client-side technologies developed in the following years. The development of Javascript parts, as we have seen, is indeed minimal.

Also, there are other frameworks, such as Vaadin, not included in Java EE, which hide client-side development, and which generally allow for less interaction with the server by fully exploiting the REST mechanisms. However, it requires more client-side memory. Choosing the right framework is always to be attributed to the environment in which you are and to the level of use.

This is the end of the section on web development in WildFly. At this point, we have a complete view of everything that WildFly provides and that we can use for our future developments, and we can use the right technology as needed.
The next part will be about cluster configuration, one of the application server's battle horses.

15
Sharing the Web Sessions

Earlier, in Chapter 7, *Implementing WebSockets*, Chapter 13, *Working with Servlets and JSP*, and Chapter 14, *Writing a JSF Application*, we focused on the Web, where we showed the web session. The web session is a temporary memory where we share the information tied to a single user, such as the navigation on the site, the login information, and all the information of the application important to give a good interaction between the user and the application. In this chapter, we will introduce the concept of clustering, and we will cover the following:

- Clustering definition
- WildFly configuration
- Introduction to Infinispan
- Deploy and develop distributable web applications
- Monitor the clustering through the web console

Clustering

Clustering is the focal point in the application servers. An application server is not only chosen because it provides developing tools to make the creation of Java client-server applications simpler. An application server can guarantee the data of the applications to be durable in the time, and mostly, they must not be loose.

The clustering technique is done to provide maximum security of the data. The data is present in a database. What happens if the database crushes and it is not recoverable? Clustering can resolve this problem.

A cluster is a set of nodes containing replicated data in a net. The number of nodes depends usually on the available machines and on the quantity of the use of the applications on the internet. The number can change from 2 nodes to 1000 nodes and more using the right clustering technique. If a node is destroyed, there must always be another parallel node to take its place. Clustering is created to resolve two issues:

- **Failover**: The failover guarantees against the loss of the data in case of problems on the machines. Once a machines crashes, automatically another machine takes its place in a transparent mode. If this happens when a user is working on the application, he should not notice it.
- **Load balancing**: Clustering must not only guarantee not losing of data but also ensure the data is balanced. Even if a machine does not crush it, it may not be suitable for use at a certain time because the memory might run out of too many connections. In this case too, data operations need to be passed to another machine at that larger time. This type of work is called load balancing. Load balancing configuration is more complex than failover because each machine needs to assign a load per minute and many other options to find the machine that best suits the need.

Infinispan

The clustering in WildFly 10 is managed by Infinispan 8.2.4. This project was born in the JBoss community; when it started, it was called JBoss Cache. JBoss Cache/Infinispan has been the cluster library of the JBoss application server since the JBoss 4.x version.

Infinispan is a distributed cache project. It is based on an internal memory in which we can put some kind of data so that it can be distributed in a wide net of nodes where Infinispan is installed and configured.

By default, Infinispan connects all nodes in the same subnet in one group of data. The same achievement happens in WildFly. As an example, we can try to start WildFly 10 in different nodes using the `standalone.sh` command, deploy a web application, and monitor what happens.

The `standalone.sh` file in the bin directory of WildFly allows us to choose a starting configuration. We will start an initial WildFly instance with the `./standalone -c standalone-ha.xml` command.

`standalone-ha.xml` is the configuration file containing a default configuration of the cluster. HA is for high availability; it's the condition the cluster has to guarantee.

The second instance of WildFly can be started on a different machine inside the same subnet with the same command. Alternatively, for those who cannot use multiple machines, often when running application tests, you can launch a second WildFly instance on the same machine as the first by adding the following argument to the launch script:

```
-Djboss.socket.binding.port-offset=1000
```

This property allows a WildFly instance to start with a configured subset of ports. Changing the subset of ports allows us to start different instances of WildFly on the same machine because we will avoid the conflicts with the ports that WildFly has to open before starting.

The number 1000 says that the subset of ports must be 1000 more than the default. For example, if the default web port is `8080`, WildFly will start the web connector using the port number `8080` + `1000`, becoming `9080`. Now, we have started two WildFly instances, and we need to deploy a web application.

Distributable applications

Web applications in Java EE don't work in a distributable system by default. The specification provides a special tag to put in the `web.xml` descriptor file of the web application--the distributable. Here's a sample of a distributable application:

```
<web-app xmlns="http://xmlns.jcp.org/xml/ns/javaee"
xmlns:xsi="http://www.w3.org/2001/XMLSchema-instance"
xsi:schemaLocation="http://xmlns.jcp.org/xml/ns/javaee
http://xmlns.jcp.org/xml/ns/javaee/web-app_3_1.xsd" version="3.1">
    <distributable/>
</web-app>
```

Now we will put a test servlet in the application:

```
@WebServlet("/SessionServlet")
public class SessionServlet extends HttpServlet {
    ...
    private final static String SHARED_ATTRIBUTE = "shared_attribute";

    @Override
```

```
    protected void doGet(HttpServletRequest request, HttpServletResponse
response) throws ServletException, IOException
    {
      HttpSession session = request.getSession();
      PrintWriter write = response.getWriter();
      Boolean attribute = (Boolean) session.getAttribute(SHARED_ATTRIBUTE);
      write.println("before: " + attribute);
      if (attribute == null)
      session.setAttribute(SHARED_ATTRIBUTE, true);
      write.print("after: " + session.getAttribute(SHARED_ATTRIBUTE));
    }
}
```

This simple servlet monitors the insertion of an attribute in the web session so that we can monitor whether the attribute is available in both the started application servers.

As the final operation before testing the servlet, we have to deploy the web application. The configuration of WildFly that we started is very basic, so we need to deploy the application in all the available nodes of the cluster. More sophisticated configurations will be seen in the next section *Cluster domains*.

Once we deploy the application in our WildFly instances a log as it will start on the log:

```
19:41:10,054 INFO
[org.infinispan.remoting.transport.jgroups.JGroupsTransport] (MSC service
thread 1-5) ISPN000078: Starting JGroups channel web
19:41:10,054 INFO
[org.infinispan.remoting.transport.jgroups.JGroupsTransport] (MSC service
thread 1-4) ISPN000078: Starting JGroups channel hibernate
19:41:10,055 INFO
[org.infinispan.remoting.transport.jgroups.JGroupsTransport] (MSC service
thread 1-8) ISPN000078: Starting JGroups channel server
19:41:10,055 INFO
[org.infinispan.remoting.transport.jgroups.JGroupsTransport] (MSC service
thread 1-6) ISPN000078: Starting JGroups channel ejb
```

Four channels are configured in the `standalone-ha.xml`. The first channel we see in the log is for the web sessions. Now, connect to the servlet of the first node. We will get this:

Four channels are configured in the `standalone-ha.xml`. The first channel we see in the log is for the web sessions. Now, connect to the servlet of the first node. We will get this:

Try the same thing on the other node. The web session is replicated!

```
before: true
after: true
```

Cluster domains

We have seen a simple cluster working with nodes of the same data in the earlier chapters. In more sophisticated clusters, we need to group the nodes. For example, we need a group containing and sharing content data, another group only sharing page data, while yet another can contain only data for inventory. Each group can have a different cluster configuration according to necessity, so it's important to divide the clustered data into sections. A cluster domain represents a group of nodes in a cluster.

WildFly provides a default configuration of a domain. It can be started through the `domain.sh` command situated in the bin directory of WildFly. Try to start it and analyze the web console. The first thing to note is a new tab in the web administration console:

From the web administration console, we can see the domain configuration. In this case, this domain contains a host called **master**. This host collects three instances of WildFly, called **server-one**, **server-two**, and **server-three**.

The domain is divided into two groups of nodes that we can see in the **Server Groups** tab:

The groups are **main-server-group**, containing the instances **server-one** and **server-two**, and the **other-server-group** containing the **server-three** instance:

This console can stop, start, and restart each instance. We can deploy distributable applications for each server group. Automatically, the deployed application will be available for all the instances of the group. For example, if we deploy the test session in the **main-server-group**, we have deployed it in both the **server-one** and **server-two** instances. The deployed applications can be seen in the web console.

Here's the distributable application seen in the preceding paragraph:

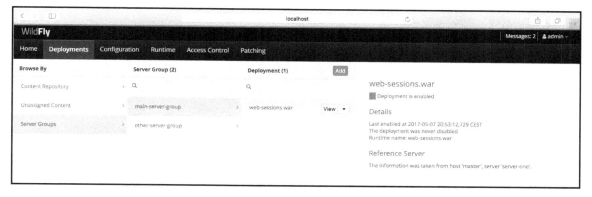

Customize the domains

A domain can be customized through the `host.xml` descriptor file in the `directory /domain/configuration` of WildFly. Here, we can see the default configuration:

```
<servers>
 <server name="server-one" group="main-server-group">
 <!--
 ~ Remote JPDA debugging for a specific server
 ~ <jvm name="default">
 ~ <jvm-options>
 ~ <option value="-
agentlib:jdwp=transport=dt_socket,address=8787,server=y,suspend=n"/>
 ~ </jvm-options>
 ~ </jvm>
 ~
 -->
 </server>
 <server name="server-two" group="main-server-group" auto-start="true">
 <!--
 ~ server-two avoids port conflicts by incrementing the ports in
 ~ the default socket-group declared in the server-group
 -->
 <socket-bindings port-offset="150"/>
 </server>
 <server name="server-three" group="other-server-group" auto-start="false">
 <!--
 ~ server-three avoids port conflicts by incrementing the ports in
 ~ the default socket-group declared in the server-group
 -->
```

```
    <socket-bindings port-offset="250"/>
    </server>
    </servers>
```

We can combine the association through servers and groups as we wish.

Summary

In this chapter, we saw the main configuration of the cluster present in WildFly, and we tested the web sessions in a very simple mode. We are now ready to create our nodes and test our distributed applications. Many applications need many nodes, so they become expensive. For testing, we can use OpenShift, which offers free nodes to install and execute our applications.

In subsequent chapters, we will show you how to work with WildFly in a cloud environment OpenShift and deep configurations starting with WildFly until the Infinispan deployment descriptors.

16
WildFly in Cloud

Cloud is the new generation technology to manage the application environment. Before Cloud, the servers needed to be hosted on internal machines. If they wish to purchase a number of different machines, customer must host them in a server room and manage them. The cost of maintenance of the machines is often very high.

In addition, the customer must be able to support a team for machine maintenance and problem solving. Sometimes, a machine deteriorates and needs to be repackaged. This management work is avoided by using Cloud technologies.

Cloud can be defined as a web management of virtual machines. Those who work with a Cloud system have virtual machines at their disposal. The administrator can add machines to its cluster, move them, and operate them; for example, they can stop, start, or restart the machine, connect through SSH to the machine, and configure it as if he were the real owner.

Cloud providers provide tools for an administration system so that they can be independent and manage the virtual machines as they want. A famous Cloud provider is Amazon AWS. Each provider has its costs, so there is a developing concurrency between the Cloud providers.

Open source is in the Cloud technologies too. Red Hat purposes OpenShift, a very good Cloud system. In this chapter, we will show the following:

- The basics of OpenShift
- Installation of a WildFly cluster on OpenShift
- Test distributable applications and REST services

OpenShift

OpenShift is provided by Red Hat, and it can be used by the developer for free. In fact, Red Hat offers temporary virtual machines, where you can install your own applications and test them on a complete cluster. We are free to create our machines on the OpenShift net through tools provided by Red Hat. In the following section, we will configure a domain cluster with WildFly, as seen in Chapter 15, *Sharing the Web Sessions*.

WildFly installation

Here, we show the step-by-step installation of WildFly in OpenShift:

1. First, we have to connect to open shift clicking on https://manage.openshift.com. If we don't have a Red Hat account, we must to create it. The procedure is very simple, so we will not show the account registration in this chapter. Once we are logged in, we will get a page as follows:

2. Click on the **FREE** button and select **Cluster Regions**:

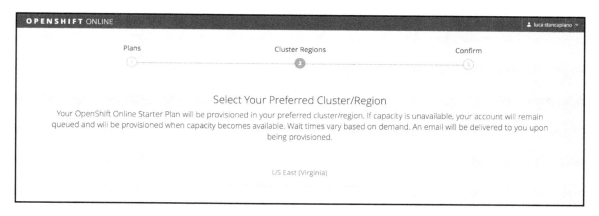

3. This page shows the available machines and their positions. For tests, only machines from the Virginia state are available. Clicking on the button the third step compares:

4. You should receive a confirmation mail with a promo code on the mail you registered. If this happens, open your mail, take the confirm code, put the promo code on the input text of the page, and then click on **Confirm Subscription**. Otherwise, just click on the **Confirm Subscription** button. Once the confirmation is done, we are ready to start our installation. Wait for a few minutes as your environment is automatically created:

After a few minutes, you will receive a confirmation mail with the link to connect to, in order to start using OpenShift. It can be something like `https://console.starter-us-east-1.openshift.com/`:

1. Here's the first step to follow:

2. Now, create the **New Project** by clicking on the button and set the ID, ***Name**, and **Description** of our application to test in OpenShift:

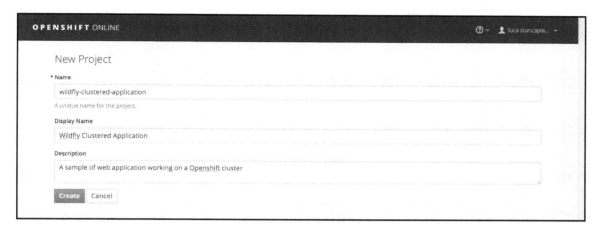

3. OpenShift provides a wide set of programming languages to use. Here, you can see a list. Simply click on your preferred language to continue:

4. Of course, we choose Java applications:

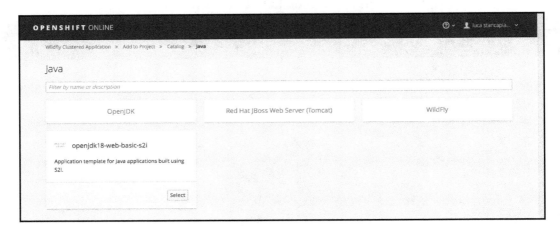

5. Also, we choose a WildFly application server with version 10.1:

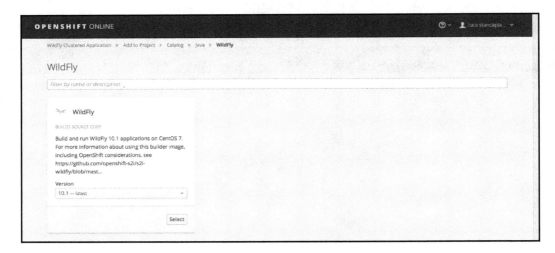

6. If your application is published on a GIT repository as, for example, GitHub, it can be very convenient to install the sample application on your WildFly in OpenShift. All operations of building, installation, and deploying will be done automatically by OpenShift, only providing the Git URL repository of the application. As an example, we will put a default Java EE test application provided by OpenShift:

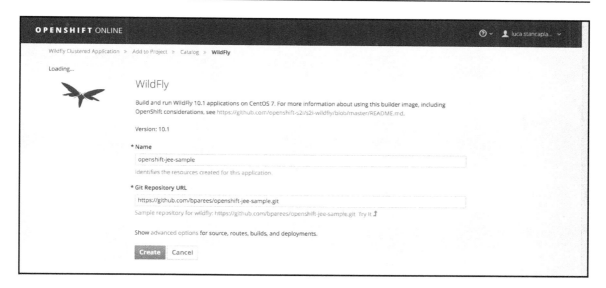

7. The application is deployed; now we have two options. We can use the web console to install and deploy other applications, or we can download the OC manager command-line tools to work in a complete mode by command line. The OC manager is downloadable, and being a standalone Java application, it works on all operative systems. To download the OC tool, simply follow the wizard on the web console:

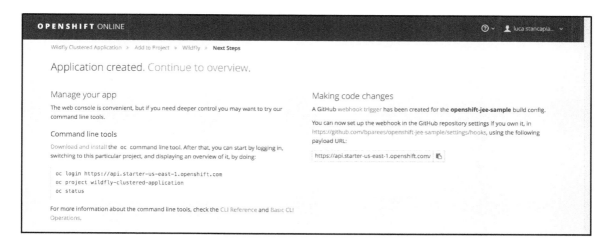

8. Here's the web console:

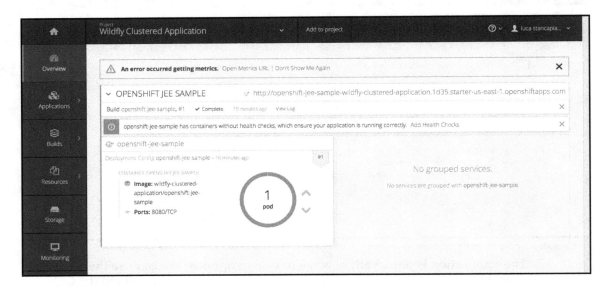

Many configurations are available on this platform.

Command-line tools

To download the command-line tools, you only have to click on your preferred operative system:

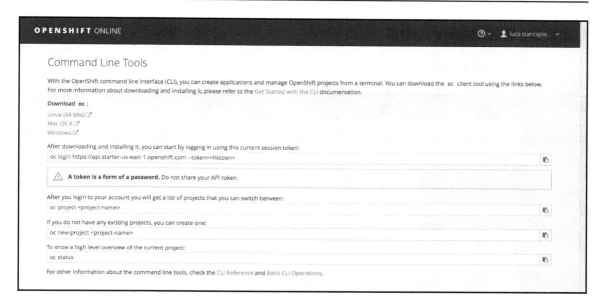

You will receive a OC.tar file; so, uncompress it. You will get a script file to execute. By following the internal guide, you will be able to manage additional applications in your OpenShift clustered instances.

Exposed services

1. Now, go to the **Applications** | **Services** tab:

2. Here, we have the list of exposed services. Actually, one service is installed by the web application. Click on the URL, and you can navigate around your automatically deployed web application:

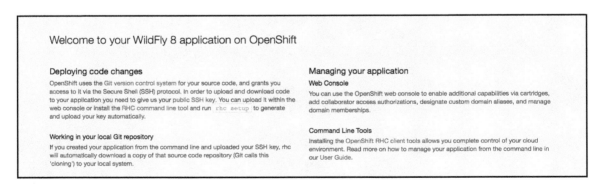

Summary

We now understand how to use an application server within Cloud technologies. We are ready to distribute our services on this new technology. Customers will have more chances to evaluate costs and decide whether to use machines on site or rely on external server images. We're now ready to go deeper into Infinispan and see how to share persistent data on our data cluster. In addition, we will show the main subprojects of Infinispan.

17
Share your Data

In the earlier chapters, we focused on cluster configuration and cloud support for WildFly. In this chapter, we resume from `Chapter 15`, *Sharing the Web Sessions*, deepening the internal replication mechanism of WildFly provided by Infinispan.

Infinispan manages the data in a replicable mode. It provides a good configuration toolkit, and it can replicate all data inside a configured network. In this chapter, we will see the following topics:

- Configuration of Infinispan
- Introduction to JGroups
- Singleton HA services

Infinispan and the cluster

A starting configuration of Infinispan can be found in the `standalone-ha.xml` descriptor file of WildFly. Here's how Infinispan is configured to replicate the web sessions seen in `Chapter 15`, *Sharing the Web Sessions*:

```
<cache-container name="web" default-cache="dist"
module="org.wildfly.clustering.web.infinispan">
    <transport lock-timeout="60000"/>
    <distributed-cache name="dist" mode="ASYNC" l1-lifespan="0" owners="2">
      <locking isolation="REPEATABLE_READ"/>
      <transaction mode="BATCH"/>
      <file-store/>
    </distributed-cache>
    <distributed-cache name="concurrent" mode="SYNC" l1-lifespan="0"
owners="2">
        <file-store/>
```

```
        </distributed-cache>
     </cache-container>
```

Infinispan, in addition to working internally to the container, can also be run in standalone with the same configuration. A module is a set of classes with particular features. Each module is represented by the name of the main package. In this case, the classes of the module `org.wildfly.clustering.web.infinispan` are prepared to manage the web session.

Infinispan is a set of tree nodes. Being a tree, each node representing a data is easily reachable. A lock timeout can be set for each node, so if the resource takes more time than the declared 60 seconds, an exception will be thrown.

This module is made up of two distributed caches: one (the dist) asynchronous and one (the concurrent) synchronous. These caches will be called internally by the module according to the need. The *mode* attribute establishes the type of replication, synchronous or asynchronous.

The **concurrent** cache is used for the replication between the nodes of the cluster. For example, when we put an attribute in the session, the attribute will be replicated instantly in a synchronous mode in the cluster.

The **dist** cache is used for long operations on the web sessions. Long operations make elongate the waiting time, so an asynchronous replication would be better. The transaction mode of the `BATCH` type is for long asynchronous operations. A locking isolation is configured as the `REPEATABLE_READ` type. For the types of isolation, you can refer to the *Isolation violations* section in `Chapter 5`, *Working with Distributed Transactions*.

The file-store tag specifies that the cache is persisted temporarily by filesystem. Another option can be the database.

The `l1-lifespan` attributes configure the maximum time that a data can be inside the cache. The value 0 means that the data has no limit time to expire in the cache.

The owners tag establishes that a single data must be replicated only twice at the maximum even if the cluster is made by more than two nodes. It is useful to make the traffic of data lighter.

LRU and LIRS

An important historical feature of Infinispan is the management of **Eviction**. An eviction policy is the ability to remove items within a cache that is no longer used or that they tend to not be used in the future.

There are two very specific algorithms that we will show in this section.

Infinispan allows you to choose the algorithm to use, but even custom algorithms can be implemented for it. Just use a class that represents the algorithm and declare it in the configuration file.

Let's see the two examples of Eviction:

- **LRU (Last recently used)**: It's a simple algorithm that evaluates the most used data within a cache. The most used data will be stored in a queue and kept, while the less used will be removed according to the percentage of usage. The least used will be the first to be emptied so as to keep cache ever lighter. It's the default algorithm in Wildfly.

- **LIRS (Low Inter-reference Recency Set)**: This is very similar to LRU with the difference that it does only not count the amount of data but also the time by which items are cached from the cache. For example, if an element is called often but in a much wider range, it may be put into the background or even eliminated.

To choose the algorithm, simply update the Wildfly XML configuration file. Here's a sample of Infinispan Eviction configuration in the cache of the JPA container:

```
<cache-container name="hibernate" default-cache="local-query"
module="org.hibernate.infinispan">
    <transport lock-timeout="60000"/>
    <local-cache name="local-query">
<eviction strategy="LRU" max-entries="10000"/>
        <expiration max-idle="100000"/>
    </local-cache>
    <invalidation-cache name="entity" mode="SYNC">
        <transaction mode="NON_XA"/>
<eviction strategy="LRU" max-entries="10000"/>
        <expiration max-idle="100000"/>
    </invalidation-cache>
    <replicated-cache name="timestamps" mode="ASYNC"/>
</cache-container>
```

In this configuration, both the JPA named queries and the entities use an LRU algorithm to remove the less important queries or entities in the second-level cache. To change the configuration using a LIRS algorithm, simply change the name of the algorithm as shown:

```
<eviction strategy="LIRS" max-entries="10000"/>
```

JGroups configuration

Infinispan provides a very wide configuration of the network too. The network configuration is a very important part in a cluster. Network environments can be very complex depending on the requested security level. JGroups is the product delegated by Infinispan to represent the low-level configuration network.

With JGroups, for example, we can decide what network protocol is used to send the messages of the replication. This is how the network is configured in the standalone-ha.xml descriptor file of WildFly:

```
<subsystem xmlns="urn:jboss:domain:jgroups:4.0">
 <channels default="ee">
    <channel name="ee" stack="udp"/>
 </channels>
 <stacks>
    <stack name="udp">
       <transport type="UDP" socket-binding="jgroups-udp"/>
       <protocol type="PING"/>
       <protocol type="MERGE3"/>
       <protocol type="FD_SOCK" socket-binding="jgroups-udp-fd"/>
       ...
    </stack>
```

The following is the configuration for the TCP protocol:

```
<stack name="tcp">
    <transport type="TCP" socket-binding="jgroups-tcp"/>
    <protocol type="MPING" socket-binding="jgroups-mping"/>
    <protocol type="MERGE3"/>
    <protocol type="FD_SOCK" socket-binding="jgroups-tcp-fd"/>
    <protocol type="FD"/>
    ...
</stack>
</stacks>
```

In these configurations, we enabled the protocols that must be used to replicate the data. All parts of the TCP and UDP can be configured in JGroups.

Singleton HA Services

In the earlier chapters, such as `Chapter 2`, *Working with Dependency Injection*, and `Chapter 4`, *Implementing Business Logic*, we have seen Singleton and how to use it within a Java virtual machine.
WildFly is able to use the Singleton mechanism even among several nodes of a cluster. WildFly can instantiate Singleton on a node and ensure that it is used within all nodes of the same cluster. This mechanism is called **HA Singleton**.

Since HA Singleton is physically instantiated on a single node, operations are performed exclusively on that node. If the cluster node breaks or stops, WildFly plans to move Singleton to a nearby node, thereby ensuring high availability of the service.

Infinispan allows Singleton to be replicated on the different nodes of the Cluster and guarantees some transparency to the clients that use it. The client, which can be an EJB, a Servlet, or a mere Java class, knows nothing about Singleton's position. Here, we can see the configuration of the replicable Singleton cache:

```
<cache-container name="server" aliases="singleton cluster" default-
cache="default" module="org.wildfly.clustering.server">
   <transport lock-timeout="60000"/>
   <replicated-cache name="default" mode="SYNC">
      <transaction mode="BATCH"/>
   </replicated-cache>
</cache-container>
```

As you can see, there is nothing of new respect the other containers. Infinispan is the replication engine, and all replicable instances and services are managed directly by it.

Here, we can see the configuration that guarantees a failover:

```
<subsystem xmlns="urn:jboss:domain:singleton:1.0">
   <singleton-policies default="default">
      <singleton-policy name="default" cache-container="server">
         <simple-election-policy/>
      </singleton-policy>
   </singleton-policies>
</subsystem>
```

When a node fails, the `simple-election-policy` is used to select a new node as Singleton master so that the service is not loose.

Writing the Service

See now how write a simple HA Singleton service. **JBoss MSC** (Modular Service Container) 1.2.6.Final is the library that handles services within Wildfly and provides APIs to write custom services. Here you can see an example of a service that returns the server environment inside a node of Wildfly:

```
public class HAService implements Service<Environment> {
    private final Value<ServerEnvironment> env;
    private final AtomicBoolean started = new AtomicBoolean(false);
    public HAService(Value<ServerEnvironment> env) {
       this.env = env;
    }
    @Override
    public Environment getValue() {
       if (!started.get()) {
           throw new IllegalStateException();
       }
       return new Environment(env.getValue().getNodeName());
    }
    @Override
    public void start(StartContext context) {
       this.started.set(true);
    }
    @Override
    public void stop(StopContext context) {
       this.started.set(false);
    }
}
```

By definition a service is something made available and has an automatically run life cycle through start and stop operations.

The service must implement JBoss MSC, *org.jboss.msc.service.Service* interface and implement the following methods:

- **start**: It's the start of the service. By default it will be started during the start of Wildfly.
- **stop**: It's the stop of the service. By default it will be started during the shutdown of Wildfly.
- **getValue**: It's the result of the service when it will be called. Anything can return by this method, simply filling the type specified in the Service interface implementation. In this case we choose a simple Environment object declared by the *Environment* class containing the name of the current node.

Here the Environment class:

```
public class Environment implements Serializable {
    ...
    private final String nodeName;
    public Environment(String nodeName) {
        this.nodeName = nodeName;
    }
    public String getNodeName() {
        return this.nodeName;
    }
}
```

The constructor of the service receives as input a simple wrapper object *org.jboss.msc.value.Value* typed with the *org.jboss.as.server.ServerEnvironment* class. This last contains all the informations of the Wildfly node where we will extract the current node name property.

Writing the Activator

To install the service in our Wildfly nodes we need to write an activator class. Here an example of Activator class:

```
public class HAServiceActivator implements ServiceActivator {
    @Override
    public void activate(ServiceActivatorContext context) {
        ...
    }
}
```

The **activate** method is started during the start of Wildfly. An activator class must implement the *org.jboss.msc.service.ServiceActivator* interface. Here a sample of activate implementation:

```
...
ServiceTarget target = context.getServiceTarget();
try {
 SingletonServiceBuilderFactory factory = (SingletonServiceBuilderFactory)
context.getServiceRegistry()
 .getRequiredService(BUILDER.getServiceName("server")).awaitValue();
    install(target, factory, DEFAULT_SERVICE_NAME, 1);
    install(target, factory, QUORUM_SERVICE_NAME, 2);
} catch (InterruptedException e) {
 throw new ServiceRegistryException(e);
}
```

In this sample we take the *org.jboss.msc.service.ServiceTarget* instance through the injected context *org.jboss.msc.service.ServiceActivatorContext*. Through the ServiceTarget we take the *org.wildfly.clustering.singleton.SingletonServiceBuilderFactory* instance passing the default name for the Wildfly instances, **server**. This factory is responsible for the creation of the HA Singletons.

Through a custom **install** method we will install two HA Singletons (default and quorum) called through the *org.jboss.msc.service.ServiceName* interface. Here the declarations of the two services:

```
public static final ServiceName DEFAULT_SERVICE_NAME = JBOSS.append("test",
"haservice", "default");

public static final ServiceName QUORUM_SERVICE_NAME = JBOSS.append("test",
"haservice", "quorum");
```

Here the install method:

```
private static void install(ServiceTarget target,
SingletonServiceBuilderFactory factory, ServiceName name,int quorum) {
 InjectedValue<ServerEnvironment> env = new InjectedValue<>();
 HAService service = new HAService(env);
 factory.createSingletonServiceBuilder(name, service)
 .electionPolicy(new PreferredSingletonElectionPolicy(new
SimpleSingletonElectionPolicy(),new NamePreference(PREFERRED_NODE)))
    .requireQuorum(quorum).build(target).addDependency(SERVICE_NAME,
ServerEnvironment.class, env).install();
}
```

Through the **SingletonServiceBuilderFactory** we:

- Create the default Singleton Service Builder represented by the *org.wildfly.clustering.singleton.SingletonServiceBuilder* interface through the **createSingletonServiceBuilder** method.
- Can customize the election policy shown over declaring an alternative policy class through the **electionPolicy** method.
- Declare the the minimum number of members required before a singleton master election will take place through the **requireQuorum** method.
- Build the service through the **build** method
- Add additional class dependencies through the **addDependency** method. In this case we add the ServerEnvironment class useful to the service to receive the server node informations
- Install the service through the **install** method.

Client for the Service

If we start two nodes of Wildfly through the standalone-ha configuration and deploy our example in both the nodes we can test the HA Singleton. In this section we write an Arquillian client that calls our custom HA Service and test it on both the nodes of Wildfly emulating the start and stop of the nodes.

The Wildfly testsuite shared library allows a client to connect to a Wildfly node and query a HA Singleton service. All we need is the import of this library in our maven XML configuration file pom.xml:

```
<dependency>
    <groupId>org.wildfly</groupId>
    <artifactId>wildfly-testsuite-shared</artifactId>
    <version>10.1.0.Final</version>
</dependency>
```

and a simple class with a main method. Here the implementation:

```
URL baseURL1;
...
try (CloseableHttpClient client = promiscuousCookieHttpClient()) {
 HttpResponse response = client.execute(new HttpGet(createURI(baseURL1,
DEFAULT_SERVICE_NAME, NODE_1)));
}
...
```

This example will deploy a default Arquillian war application in the Wildfly node and it will call the HA Singleton through the HTTP protocol returning as response the Environment object we have seen in the previous section *Writing the Service,* specifying the name of the node NODE_1 and the name of the service. Here we can see start and stop methods to simulate the start and the stop of the node:

```
public static void start(ContainerController controller, String...
containers) {
    for (String container : containers) {
        try {
            controller.start(container);
        } catch (Throwable e) {
        }
    }
}

public static void stop(ContainerController controller, String...
containers) {
    for (String container : containers) {
        try {
            controller.stop(container);
        } catch (Throwable e) {
        }
    }
}
```

You can enjoy playing with start and stop methods and you will see that the service will always be invoked. The important thing is that at least one of the two knots remains.

In *Chapter 1: Introducing Java EE and Configuring the Development Environment* in the section *Debug exercises* we saw how to debug a test case. Since we are in a clustered environment, the debugging parameters are slightly different because we need to specify the name of the node to be tested.

Here's an example of scripts to launch a test in debug mode:

```
mvn test -Djboss.node0.options="-Xdebug -
Xrunjdwp:transport=dt_socket,address=8001,server=y,suspend=y" -
Djboss.node1.options="-Xdebug -
Xrunjdwp:transport=dt_socket,address=8002,server=y,suspend=y"
```

We need to specify a different port for node otherwise we will receive a port conflict starting a server test connection on the same port. So simply specify the new java properties jboss.node0.options and jboss.node1.options valued with a different number of port.

Summary

We have ended the part of the book dedicated to clustering. Now we know where to put our hands in case of configuration in a clustered environment. With this chapter, we end the discussion on clustering. The next part deals with class management, and we will see how WildFly handles them through its internal mechanisms.

18
Deployment

With this chapter, we begin part 6 of the book, showing some internal mechanisms of Wildly to manage the classes. Each application server is pushed by the enterprise specification to implement its own deployment mechanism. Deployment is the basic operation to install enterprise applications. Apart from the SPI interfaces provided by the enterprise specifications, the application servers are free to manage, in an independent mode, the memory and the clustering, providing proper mechanisms and frameworks. The application servers provide their tool to make this operation very simple. In this chapter, we'll get on with the following topics:

- The available package we can deploy
- Tools provided by the internal implementations of WildFly

Deployment types

Many types of packages can be installed in WildFly. In this section, we will collect all the available packages implemented by the specifications and also, the other extensions typical in JBoss/WildFly. Now we start with the packages dependent on the specifications.

Enterprise packages

Here, we collect all the packages that are defined in the Java EE specifications and completely supported in WildFly.

Web archive

The web archive (**WAR**) is the most common package used in enterprise applications. It is used to install the web applications using technologies such as Servlet, JSF, or more client-oriented ones like the most recent frameworks AngularJS or Vaadin. To deploy a WAR, it is mandatory to add the `web.xml` descriptor file in the `WEB-INF` folder.

In the web archive, we can also install REST services and WebSocket. The `web.xml` is never useful in these cases, but it's a good rule to release it for customization.

As shown in `Chapter 14`, *Writing a JSF Application*, we need a `faces-config.xml` descriptor file in the `WEB-INF` folder to install JSF applications.

Other useful deployment descriptors to put in the `WEB-INF` folder are as follows:

- `*.taglig.xml`: Descriptor file containing custom tags and functions. It can be named by any name. The only rule is that the filename ends with the `.taglib.xml` extension.
- `beans.xml`: It is mandatory to use CDI inside a web/REST application.

Details on the packaging can be seen in `Chapters 6`, *Creating REST Services*, `Chapter 7`, *Implementing WebSockets*, `Chapter 10`, *Asynchronous REST*, and `Chapter 13`, *Working with Servlets and JSP*, where the web is deeply shown.

Another special folder is the `lib` inside the `WEB-INF` folder. All the external dependencies used by the application must be in this folder. A good rule is not replicate the dependencies just installed in WildFly. WildFly provides a wide set of libraries that can be used in the applications.

The last specifications provide all the other components too, to put in a WAR. The extension of the package is not important since several years because the annotations have simplified much of the configuration of the components. So, if a class is annotated as an EJB, this component will automatically be installed as an EJB and the application server will not care about the extension name of the descriptor file present inside the package. In this chapter, to maintain a right complete order, we will continue to show the extension files and the descriptor files inside the packages.

Java archive

JAR (**Java ARchive**) can be used to deploy three types of applications. These extensions end with the `.jar` suffix.

EJB

The package will deploy EJB if a `ejb-jar.xml` descriptor file is inside the `META-INF` folder. Also, the `beans.xml` file can be important in this folder to enable the CDI. Without CDI, we can do the injection only for the classes annotated with the annotations in the `javax.ejb` package of the EE API. Unlike the web, the descriptor file is not mandatory.

Client application

A client application is a special application containing all the interfaces needed to make a connection to the EJB. An EJB provides its home and local/remote interface used to communicate with the clients. In this package, all the interfaces will put together a particular descriptor file, `application-client.xml`, inside the `META-INF` folder. The same package can be provided directly to a remote client also if it doesn't run inside containers. Here's a sample of `application-client.xml`:

```xml
<?xml version="1.0" encoding="UTF-8"?>
<!DOCTYPE application-client PUBLIC "-//Sun Microsystems, Inc.//DTD J2EE
Application Client 1.2//EN"
"http://java.sun.com/j2ee/dtds/application-client_1_2.dtd">
    <application-client id="Application-client_ID">
        <display-name>basiccalc-client</display-name>
        <description>Basic Calculator Client Sample</description>
        <ejb-ref>
            <ejb-ref-name>ejb/BasicCalculator</ejb-ref-name>
            <ejb-ref-type>Session</ejb-ref-type>
            <lookup-name>java:global/deployment-ear/basiccalc-
ejb/BasicCalculatorSessionBean!net.wasdev.sample.basiccalc.ejb.BasicCalcula
torSessionBeanRemote</lookup-name>
            <remote>
it.vige.classloading.deployment.ejb.BasicCalculatorSessionBeanRemote</remot
e>
        </ejb-ref>
</application-client>
```

Simple Java library

Simple JARS are always accepted in the application servers, so they can be used as external dependencies for enterprise applications. It's important that these libraries are visible to the other application, otherwise they will be of no use inside the application server. The descriptor file managing these libraries is the Java MANIFEST.MF inside the META-INF folder. In this file, we have to state what to expose to external applications. Here's a sample of MANIFEST.MF with the shared classes:

```
Dependencies: org.some.module, org.another.module
```

Resource adapters

The resource adapters are particular enterprise components used to connect to external resource managers. Examples of resource managers are databases, ERP systems, and something done to manage resources. These adapters must have the .rar (resource archive) suffix. A resource archive must have a META-INF folder and a ra.xml descriptor file. The following is a sample of ra.xml:

```
<managedconnectionfactory-class>
com.sun.connector.blackbox.LocalTxManagedConnectionFactory
</managedconnectionfactory-class>

<connectionfactory-interface>
javax.sql.DataSource
</connectionfactory-interface>

<connectionfactory-impl-class>
com.sun.connector.blackbox.JdbcDataSource
</connectionfactory-impl-class>

<connection-interface>
java.sql.Connection
</connection-interface>

<connection-impl-class>
com.sun.connector.blackbox.JdbcConnection
</connection-impl-class>
```

In this sample, we specified the interfaces for connection factory and the connection and relative implementations to connect to an external resource manager. This configuration file, despite being fully supported in WildFly, tends to be used less and less because the extensions are faster to configure.

Extension packages

Despite WildFly supporting all Java EE 7 specifications and related packages, it supports its extension packages to allow for greater ease of configuration and use. We will see a list of packages and descriptor files supported only in WildFly shortly.

Datasources

Datasources can be considered a part of the resource adapters. In the old JBoss application server, there existed a RAR package declaring a JDBC connector configurable by datasource connector files with a -ds.xml. Now the WAR package is moved with the IronJacamar extension configured directly in the standalone.xml files. For more information on resource adapters and IronJacamar, refer to Chapter 3, *Persistence*, and Chapter 5, *Working with Distributed Transactions*.

-ds.xml files can be deployed as single files or inside other enterprise packages. Inside the packages, you only need to put in the META-INF folder.

Service archives

The service archives represented by the sar suffix are historical archives in the JBoss world, and they are still supported by WildFly. A service archive is used to deploy services using the JMX technology (Java management extensions). A sar is deployed along with a jboss-service.xml in the META-INF folder that declares the services under JMX classes.

JMX is used in addition to adding additional internal services, and also to monitor containers and all the modules of the application server. Through the Java console, we can connect to an instance of WildFly and monitor everything that happens inside it in real time.

Deployment tools

Deployment in WildFly can be done in different modes according to how comfortable it is for the administrator or the developer.

Administrator tools

The packages can be deployed by the administrators directly to the filesystem under the `deployment` directory of WildFly or through the web console. Here's an example of deployment of an application in the web console:

By clicking on the **Next>>** button, we choose the application and make the upload:

Finally, we can decide whether to enable the application immediately or to do it later:

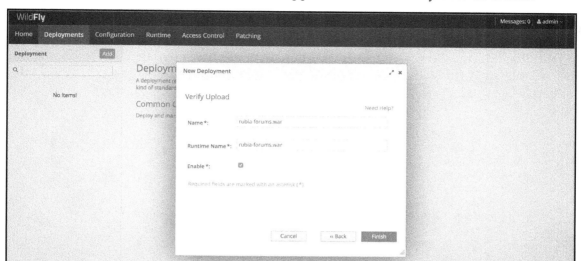

HA deploy

By starting Wildfly with a clustered configuration, for example, the `standalone-ha.xml`, `standalone-full-ha.xml`, or `domain.xml`, we automatically import the HA deployment feature. This feature means that once you deploy an application on a node in a cluster, the next nodes that will be put in place will import the application by also deploying them. This mechanism is called **HA** (**high availability**) deploy.

 By default, HA deploy does not intervene on nodes that are already standing. If you want the application to be deployed on a node that is already active, you will need to restart the node.

Development tools

When you develop, it can be very boring to deploy your application through the web console each time, or copy the package in the directory after a manual build of the application. Maven allows you to do everything with only one operation. A Maven plugin is available for WildFly. Here's a sample of Maven configuration in the pom.xml file of the project:

```
<plugin>
    <groupId>org.wildfly.plugins</groupId>
    <artifactId>wildfly-maven-plugin</artifactId>
    <version>1.0.2.Final</version>
    <executions>
      <execution>
        <id>add-securitydomain</id>
        <phase>install</phase>
        <goals>
            <goal>add-resource</goal>
        </goals>
        <configuration>
            <address>subsystem=security,security-domain=rubia-
domain</address>
            <resources>
                <resource>
                    <properties>
                        <cache-type>default</cache-type>
                    </properties>
                </resource>
            </resources>
        </configuration>
      </execution>
    </executions>
</plugin>
```

A security domain will automatically be installed in WildFly when, with this configuration, we build the application through the maven command:

```
mvn clean install
```

Summary

Now we know all the package types we can install in WildFly 10. A wide baggage of application type gives a better choice and better work. Now we can decide which application we should use according to our needs. Another type of deployment not dependent on the EE specification can be done through OSGi. We are ready to show this technology in the next and the final chapter, Chapter 19, *Working with OSGi*.

19
Working with OSGi

Since the development of JBoss 7, WildFly has a modular structure. External libraries can be installed in different modes in a application server. The preferred mode in WildFly is through the modules. This chapter is divided into two sections:

- Modules management
- OSGi management

Modules

A module is a library with its own life cycle. By default, a module is started at the start of WildFly and stopped at the stop of WildFly. A module is loaded in a lazy mode only when it is required by an application.

WildFly loads the dependencies with the following priorities:

- Libraries inside the application
- Modules
- Libraries inside other external applications

JBoss module 1.5.2.Final is the product managing the modules in WildFly. All WildFly dependencies are modules, and they are situated in the `modules/system/layers/base` folder. Now, let's see an example of a module representing hibernate.

From the `modules` folder, there is the `org/hibernate/5.0/module.xml` descriptor file. The following is the content to transform the hibernate library into a module:

```
<module-alias xmlns="urn:jboss:module:1.3" name="org.hibernate" slot="5.0"
  target-name="org.hibernate"/>
```

This code says that all Java packages starting with the `target-name` as `"org.hibernate"` will be part of the newly created `org.hibernate` module. That is enough to add this file and all library JARS to the same folder.

If your project needs to work with hibernate, only put this code in your `pom.xml` Maven descriptor file and use the newly imported hibernate packages in the code of your application. The dependency will be found automatically:

```
<dependency>
  <groupId>org.hibernate</groupId>
  <artifactId>hibernate-core</artifactId>
  <version>5.0</version>
  <scope>provided</scope>
</dependency>
```

The 5.0 is provided in WildFly. If you are not satisfied with this hibernate version, you can override it. Remember that it will not come from the module, so it must be installed as an internal dependency of your application with a similar script that overrides the version of the product and uses the scope runtime as default:

```
<dependency>
  <groupId>org.hibernate</groupId>
  <artifactId>hibernate-core</artifactId>
  <version>5.1.0.Final</version>
</dependency>
```

Alternatively, you can create a new hibernate module following the example we saw.

JBoss modules provides a good framework to manage the dependencies.
However, someone accustomed to other types of standards might be better off using other protocols. WildFly provides an external tool to make the dependencies through OSGi.

OSGi in WildFly

Increasing complexity in a software product, whether embedded, client or server, requires modular code, but also systems that are dynamically extensible. The OSGi framework aims to implement a complete and dynamic component model that is missing from the Java environment. In fact, Java language provides some mechanisms that allow us to create a component model, but they are still low-level solutions, resulting in the risk of introducing code errors as well as becoming an ad-hoc solution. OSGi solves many of the problems associated with poor Java support in modularity and dynamism through some key concepts:

- Automatic dependency management
- Definition of the module concept (bundle)
- Code life cycle management (dynamic configuration and distribution)

In summary, you can regard OSGi technology as follows:

- A dynamic system that allows you to install, start, stop, and remove runtime modules without having to restart
- A modular system for the Java platform
- Services oriented, which can be dynamically recorded and used in the Java virtual machine

JBoss OSGi, initially integrated in JBoss 7, is an alternative to JBoss modules to manage the dependencies through OSGi. It's an extension of JBoss modules, so it's very simple to install it. Let's now see how to install it in WildFly and how to work with it.

Installation

It can be downloaded from https://repository.jboss.org/nexus/content/repositories/releases/org/jboss/osgi/distribution/jbosgi-installer/2.5.2.Final/jbosgi-installer-2.5.2.Final-installer.jar.

Once downloaded, launch the following Java command to start the installation:

```
java -jar jbosgi-installer-2.5.2.Final-installer.jar
```

Once started, simply follow the wizard by setting a default folder to contain the OSGi core base and by setting your WildFly home.

Deployment of bundles

Now we are ready to deploy OSGi bundles. When we installed OSGi, a default bundles folder was created in the root of WildFly. It contains the base bundles, so we can work with JBoss OSGi. Here's the bundle list:

- **Felix**: Apache is the default OSGi repository. All deployed bundles will be installed and managed in this product.
- **Aries**: It's a set of API to write OSGi applications compliant with Java EE.
- **JBoss Logging OSGi**: The OSGi version of the default logging system of WildFly used to log in to OSGi applications.

Also, a new WildFly configuration is created; so, we must start WildFly through this command:

```
./standalone.sh -c standalone-osgi.xml
```

It will start WildFly with the new OSGi support. In the log, we can see the installation of the new bundles:

```
18:53:42,421 INFO [org.jboss.osgi.framework] (MSC service thread 1-3)
JBOSGI011001: Bundle installed: org.apache.felix.log:1.0.1
18:53:42,424 INFO [org.jboss.osgi.framework] (MSC service thread 1-3)
JBOSGI011001: Bundle installed: jboss-osgi-logging:1.0.0
18:53:42,426 INFO [org.jboss.osgi.framework] (MSC service thread 1-3)
JBOSGI011001: Bundle installed: org.apache.felix.configadmin:1.8.8
```

Now, a bundle can be deployed just like any other enterprise application in the `deployments` folder or through a web console. See the properties an OSGi bundle must have. If we open the `felix` admin bundle, we can see a `META-INF/MANIFEST.MF`, as shown:

```
Manifest-Version: 1.0
Bnd-LastModified: 1438908406824
Build-Jdk: 1.7.0_71
Built-By: cziegeler
Bundle-Activator: org.apache.felix.cm.impl.ConfigurationManager
Bundle-Category: osgi
Bundle-Description: Implementation of the OSGi Configuration Admin Servi
  ce Specification 1.5
Bundle-DocURL: http://felix.apache.org/site/apache-felix-config-admin.ht
```

```
ml
Bundle-License: http://www.apache.org/licenses/LICENSE-2.0.txt
Bundle-ManifestVersion: 2
Bundle-Name: Apache Felix Configuration Admin Service
Bundle-SymbolicName: org.apache.felix.configadmin
Bundle-Vendor: The Apache Software Foundation
Bundle-Version: 1.8.8
Created-By: Apache Maven Bundle Plugin
DynamicImport-Package: org.osgi.service.log;version="1.3"
Embed-Dependency: org.osgi.core;inline=org/osgi/util/tracker/ServiceTrac
 ker*|org/osgi/util/tracker/AbstractTracked.class
Export-Package:
org.apache.felix.cm;version="1.1",org.apache.felix.cm.file;uses:="org.apach
e.felix.cm,org.osgi.framework";version="1.0",org.osg
 i.service.cm;uses:="org.osgi.framework";version="1.5"
                              Export-Service:
org.osgi.service.cm.ConfigurationAdmin;service.descripti
 on="Configuration Admin Service Specification 1.5
Implementation";service.pid="org.osgi.service.cm.ConfigurationAdmin";servic
e.vendor="Apache
 Software Foundation",org.apache.felix.cm.PersistenceManager;service.des
 cription="Platform Filesystem Persistence Manager";service.pid="org.apa
 che.felix.cm.file.FilePersistenceManager";service.vendor="Apache Softwa
 re Foundation"
Import-Package: org.apache.felix.cm;version="[1.1,1.2)",org.apache.felix
 .cm.file;version="[1.0,1.1)",org.osgi.framework;version="[1.4,2)",org.o
 sgi.service.cm;version="[1.5,1.6)",org.osgi.service.log;resolution:=opt
 ional;version="1.3"
Import-Service: org.osgi.service.log.LogService;availability:=optional;m
 ultiple:=false
Tool: Bnd-1.50.0
```

All definitions of the OSGi bundles are in the Java `MANIFEST.MF` descriptor file. Here, you need to put all properties to identify a bundle, along with the dependencies' information.

Maven bundle plugin

Often, it can be particularly challenging to configure the manifest by hand, so many OSGi utilities can be found to create this file automatically.

A maven plugin is provided to do it. You just have to add code into your project, similar to the one shown as follows in your project and, automatically, your package will become an OSGi bundle to be deployed in an OSGi repository:

```
<plugin>
<groupId>org.apache.felix</groupId>
<artifactId>maven-bundle-plugin</artifactId>
<extensions>true</extensions>
<configuration>
<instructions>
<Export-Package>org.foo.myproject.api</Export-Package>
<Private-Package>org.foo.myproject.*</Private-Package>
<Bundle-Activator>org.foo.myproject.impl1.Activator</Bundle-Activator>
</instructions>
</configuration>
</plugin>
```

Summary

In this chapter, we looked at dependency management in WildFly 10. A good practice to guarantee solid work is to always use the existing frameworks if they are sufficient meet your needs. If you want your library to be shared on more applications, it is a good practice to transform it into a module. The book is now complete. We hope you liked it and found it comfortable to read and execute the examples. The world of application servers is very broad and includes many technologies that have increased over the years. In addition, there are many other products that can be used with WildFy. Typical examples are portals and ECMs.

A complete display of all is impossible in one book, but now the reader knows what the available technologies are and can choose the one he needs and can also try them out using more specific books and guides. Wishing you happy working; do continue to follow us.

Index

C

X

www.ingramcontent.com/pod-product-compliance
Lightning Source LLC
Chambersburg PA
CBHW060920060326
40690CB00041B/2826